25 BRAVE MEN

25 BRAVE MEN

Tales from an Arctic Journey

James Urness

Edited by Donald Kvamme

25 Brave Men: Tales from an Arctic Journey

Published by Wheatmark®
1760 East River Road, Suite 145
Tucson, Arizona 85718 U.S.A.
www.wheatmark.com

ISBN: 978-1-62787-034-4 (paperback)
ISBN: 978-1-62787-039-9 (ebook)
LCCN: 2013946454

Contents

Acknowledgment

I WOULD LIKE TO give a special thank you to Don Kvamme. He reviewed each chapter of the book after I had compiled it, checking for grammatical errors, reviewing content, and making suggestions to help me in my endeavor. His assistance over the years was of tremendous value. Thank you Don.

25 BRAVE MEN

Prologue

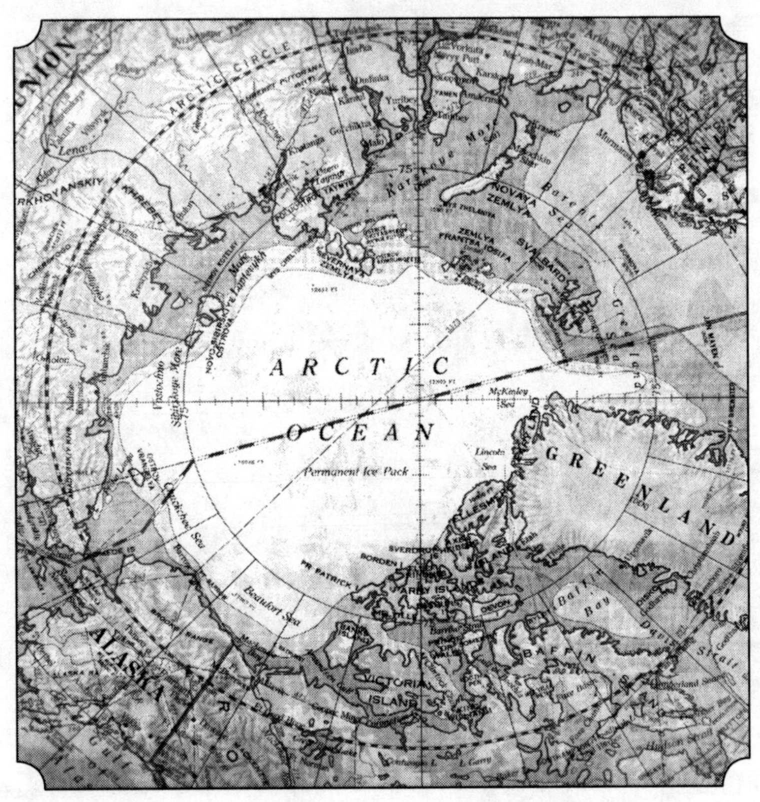
ARCTIC CIRCLE
ARCTIC
OCEAN
Permanent Ice Pack
GREENLAND
ALASKA
NOVAYA ZEMLYA
SVALBARD
Lincoln Sea
McKinley Sea
Beaufort Sea
BAFFIN
VICTORIA ISLAND
Baffin Bay

Mankind has always had a desire to explore. We want to see what is over the next hill. We continually develop means to get a better look at distant stars and planets, as well as finding out what is beyond the sea. The Viking Lief Erickson traveled northwest to what we know now as Greenland over a thousand years ago. In a quest to find a shorter route to the Orient, Christopher Columbus set sail to the west and ended up discovering the islands off the coast of the Americas. Each of these explorers took great risks in his pursuits.

The astronauts of the past fifty years are no different. They explored at great personal risk. Some of them have come back as heroes, while others have perished during their journeys. While some may perceive them as glory seekers, they are really brave men and women. The risks that they took upon themselves outweigh any hope of glory that they may have received. This story is about the brave men who journeyed to the far north during the period 1881 to 1884 in order to establish a permanent outpost for explorations, monitor weather conditions, make observations, and generally improve weather forecasting and navigational capabilities. Most, if not all, of these men recognized the great risks involved, yet they volunteered for the duty.

John Davis sailed from England in quest of the Northwest Passage over four hundred years ago. He rediscovered Greenland and may have discovered Smith Sound, a route to the North Pole. On successive voyages, Davis ventured up the western coast of Greenland and reached a point about fifty miles south of the present location of Upernivik. The latitude over 72° north, which Davis reached in the late 1500s, was a record at that time.

Some twenty-five years later, in 1616, William Baffin sailed up Smith Sound and eventually reached a latitude over 77° north, a record that was to stand for 236 years. For nearly two centuries the areas of Smith Sound where Baffin sailed were mostly forgotten, and the explorations of the north were discontinued.

In 1818 John Ross and William Parry sailed up Smith Sound, reaching a latitude over 76° north, and sighted many of the landmarks that Baffin had described on his journey. Other explorers included Admiral Inglefield in 1852 and an American, Elisha Kane, who traveled northward from New York in 1853, reaching a point beyond latitude 78° degrees north. Morton reached beyond 80° north that same year. During the 1870s several explorations were made up the coast of Greenland and Smith South. Our story begins in 1879.

1

The Lady Franklin Bay Expedition

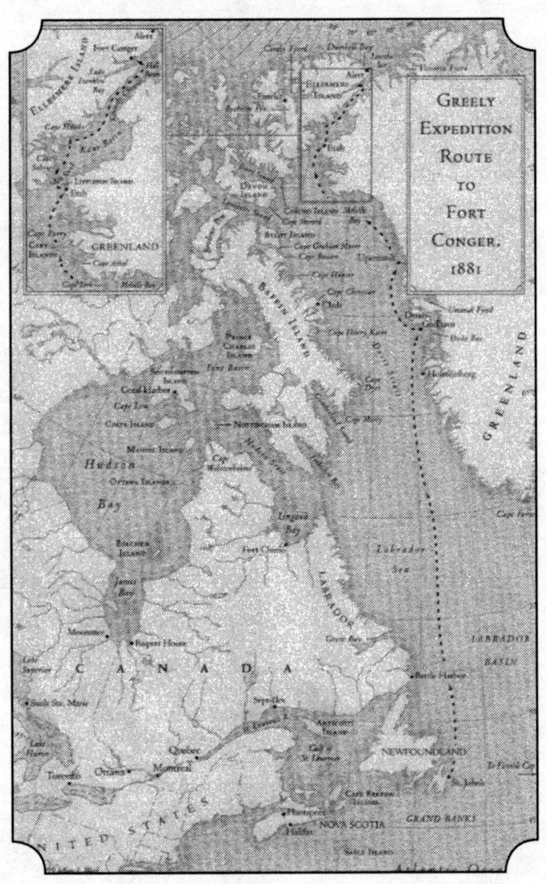

AN INTERNATIONAL CONFERENCE met in 1879 and again in 1880 in Europe to discuss the idea of establishing permanently manned stations at different points around the polar areas. There were multiple purposes for the stations. Earlier expeditions had no staging places in which to prepare for further expeditions toward the poles. These manned stations would provide for staging as well as refuge points upon the return of the expeditions. Secondarily, manned stations could gather all sorts of meteorological, terrestrial magnetism, weather, and temperature data, which would aid further expeditions. It was determined that twelve stations should be erected as observation posts, eight in the northern polar region and four in the southern polar region. Two of these stations were to be located in North America in areas close to the North Pole.

As early as 1877, Captain Henry W. Howgate of the United States Army had an interest in establishing an arctic colony at Lady Franklin Bay. It is located on the eastern coast of Grinnell Land, across Kane Basin from Greenland, about twenty-four hundred miles north of St. John's, Newfoundland, and a little more than six hundred miles south of the North Pole. Captain Howgate succeeded in having Lady Franklin Bay designated as one of the points in North America to be occupied by the United States Signal Service as a permanent polar station. A second station under the control of the United States was to be established at Point Barrow, Alaska.

Neither President Garfield nor his secretary of war, Robert Todd Lincoln, the son of Abraham Lincoln, considered this venture worthwhile. Congress, however, approved of an expedition to Lady Franklin Bay in an act passed on May 1, 1880, but did not appropriate funding for this project. Captain Howgate was put in charge of establishing the permanent station at Lady Franklin Bay. It was understood that costs for the expedition would come from private funding by Captain Howgate. He contracted the British steamship *Gulnare* for the journey and loaded her with supplies including material to build quarters for the party, all of this reportedly from his own funds. He would later be convicted of misappropriating government funds for this use.

Howgate assigned Lieutenant Adolphus W. Greely and two other officers of the United States Army to lead this team. Dr. Octave Pavy was employed as surgeon, and Henry Clay, grandson of the great statesman, would join them as volunteer aide of the expedition. George W. Rice was to go as the official photographer. The plan called for a permanent depot to be set up off Smith Sound at latitude 81° 44' north (Lady Franklin Bay), leaving supplies and extra men there and returning in the fall for another load. When the returning ship again reached Smith Sound she would exchange men, and, as by this time the first group of men would be acclimated, they would be taken to a point still farther north, where a second station was to be established. Returning to station number one, the second group of men would be taken to a third station, to be established at still a higher latitude than the second station, and thus, by gradual approach, it was hoped that the North Pole might finally be reached.

Lieutenant Greely refused this command after the Navy Department determined that the *Gulnare* was not sufficiently seaworthy for the expedition. But Captain Howgate was determined to send the ship on the expedition anyway. The ship sailed in June 1880 with a party led by Lieutenant Gustavus Cheyney Doane and Lieutenant Howe. Dr. Pavy, Mr. Clay, Mr. Rice, and Mr. Jewell accompanied the rest of the crew on this journey. They proceeded to Disco, Greenland. The *Gulnare* became disabled and was forced to return home. Dr. Pavy and Henry Clay remained in Greenland with the expectation that another ship would be brought up the next year.

In action by Congress on May 3 of the following year, authorization was given to charter a steam sealer or whaler to transport the party to Lady Franklin Bay. Lady Franklin Bay was to be the northernmost of all of the eight permanent stations in the northern hemisphere, located at latitude 81° 44' north and longitude 64° 45' west, off the coast of Ellsmere Island. It was about six hundred miles from the North Pole. Lieutenant Adolphus W. Greely was designated to prepare for and lead the expedition. The expedition was to be assembled at Washington, DC, no later than May 15, 1881, and at St. John's, Newfoundland, no later than June 15, 1881.

Three officers and twenty-one enlisted personnel were assigned to duty by the War Department as the expeditionary force to Lady Franklin Bay. The other two officers were second lieutenants Frederick F. Kislingbury and James B. Lockwood.

The enlisted men consisted of sergeants Edward Israel, Winfield S. Jewell, George W. Rice, David C. Ralston, Hampden S. Gardiner, William H. Cross, David L. Brainard, and David Lynn; corporals Daniel C. Starr, Paul Grimm, Nicholas Salor, and Joseph Ellison; privates Charles Henry Buck (alias Charles B. Henry), Maurice Connell, George Layerzapf (alias Jacob Bender), Franz Joseph Lang (alias Francis Long), William Whisler, Henry Bierderbick, Julius Frederick, James Ryan, and William A. Ellis. Private Roderick R. Schneider replaced Corporal Paul Grimm prior to departure.

Lieutenant Lockwood gathered together in Baltimore sergeants Brainard, Israel, Lynn, Jewell, Cross, and Starr; corporals Salor and Ellison; and privates Frederick, Long, Whistler, Henry, Ellis, and Bierderbick. They sailed on the Allan Line steamer *Nova Scotia* for St. John's on June 14, 1881. The other members of the expedition gathered with Lieutenant Kislingbury. They were sergeants Rice and Ralston and privates Gardiner, Ryan, Connell, Bender, and Schneider.

The two parties united in St. John's, where Lieutenant Greely was preparing for the expedition. They helped with the loading of the *Proteus*, the steamer that had been procured to take them, along with their provisions, to Lady Franklin Bay. They departed St. John's at noon on July 7, 1881, heading northward toward Greenland. Two major stops were made along the journey, at Godhavn and Upernivik in Greenland. Dr. Octave Pavy and two Eskimos, Thorlip Frederik Christiansen and Jens Edward, as well as Henry

Clay, boarded at these stops. Dogs and sleighs that Dr. Pavy and Mr. Clay had procured to be used on the expedition were also loaded.

On August 10, 1881, a little over a month since they left St. John's, they docked at Lady Franklin Bay. After three days of unloading, the *Proteus* was ready to return to St. John's. Henry Clay and two of the expedition members, Corporal Starr and Private Ryan, who were relieved of duty with the expedition because of physical ailments, returned to St. John's with the *Proteus*. Lieutenant Kislingbury, who had a disagreement with Lieutenant Greely, was relieved of duty and went to shore, planning to return with the *Proteus*; however, the *Proteus* had pulled out just before he got there. He was destined to stay with the expedition.

The station was named Fort Conger, in honor of Senator Omar Dwight Conger. Senator Conger was very much interested in the expedition and had enough authority to help push the funding for it through Congress. After unloading all the supplies, the men began building their quarters. The men lived in tents until near the end of August, when some of them began moving into the quarters. By this time temperatures had dropped below freezing several times. The building, which housed the party of twenty-five, was sixty by seventeen feet—about one thousand square feet. Each person was assigned a bunk. Except for Dr. Pavy and the three officers, the bunks were two-tiered, areas being established for each person or group of people. Biderbick, Connell, Henry, and Whisler shared an area. Ellison, Schneider, Cross, and Lynn shared another area. Salor, Long, Bender, and Ellis shared a third area. Brainard, Frederick, Ralston, and Gardiner shared a fourth area. Jewell, Israel, and Rice shared the fifth area, and the Eskimos, Christiansen, and Jens shared area six, somewhat separated from the other men. Dr. Pavy and the officers were together in a separate room, seventeen by fifteen feet.

General W. B. Hazen, the chief signal officer of the United States Army, provided the leader, Lieutenant Greely, with the following plan: The fort should be visited in 1882 and again in 1883 by some vessel that would bring supplies and such additions to the present party deemed necessary. The plan stipulated that in case the vessel sent in 1882 did not reach the permanent station (Fort Conger), a portion of her supplies and all of her letters and dispatches would be cached at the most northerly point she attained on the east coast of Grinnell Land. A small depot at Littleton Island would also be established. Notices of the locations of such depots were to be left at one or all of the following places: Cape Hawks, Cape Sabine, and Cape Isabella. In the event that no vessel reached the permanent station in 1882, the vessel sent in 1883 would remain in Smith Sound until there was danger of its closing by ice, and on leaving would land all her supplies and a party at Littleton Island, which party would be prepared for a winter's stay, and would be instructed to send sledge parties up the east side of Grinnell Land to meet this party. If not visited in 1883, Lieutenant Greely would abandon his station not later than September 1, 1883, and would retreat southward by boat, following closely the east coast of Grinnell Land until the relieving vessel was met or Littleton Island was reached.

The first test of the plan came in May 1882. Congress had not allocated funds for any relief vessels to visit Fort Conger. General Hazen was beside himself because he felt that action should start soon. It was not until June 19 that $33,000 was appropriated to support both Fort Conger and Point Barrow. While the *Proteus* was the best equipped for the mission, the owners wanted $26,000 to lease it, more than the available funds. Instead, the *Neptune*, a less able vessel, was selected at a cost of $6,000 a month. Replacement personnel for the Greely party were poorly selected, and four of the eight deserted before departure. The *Neptune* departed with twenty-five hundred rations, enough to feed the Greely party for about one hundred days. The person in charge of the relief was a private with a questionable background. The vessel did not leave St. John's until July 8, about a month after the desirable time.

After encountering many ice fields, they neared Littleton Island, some three hundred and fifty miles from Fort Conger, on July 26, eighteen days after leaving St. John's. The ice extended clear across Smith Sound, making it next to impossible to make any northward progress. They got to within twenty-five miles south of Littleton Island but were pushed back by the ice and gales. On August 12, while they were still attempting to move northward, the ice caused damage to the boiler of the ship. The captain of the vessel turned south to prevent further damage. They landed at Payer Harbor, a few miles south of Cape Sabine, but left no stores of food. A note was left in case Greely should land at that site. They finally were able to reach Cape Sabine and Littleton Island, where they left two hundred and fifty rations at each place, enough to feed the expedition for ten days at each place. Unable to reach Fort Conger, with two thousand of their twenty-five hundred rations still on board, the *Neptune* returned to St. John's.

The resupply and rescue attempt of 1883 was a little better equipped. For this venture, the steamship *Proteus*, the same ship that took the Greely party to Fort Conger, was chartered. Under the direction of General Hazen, chief signal officer of the army, Lieutenant Earnest Garlington was placed in charge. The instructions that Lieutenant Greely had left before his departure two years before were quite clear and were given to Garlington. Greely stated, "If the party does not reach here in 1882, there should be sent a capable, energetic officer, with ten men, eight of whom should have practicable sea experience, provided with three whale-boats and ample provisions for forty persons for fifteen months." He pointed out that Cape Sabine was to be Depot A, with caches of supplies at six other points. A crew should be left at Littleton Island to keep watch for the Greely party and intercept them. A navy ship, the *Yantic*, was to accompany the *Proteus* as far as Littleton Island.

While some of what Greely had asked for was loaded aboard, not all was met. But it really didn't matter, as the *Proteus* passed by Cape Sabine without leaving stores, the crew believing that they could get to Fort Conger. But the ship became caught in an ice jam and sunk. Only a portion of the supplies and some of the boats were salvaged. While the crew did manage to get back to Cape Sabine, very little was left that would aid the Greely party if they made it there. Garlington and the rest of the people from the *Proteus* finally made contact with the navy ship, the *Yantic*, and returned on it to St. John's without leaving a rescue crew for Greely and his party.

When no vessel appeared at Fort Conger in either 1882 or 1883, it was necessary for Greely to implement the plan to leave the fort and head toward Cape Sabine, some three hundred and fifty miles to the south, Littleton Island being some twenty-seven miles east of Cape Sabine. They had a twenty-seven-foot steam launch and two boats towed behind them, filled with rations and the expedition members. All were well and in good condition.

They departed the fort on August 8. A month later, on September 10, they abandoned the launch after it had been jammed between ice floes. They dragged their remaining supplies over the ice floes toward Cocked Hat Island. A week later, although pulling the supplies over the ice for up to fifteen miles a day, they were no closer to land than when they started. This was due to the fact that the ice floe that they were on was rotating and progress made one day was lost over the next few days. By this time they were thirty miles from Greenland to the east and nineteen miles from Cape Sabine to the west. Between the movement of the floe and the pulling of the boats, they finally landed near Cape Sabine on September 29, nearly two months after leaving Fort Conger. They had traveled over four hundred miles by boat and another hundred by foot to reach this point.

They set up camp at this point, making a cover for their tent using one of the boats. They searched for, but did not find, the supplies that they had expected to find cached there. Faintly able to see Littleton Island, some twenty-seven miles from them, they wondered if their rescue party was there.

None came—because they were not there. They spent the winter in these scant quarters, members of the party dying as time went on. When the rescue party arrived in June 1884, only seven members of the expedition had survived. One of these died on the way back to St. John's. More details of the events that transpired during these three years are chronicled in the chapters that follow.

2

Adolphus Washington Greely

(1844–1935)

ADOLPHUS WASHINGTON GREELY was born in Newburyport, Massachusetts, on March 27, 1844. He was the first child born to John Balch Greely and Frances S. Cobb Greely. His father was born in Newburyport on July 24, 1802, the son of Stephen and Betsy Greely. Adolphus's father, John Balch Greely, married Clarissa Jewett on August 12, 1823. John and Clarissa Greely had five, six, or seven children: Stephen, John Augustus, William Henry, Elizabeth, and the second William Henry; they possibly had two other children, Mary Ann and James Henry.

All the children were born in Newburyport or nearby Haverhill. Stephen was born on December 21, 1823. He died on July 11, 1846, when he was twenty-two years old.

John Augustus, the next oldest son, was born on July 31, 1825. He married Charlotte Mills Rundlett two times. First they married in Newburyport on October 28, 1846, and again in Hampton, New Hampshire, on December 14, 1846. John and Charlotte had three children. John died in Altamonte, Florida, on February 28, 1891. Charlotte lived until March 30, 1906. William Henry was born on May 6, 1827. He died as an infant.

Elizabeth was born on August 4, 1829. She married Lucius E. Hallock in Boston, Massachusetts, on August 30, 1853. They had three children. Elizabeth died on March 6, 1870.

The second William Henry was born in 1833 or 1834. William married Eliza Ann Jones on March 29, 1856. William died four years later, on December 1, 1860, from consumption.

John Balch Greely's first wife, Clarissa, died in Newburyport on May 23, 1840. She was thirty-seven years old. Two years later, on October 30, 1842, John married Frances Dunn Cobb. Adolphus was their firstborn. A sister, Mary Ellen, was born on August 17, 1845. She died in a fire on April 7, 1850, when she was only four years old. Adolphus's father died on October 9, 1864. His mother, Frances, was a widow for over thirty years, dying in Newburyport on September 13, 1901.

Adolphus graduated from the Newburyport high school. He enlisted as a private in the Massachusetts infantry on July 3, 1861. It is not surprising that he chose to join the military. His father, John Balch Greely, had been a captain in the Massachusetts militia, and his great-grandfather, Joseph Greely, served as a sergeant in the military during the American Revolution.

The list of battles he was in during his early years of service is extensive. During the remainder of 1861 he was engaged at Ball's Bluff. In 1862 he was in battles at Yorktown, West Point, Fir Oaks, Savages' Station, White Oak Swamp, Malvern Hill, Antietam, and Fredickson. At White Oak Swamp he was wounded in the leg. While at Antietam he was again wounded, this time in his side.

Adolphus rose up the ranks rapidly. By May of 1862 he had been promoted to corporal and in November of the same year to first sergeant. On March 18, 1863, he was commissioned a second lieutenant in the Colorado infantry, and he was promoted to first lieutenant on April 14, 1863. He was promoted to captain on April 4, 1865, and to brevet major of US Volunteers on March 13, 1865. He was mustered out on March 27, 1867. Two months later, on May 20, 1867, he was appointed second lieutenant in the Thirty-Sixth US Infantry. He was assigned to the Fifth US Cavalry on July 14, 1869.

During the next ten years of his military career, Greely was involved in building telegraph lines between various military facilities. It was while doing this type of duty that he met many of the soldiers that would eventually join him on the Lady Franklin Bay expedition. His duty took him to all parts of the Great Plains as well as those areas south and west of the plains. He also served in California, where in 1878 he met his bride-to-be, Henrietta Hudson Cruger Nesmith.

Henrietta was the daughter of Thomas L. Nesmith and Maria Antoinette Gale. Although she was born in Thoune, Switzerland, her parents both had ancestry of over one hundred and fifty years of life in New England. Henrietta had resided in Texas, Mexico, and California. She was living in San Diego when she met Greely. They were married in San Diego on June 20, 1878. They had relocated to Washington, DC within the year, as their first child, Antoinette, was born there on June 2, 1879.

Greely must have spent most of his time while in Washington preparing for the trip northward. He had to be concerned about how large the expedition would be and who he would like to have on the expedition—people who had the necessary skills to accomplish their mission, such as taking weather readings, providing medical care, etc. He had to determine how to get the men and supplies to the proper place to make their camp. He had to make contingency plans. These included what to do if the ship bringing supplies did not make it to the camp in either the summer following their encampment or the second year following. He had to ensure that he had medical support and dogs, sleds, and drivers of these dog teams.

He had planned to go to the Arctic region in the summer of 1880, leaving behind his wife and a one-year-old child; however, government finances had not been approved for the mission. Instead a group went that was supposedly financed by private funds and consisted mostly of nonmilitary personnel, with a ship that was damaged as it tried to break through the ice in Smith Sound. The prefabricated quarters, however, along with the expedition's doctor, remained in Greenland.

By 1881 funds were made available for another try at getting to the point where the camp was to be established on Lady Franklin Bay. A ship, the *Proteus*, was obtained for the trip to the campsite. Greely went ahead of the other members of the expedition to St. John's, Newfoundland, the site of embarkation for the expedition. His wife had had twins, a boy and a girl, on April 20, 1881, just a couple of months prior to his departure. The boy died at birth; however, the girl, Adola, survived. Now Henrietta had a two-year-old and a two month old child to rear with her husband going to the Arctic, possibly for as long as three years. She decided go to San Diego with her girls so they could be with their grandparents.

Now that the expedition had been fully planned, it was time to carry it out. His first order of business was to get the men and supplies to Lady Franklin Bay. The supplies, which were to last for three years, were loaded at St. John's, including a steamboat, powered by coal, which was christened the *Lady Greely*, named for his wife, Henrietta Greely. When the *Proteus* reached Greenland, the prefabricated living quarters, which had been dropped off the year before, were loaded. Also, Doctor Pavy and Henry Clay, who had been dropped off the year before, were added to the party. Pavy, during his yearlong stay in Greenland, had procured dogs, sleds, and Eskimo drivers for the dog teams. Now Greely had all that was needed for the expedition aboard the *Proteus*.

Since the *Proteus* made it through the ice in Smith Sound to Lady Franklin Bay with relatively few problems, it did not seem unreasonable to expect that another ship could make it to Lady Franklin Bay in the next two years to resupply or bring them back home. This, however, was not the case, the summer of 1881 being exceptional for the travel to Lady Franklin Bay. Another ship would not make it through the ice to Lady Franklin Bay for several years. The chances of the *Lady Greely*, a relatively small boat with no ice-breaking ability, traveling through Smith Sound and meeting a rescue ship, seemed to be slim. This, however, was the plan, and they did get some two hundred and fifty miles south, but much of the distance was obtained while they were floating on an ice floe, and not in the *Lady Greely*, which they were forced to abandon.

Once up in the Arctic at Lady Franklin Bay, Greely's control over his troops was tested. He had learned over the past twenty years of military service, including being involved in battles during the Civil War and the Indian Wars that followed, that it was necessary for the commanding officer to maintain control of his troops. The first decision involving personnel probably was to return two of the men, Corporal Starr and Private Ryan, to the States because of ill health. Then there seemed to be a dispute between Henry Clay and Doctor Pavy. Greely decided to send one of them back on the *Proteus* and decided that the doctor was more important to the mission, so he chose him to stay with the expedition. Henry Clay later (in September 1884) was killed in a gun battle outside a saloon in Louisville, Kentucky. When Lt. Kislingbury, the second-in-command, did not concur with the time that Greely set for him to arise from his sleep, Greely relieved him from the expedition and told him he could go back home; however, he missed the boat and had to stay with the expedition. With Kislingbury removed from his position as second-in-command, Lockwood was now Greely's deputy. Lockwood would be assigned to lead and help decide which functions he would participate in and, in many cases, select whom he would have participate with him. Kislingbury was left hanging.

Brainard was the type of first sergeant that all commanders wish they had. He held discipline over the enlisted men and related problems to the commander. Greely felt that he could really count on him. Pavy was a problem for Greely. Pavy was given a temporary commission as a lieutenant while on the expedition. He was the doctor, and from Greely's standpoint, his job was to make sure that the expedition members were kept healthy. But Pavy did not perceive himself as just the doctor. He was interested in polar exploration. He felt that he was in the Arctic for that reason. He did not see himself as subordinate to Greely, but only as a doctor and explorer. Greely felt he had to hold the reins on Pavy. This resulted in friction between the two of them.

Greely, while he was not one of the expedition members that reached the "farthest north," certainly helped plan it and ensured that those who were on the journey had all the supplies they needed and that it was prudent for them to go on such a journey.

The plan for the expedition was that a resupply or rescue ship would reach their fort in the summers of 1882 and 1883. If the ship was unable to reach them in either of the years, the plan was for them to abandon the fort and attempt to go south where a rescue ship and/or supplies would await them.

Pavy offered to take a team and go overland to check out the area they would be trying to reach. He was planning on checking how many supplies were cached there, hunting conditions, etc. This was not in Greely's plan, and as such, he declined the offer. It would have been a long and dangerous trip and might not have changed the final outcome.

Possibly one of the hardest decisions Greely had to make was to order the shooting of Henry. But after warning Henry of the consequences of his theft of their meager food supply, and when Henry did not respond to the warning, Greely felt that in order to keep order among the expedition members, he must take such action against him.

Meanwhile, Greely's wife, Henrietta, had moved back to Washington, DC. She was active in the DAR (Daughters of the American Revolution). For at least one year she was vice president of the organization. Many elite people were members of the DAR, including Clara Barton.

When the two ships, the *Neptune* in 1882 and the *Proteus* in 1883, did not make it to Lady Franklin Bay, many in the Washington, DC, political arena concluded that there was no use in spending any more money in trying to rescue Greely and the rest of the party. It was pretty much concluded that sending another ship would likely fail and that the party probably had not survived even if a ship did get through. Henrietta, even though she had opposition from many in Washington, continued to push for support in trying to rescue her husband and the rest of the party. She was quite successful in this endeavor, and had she not been, it is likely that not one of the expedition members would have survived.

Three ships, the *Bear*, the *Thetis*, and the *Alert*, finally reached them at their makeshift camp called Camp Clay. Only seven of the expedition members were still alive when they were rescued. One of the seven died on the way home. The party received a great welcome when they arrived at St. John's, and they were received at Portsmouth, New Hampshire, with the same enthusiasm. From Portsmouth the ship took them to Washington, DC, where they had another large welcome.

The survivors of the expedition were all greeted as heroes, and they were welcomed by all. This continued until the story broke that there may have been cannibalism during the expedition, and the fame began to wane. Even though much had been accomplished during the expedition, such as mapping areas that had not been mapped and adding to the knowledge of the climate in the Arctic, the excitement did not last for long. The survivors were placed in medical facilities for about a month so they could recover from their ordeal.

Greely remained in Washington, DC, throughout the following years, and his home base would be there. He was promoted to captain in June 1886. He became, by order of President Grover Cleveland, a brigadier general and chief of the United States Army Signal Corps in March of the following year. In that post, he was responsible over the next twenty years for the construction of tens of thousands of miles of telegraph lines and submarine cables in Puerto Rico, Cuba, the Philippines, Alaska, and elsewhere, and for the army's earliest adoption of wireless telegraphy. He was also head of the weather bureau until it was transferred to the Department of Agriculture in 1891.

He was a delegate to the International Telegraph Conference in London and the International Wireless Telegraph Congress in Berlin in 1903. In February 1906 he was promoted to major general and placed in command of the Northern Division. He was later transferred to the Pacific Division and there oversaw relief operations following the San Francisco earthquake in that year. He retired from the army in 1908.

Greely was awarded the Medal of Honor by Congress on March 27, 1935, his ninety-first birthday, for his part in the Lady Franklin Bay expedition. He died that same year and is buried alongside his wife in Arlington National Cemetery. His wife, Henrietta Nesmith Greely, had died some seventeen years earlier, on March 15, 1918.

Greely's family expanded greatly after his return from the Arctic. Besides his two daughters, Antoinette and Adola, who were born prior to his Arctic adventure, he and Henrietta had two more daughters and two sons. John Nesmith Greely was born on June 6, 1885; Rose Isabel was born on February 18, 1887; Adolphus Washington Jr. was born on January 2, 1889; and Gertrude Gale was born on September 26, 1891.

Antoinette Greely worked for many years in social services. She never married. Born in Washington, DC, she traveled on more than one overseas trip with her parents. After living and working in New

Hampshire, she relocated to Texas. She died in Victoria, Texas, on August 5, 1968, at the age of eighty-nine.

Greely's second daughter, Adola, married Reverend Charles Lawrence Adams in Washington, DC, on April 24, 1906. Greely was on his way to attend the wedding but had to forgo going to Washington, DC, because he was needed for the San Francisco earthquake disaster. Charles and Adola had two children. One of them died at birth, and the other died when she was about a year old. Charles died in 1933. Adola was still living in 1957.

John Nesmith Greely, the older son of Adolphus and Henrietta, married Marian Chapman on December 24, 1920. Like his father, he was well educated, and he was commissioned a second lieutenant in 1908. He advanced to the grade of brigadier general in 1841. He died on June 13, 1965. Marian died in 1973. They were parents of a son.

Rose Isabel Greely, the next daughter, lived out her life in Washington, DC. She never married, and she worked as a landscape architect. She died on May 21, 1969.

Adolphus W. Greely Jr., their other son, also served in the army. He rose to the grade of major. He married Anna Louise Sponsler on October 20, 1917, in Harrisburg, Pennsylvania. He died at Martinsburg, West Virginia, on September 22, 1956. He is buried in Arlington National Cemetery. Louise died four years later, on April 2, 1960. She is buried alongside her husband at Arlington National Cemetery. They had no children.

Gertrude Gale Greely married Lt. Commander James C. Kress on August 16, 1919. The marriage was short-lived, as James died three months later. Kress was either retired or about to be retired from the navy. Gertrude married a second time, to George Harold Shedd, on December 23, 1926. They were married in New Canaan, Connecticut. They made their home in North Conway, New Hampshire, where George was a doctor. They had three children. George died sometime after 1942, and Gertrude died in August 1969.

3

James Booth Lockwood

(1852–1884)

JAMES BOOTH LOCKWOOD represented the seventh generation of the Lockwood family, the first generation having emigrated from England and settled in Delaware. These generations included many prosperous people, including one who was judge of the Supreme Court of Maryland. Indeed, James's father was a graduate of West Point and had distinguished himself in many ways, including becoming a professor who taught at many military academies. His father retired after having served also as a brigadier general in the United States Army.

James was born at the Naval Academy at Annapolis, Maryland, where his father was then teaching, on the ninth of October, 1852. He was the second son and the third child born to Henry Hayes Lockwood and Anna (Booth) Lockwood. An older brother had died as an infant. His older sister was Eliza Rogers Lockwood. His four younger sisters were Anna, Caroline, Julie, and Mary Murray Lockwood. He also had a younger brother, Henry.

The childhood of James was much like that of any military youngster. His father was relocated many times and, as such, so was the family. They lived at Annapolis until James was about nine years old, the family relocating to Newport, Rhode Island. Soon after, the family moved to Virginia, then to Harper's Ferry, West Virginia, and later to Baltimore.

When James was about twelve years old, he was sent away from home to a boarding school in Bethlehem, Pennsylvania. After a year or two he returned to Annapolis, where his father was now located, and the fourteen-year-old boy was enrolled at St. John's College, a military academy located in the vicinity. Later his father was reassigned to the National Observatory in Washington, DC. James dropped his education at St. John's College and moved to Washington with his family. Soon it was decided that James should return to Annapolis and take charge of his father's farm until he could find other employment.

James soon fixed his mind on engineering work in connection with the railroads. He joined a corps on the Texas and Pacific Railroad line and went to Texas, where he drove pegs and cut down bushes in the virgin wilderness. After four months, his employment was terminated by the failure of the company to go on with its enterprise.

After finding that farming and railroad engineering were not exactly the tasks he had fancied them to be, James resumed his studies under the direction of his father. Not long afterward, however, he was seized with the idea of entering the army. After going through a series of hoops and tests he was finally accepted as a second lieutenant in the Twenty-third Infantry of the United States Army. He was sent to the recruiting station at New York City for instruction.

After a service of several weeks at the recruiting station, he was assigned duty at McDowell Post in Arizona. He took a group of recruits with him to the post. Different modes of transportation were used in the journey, including marching a distance of more than 150 miles in the dusty plains. His duties at the post were quite varied.

In July 1873 he transferred with his regiment to Yuma, Arizona, a march that took two weeks to complete. Before long Lockwood was assigned duty at the barracks in Omaha, Nebraska. Many of his duties there had to do with courts-martial.

When we review the letters that he wrote home, we find them conveying a sense of dissatisfaction in the route that his life had taken. He had a real interest in horses as a young man, yet he joined the infantry instead of the cavalry. He was sorry for this decision. Promotions were slower than he had expected, and some of the work he found mundane or boring. By June 1875 it would seem as if something like homesickness was weighing down his spirits, for he then began to write about employment in civil life. He found life at the Omaha garrison during the summer of 1875 comfortable but monotonous.

On the approach of spring, and with the expectation of obtaining a leave of absence during the coming summer, he resumed a discussion with his father about leaving the army for civil employment.

In June 1876, the monotony of his life was relieved somewhat by an order to take some convicts to the state prison near Fort Leavenworth, Kansas.

In the fall of 1876 he was given a leave of absence to visit his family. During Lieutenant Lockwood's absence on leave, his regiment was transferred to Fort Leavenworth. He returned to Fort Leavenworth, where he would serve until the spring of 1879.

By the end of this duty tour, Lockwood considered leaving the military service. He was interested in telegraphic communications and considered a position with the Signal Service. He went so far as to ask his father about the practicability of securing such a position in that corps, and desired especially to know all about the necessary qualifications. On one occasion, after alluding to the possibility of his being transferred for duty to some other place, he felt that it might be a good thing for him, as he could not remain at Leavenworth always, and yet he stated in a letter that he dreaded to be sent to some "far-distant and isolated post." Two months later, in July, he resumed with special earnestness the consideration of being detailed for a duty in the Signal Service and, with his father's approval, made the proper application. He thought the proposed transfer would be of benefit to him in many ways, and if he failed to make it so, he would very quickly be ordered back to his regiment.

In December 1878, the Twenty-Third Regiment received orders for service in the Indian Territory and a few weeks afterward entered upon its line of march. Much of Lockwood's time was spent in Colorado.

At the time the expedition to Lady Franklin Bay was being organized in Washington, Lieutenant Lockwood was visiting his parents in Washington. Taking a special interest in the operations of the Signal Service Bureau, he volunteered for the proposed expedition and was accepted for it by the secretary of war.

In May of 1881 he was appointed acting signal officer with

orders to report to the chief signal officer for special service, which was the Lady Franklin Bay expedition. Lockwood left Washington with fifteen enlisted members of the expedition and went to Baltimore, where he and the rest of the men boarded a steamer for St. John's, Newfoundland.

The expedition left St. John's for Lady Franklin Bay on Thursday, July 7, 1881, on the steamer *Proteus*. Nine days later the steamer reached the coast of Greenland. In Greenland they picked up all their supplies, including the prefabricated quarters, which were left there by the 1880 expedition ship that failed to reach Lady Franklin Bay. They also picked up sledge dogs and two Eskimos, Jens and Fredericks, who would be used as sledge drivers. Doctor Pavy and Henry Clay, who had stayed in Greenland after the failed 1880 expedition, were added as members of the expedition.

They departed Greenland on the *Proteus* on July 29, heading through the ice-filled waters toward Lady Franklin Bay. On August 10 they reached their destination, establishing their station as near as possible to the coal mine on Watercourse Bay. They unloaded the ship and started construction on the quarters. While this was going on, Lieutenant Kislingbury, the second-in-command of the expedition after the commander, Lieutenant Greely, was asked to be relieved of duties and allowed to return to St. John's on the *Proteus*. Thus he was relieved of his duties; however, the *Proteus* had departed before he could board it. Lieutenant Kislingbury was relieved of duty until he could return to the United States for further assignment. Lieutenant Greely remarked that if anything should happen to him, he desired that Lieutenant Lockwood should have command of the expedition.

On August 27, the building in which the expedition members would live was entirely finished. Lieutenant Greely commemorated the opening of the quarters by issuing an order that the exploring expedition along the northern coast of Greenland was to be placed in command of Lieutenant Lockwood. Lockwood now felt that the opportunity for doing something creditable, for his own as well as his country's reputation, was at hand.

Since the strait was very wide at Lady Franklin Bay, the plan was to go northward, where the crossing of the strait would be a shorter and easier task. The strait would have to be frozen over to allow them passage.

Lockwood immediately began planning for the trip. He established staging stations along the route that he planned to take. All during the fall, winter, and spring these staging stations were set up and supplied with provisions. The winter was long and, for Lockwood, very dull. He longed to be active and to accomplish something that would be pleasing to his father. He missed his family back in Washington.

Lockwood decided that on the first of April he would start upon his expedition to the Greenland coast. This trip occupied his mind continually. He hoped he might be successful, yet there were many chances of failure. He felt that he ought to be able to reach Cape Britannia, but that was not enough; he desired to do more. He had at his disposal any of the men to accompany him and any of them to act as support teams. It would involve moving supplies over land and sea. The land was covered with what was known as rubble-ice: ice that has been pushed out of the sea to the shore and broken up. Travel over the sea was a concern, as all of the water might not be frozen to the extent necessary to pass over it.

On April 2, 1882, the expedition to explore the northern coast of Greenland departed from Fort Conger. The advance parties carried supplies from Fort Conger to Depot A and Depot B and farther to Cape Beechy, about thirty miles north of the fort. At this point some of the party returned to the fort and some continued on, Lockwood in charge of all activities. One week later they had crossed the frozen strait, Robeson Channel, and were on the Greenland coast.

When they were about fifty miles from the fort, the runners of the sledge they would use to carry their supplies northward were worn so badly that they had no choice but to return to the fort and get new runners. Nine members of the expedition were with them at this point. Lockwood himself decided to take a dog team back to the fort, along with the Eskimo Frederik, and get the new runners. The trip of about one hundred miles was completed in fifty-four hours, just over two days, and the sledge was repaired.

The party continued to the northeast along the coast of Greenland. By April 28, they reached Cape Bryant. This was as far as

Lockwood's support party was to travel. The support party would meet them on the return of Lockwood's party. The party now consisted of Lockwood, Sergeant Brainard, and the Eskimo Frederik.

Lockwood decided to take twenty-five days' worth of rations with them. The supplies they would take, which included their rations, food for the dogs, equipment, sleeping bags, etc., weighed nearly eight hundred pounds. The explorers now turned toward Cape Britannia, over the sea ice. They reached their destination on the fifteenth of May, some seventeen days after they had left their support party. This point was measured by astronomical observations and found to be latitude 83° 24' north and longitude 40° 46' west. That placed them about four hundred and fifty miles from the North Pole, about fifty miles nearer the pole than any explorer had ever reached. They planted the United States flag—which Mrs. Greely had made and sent with them—marking the spot that they had achieved, and started back toward the support crew's location. The entire party, including the support crew, reached Fort Conger on June 1, 1882. Lockwood had traveled over a thousand miles on this trip, sometimes in strong winds with temperatures dipping below thirty degrees below zero. Lockwood had achieved honor both for the expedition members and for the United States. He knew that his father would be proud of him.

Two weeks after his return, Lockwood was ready to leave the fort on other expeditions. He was gloomy from this extremely monotonous existence. He took the steam launch, *Lady Greely*, and scouted out the area around Lady Franklin Bay, watching for any sign of a relief ship. He made treks to the west and southwest of the fort. Yet, during the summer and fall of that year, 1882, Lockwood tired of the inactivity. Lockwood wrote in his journal, "I must go on another sledge-journey to dispel this gloom."

It seemed that Lockwood's desire was to be away from that cold region, and yet he seemed determined again to explore the north Greenland coast and thought that, under favorable circumstances, he could go farther than he had already gone by at least seventy-five miles. It was Lieutenant Greely's opinion, however, that the most northerly point already attained by Lockwood would not be reached again in the present century.

Lieutenant Greely finally gave permission to Lockwood for another journey to the north. When the first of March arrived, all hands were engaged in preparing for their spring work. First in order was food and other supplies to be cached at a depot on the eastern side of the strait, and Lockwood purposed leaving soon, to convey several hundred pounds of rations to that place. Both Lieutenants Greely and Lockwood did all they could to make a success of this expedition. Lockwood was impatient to be away from the gloom that he felt at the fort and at work. He felt that if he could not go farther than on his previous trip, he could at least try, and no man could do more than his best.

On the tenth of March, 1883, Lockwood wrote in his journal, "Before I go home, I must make another 'strike' on the north Greenland coast. If the conditions of the ice are no worse, I ought to be able to discover the northeast extremity of Greenland, and add several miles to my latitude, although Lieutenant Greely thinks that my present 'farthest' will not again be reached in our day."

They departed the fort on March 27, 1883, Lockwood hoping to break his own record of the farthest north ever recorded by man. The trek did not go as well as that of the previous year. They crossed the strait, Robeson Channel, as before, reaching the Greenland coast. There they met with extreme buildups of rubble-ice, which made the traveling slow. They also encountered strong winds and temperatures near fifty degrees below zero. Finally they found that the ice on the northwest coast of Greenland was not all frozen over as it was the preceding year. They finally were forced to either place their lives in grave danger or return to the fort. Following the orders given by the commander before they departed the fort, Lockwood decided to return without reaching the point that he had the year before. This was certainly a bitter defeat for Lockwood.

Upon his return, Lockwood walked in on Lieutenant Greely like a ghost and simply said, "Well, I'm back again; open water at Black Horn Cliffs." Lockwood tried to get Lieutenant Greely to let him go out again, but Greely stated that this was to be their last year here, and that they still had the previous year's work to fall back on, and above all, that it would not be prudent.

After consulting with Lieutenant Greely, Lockwood fixed his

mind upon an exploration up and beyond the Archer Fjord. His idea was to go west, at least as far as the English had gone along the northern shore of Grinnell Land, feeling that he could hardly fail to find something of interest and would perhaps make important discoveries. Indeed, he might be able to determine the coastline at the west. As usual, he wanted the company of Sergeant Brainard and the Eskimo Frederik, and he would be content with one dog team and supplies for thirty days, with a proper supporting party for two days. His late failure had been a disappointment to himself as well as to Lieutenant Greely and the men. It seems that Lockwood's main thrust was to accomplish anything that would be pleasing to his father. That had been driving him all during the expedition.

The personal relations of Dr. Pavy and Lieutenant Kislingbury with Lieutenant Greely and himself were not what they should have been, and instead of getting better, these relations seemed to grow worse. Could he not have gone abroad on these fatiguing journeys to escape such companionship, he would have felt utterly desperate. He certainly would cheerfully take any risks during the summer rather than longer endure the existing personal troubles. Lieutenant Kislingbury's only thought seemed to be that a sledge party should be sent down to Littleton Island and Cape Sabine to leave a store of supplies, which merely reflected the latest opinion of the doctor. If this had been done, the entire expedition might have escaped the doom that followed. Greely and Lockwood were willing to take great risks to accomplish the mission and make great achievements, while Pavy and Kislingbury were more concerned with planning that would assure their safety.

Lockwood and his team started on the trip to the west on April 25, 1883. They took with them enough supplies to last them for a month. They returned a month later, as planned. The comments of Lockwood, in regard to the expedition, and how matters were at the station, were as follows: "No such word as 'failed' to write this time, I am thankful to say, but the happy reflection is mine that I accomplished more than any one expected, and more than I myself dared hope, the discovery of the western sea, and hence the western coast line of Grinnell Land."

In order to satisfy his desire to get away from the fort, Lockwood took one more trip to the northwest, a trip lasting only four days. As no relief ship had arrived, on the ninth of August, the twenty-five expedition members pushed off from shore in the *Lady Greely*, towing three boats with supplies. Fifty days later, after the *Lady Greely* had been caught in the ice and crushed and the men had experienced thirty days on an ice floe, they finally reached land again.

Arrangements were made for building out of stones and ice the necessary huts for protection during the coming winter, should it be their fate to remain there. While this work was progressing, it was decided that the daily rations would have to be reduced. Lockwood expressed the opinion that they had only three chances for their lives: first, the chance of finding an American cache at Cape Sabine; secondly, a chance of crossing the straits, here thirty-five miles wide, when their provisions were gone; thirdly, the chance of being able to kill enough game for their support during the winter. None of these chances would happen.

A small cache left by the rescue team on the wrecked *Proteus* was discovered. They not only found news about the wreck of the *Proteus*, but also a copy of the Army Register for 1883, in which appeared Lockwood's name as a first lieutenant. Rice also succeeded in discovering the English cache with two hundred and forty rations, the cache left by the *Neptune* in 1882, and the stores brought from the wreck of the *Proteus* in 1883, all of which was hailed with delight by the party.

On the twenty-fifth of November, Lockwood recorded in his journal the following: "I have intended writing a letter home recounting my experiences since leaving Fort Conger, but so far the discomforts of this life have prevented me. It is difficult to get the blubber-lamp for more than a few minutes during the day, and sometimes it can not be had at all. The lamp is blown out every evening when we are ready to retire, which is generally about eight o'clock."

Lockwood gave expression to the following: "These short rations make me feel the cold dreadfully. It is a constant effort to keep one's hands and feet comfortable, or even comparatively so. I find my spirits first up and then down. Sometimes, when I think of the months before us of this life of misery and suffering, I do not see how we can possibly pull through. At other times I feel much more hopeful; but this is a life of inexpressible misery."

Lockwood was greatly pleased to learn that his comrades had formed a high opinion of his father from what Greely and he had occasionally told them.

On the twenty-first of January, Lockwood had a talk with Greely about his own health. Lockwood, who now became despondent and apathetic, endeavored to peer into the future, and wondered whether his bones were really to be left in the Arctic regions. He mourned over the fact that he had not been as good a son or as kind a brother as he might have been, and hoped that the dear ones at home would remember him as he wished to be, and not as he had been. As to the end, he hoped it would come soon, whatever it might be.

The concluding paragraph in Lieutenant Lockwood's journal was written on the seventh of April, 1884, and allude to the sickness and death of his two comrades. In the last allusion that he makes to himself, he speaks of his excessive weakness, and of the fact that he could not rise from his sleeping bag without great difficulty. His death occurred two days later.

The next day, April 10, the last sad rites were performed over the remains of Lockwood, and he was interred with the others on Cemetery Ridge, Lieutenant Greely reading the Episcopal service.

In 1884 a rescue expedition was organized and dispatched for the relief of the Greely exploring party. That expedition was composed of a squadron of three ships, the *Thetis*, the *Bear*, and the *Alert*, under the command of US Navy Commander Winfield S. Schley. They left St. John's on the twelfth of May and, after the usual tribulations along the western coast of Greenland, reached the vicinity of Cape Sabine and discovered the Greely party at Camp Clay, on Sunday, the twenty-second of June, seventy-three days after the death of Lieutenant Lockwood. As soon as the survivors could be relieved and transferred to the ships, the remains of the dead were exhumed with care and taken to the ships for transportation to the United States, except the remains of the Eskimo Frederik, which were left at Disko.

On Thursday, the seventeenth of July, the relief expedition arrived at St. John's, Newfoundland, where they were kindly welcomed and the tidings of their arrival promptly telegraphed to the anxious multitudes in the United States. Complete arrangements were made for the continuous transportation of the living and the dead to their homes. In a dispatch sent by the secretary of the navy to Commander Schley on the day of his return, he said, "Preserve tenderly the remains of the heroic dead," and that order was duly obeyed. The bodies of the dead were placed in metallic caskets, and the squadron sailed from St. John's on the twenty-sixth of July, arriving at Portsmouth, New Hampshire, on the second of August.

The squadron then sailed for New York, and on its arrival, on the eighth of August, was received with great enthusiasm. Here the remains of the dead were delivered to the custody of the army commander at Governor's Island, by whom the final dispositions were made. The remains of Lieutenant Lockwood were forwarded to Annapolis and placed under a military guard in the church of St. Anne, the church where the young hero had been baptized and confirmed and had received his first communion. The funeral was of a military character, and the attendance was very large, consisting of all the naval, military, and civil organizations of the city. The remains of the hero lie in the beautiful cemetery of the Naval Academy, overlooking the place of his birth and the scenes of his childhood. An appropriate tomb was erected over them, bearing this inscription: "James Booth Lockwood, Lieutenant United States Army, Born at Annapolis, Maryland, October 9, 1852, Died at Cape Sabine, April 9, 1884. The sufferings of this present time are not worthy to be compared with the glory that shall be revealed in us."

The rector of St. Anne's church, William S. Southgate, said, "There is a peculiar appropriateness in the ordering of events that brings James Booth Lockwood here to be buried. Born in this parish, baptized here, confirmed in St. Anne by Bishop Whittingham, April 19, 1868, he received his first communion at this altar on Christmas day of the same year. The rector of the parish, who presented him for confirmation and administered to him the holy communion, has just been called suddenly to his rest."

When the news of Lockwood's fate was known at Fort Leavenworth, Kansas, arrangements were made, by those who had known and loved him there, to erect a tablet to his memory in the handsome post chapel at Fort Levenworth. When completed it was placed in a conspicuous position and bore the following inscription: "In Memoriam James B. Lookwood, First Lieutenant Twenty-Third Infantry, a member of the Greely Polar Expedition, Died at Cape Sabine, Grinnell Land, April 9, 1884." This tablet was erected chiefly at the expense of Lockwood's old regiment.

On the twentieth of July, 1884, the Rev. Dr. John S. Lindsay, of St. John's Church in Georgetown, delivered a sermon in which he alluded to the return of the Greely Expedition, and especially to Lieutenant Lockwood, who had been one of his parishioners.

James Booth Lockwood was truly a brave man. While much of his drive may have come from his desire to please his father and make him proud of him, nonetheless he put himself at all kinds of risk to accomplish any task assigned to him. Even though he felt that he was in desolate places when stationed in the desert and in the prairie land, he still volunteered for the duty in even a more isolated place. His devotion to duty, and his willingness to support the desires of his commander, certainly contributed to his demise. Even though he was suffering from rheumatism and apparently circulatory problems in his feet, he still insisted that he should do things reflecting favorably on the expedition.

His father and the rest of his family were certainly proud of James Booth Lockwood. His father died in 1899, some eighteen years after James's death. His mother died in 1894, five years before his father's death. His sister Eliza lost her husband, Charles Sigsbee, in 1923, and she herself died in 1926. All the rest of her family married and had children, except for Mary Murray. More than one of James's nephews were honored with the name of James Booth. James's brother, Henry, named his son James Booth Lockwood, and he in turn named his son James Booth Lockwood, Jr., and then came James Booth Lockwood III. What an honor Lieutenant James Booth Lockwood brought to his family and his country.

4

Frederick Foster Kislingbury

(1846–1884)

FREDERICK FOSTER KISLINGBURY was born in East Ilsley, Berkshire, England, on December 25, 1846. He was the third of ten children born to John and Maria Chenery Kislingbury.

Frederick's father, John Kislingbury, was born on October 11, 1814, in Kintbury, Berkshire, England. Frederick's mother was born in Malton, Suffolk, England, about 1821. Frederick's parents, John and Maria, were married on September 20, 1840, at the Christ Church on Newgate Street in London, England.

Frederick's older brother, Frank, was born about 1842 in East Ilsley. His older sister, Ellen, was born about 1845 in East Ilsley. Two of his younger brothers, John and Harry, were born in East Ilsley, John about 1847 and Harry about 1850, as well as two younger sisters, Jessie about 1852 and Ada sometime before 1855.

About 1856 the family moved to the United States, settling in Rochester, New York. A sister-in-law, Margaret Kislingbury, who was a widow, and her daughter, Maria, had settled in Rochester a year or two ahead of them. Margaret was a witness at Frederick's parents' wedding in London. Frederick's youngest brother, William, and two more sisters, Harriet and Kate, were born in Rochester: William about 1857, Harriet about 1858, and Kate about 1859. Frederick's father's occupation in Rochester was that of a house painter.

Frederick received a common school education and began a mercantile career. He was employed by Smith, Perkins & Company, occupying a responsible position in their store. This career was cut short on July 26, 1864, as he volunteered for service with Company E of the Fifty-Fourth Regiment of New York at Rochester, New

York, for a period of one hundred days. He was assigned the rank of private. He was mustered out at Rochester on November 10, 1864, after being on the sick list for the latter six weeks.

The following year, on June 3, 1865, Frederick enlisted again in the army. This time he was assigned to Company D of the Fourth US Infantry. At the end of the Civil War he was stationed at Detroit, Michigan, with duty as chief clerk of the Department of the Lakes. On March 1, 1866, Frederick married Agnes Struther Bullock. Agnes was born in Amherstberg, Ontario, Canada, in 1843, the daughter of George and Agnes Findley Bullock. She lived in Windsor, Ontario, Canada, which is just across the river from Detroit, at the time of their marriage.

Agnes was the third of nine children, having four brothers and four sisters. Her father was a British major and her mother was of Scottish heritage. Probably the most famous of her brothers was Seth. He went to Helena, Montana Territory, in 1867 and ran for the Territorial Legislature. He was defeated. He did not give up, and in 1871 he was elected as a member of the Territorial Senate. During this time in the Senate, Seth was instrumental in creating Yellowstone National Park, the first ever United States National Park. After serving in the Senate, Seth was elected sheriff of Lewis and Clark County in 1873. He entered the hardware business and relocated to Deadwood, South Dakota in 1876. The day after his arrival, Wild Bill Hickok was shot in Deadwood. In 1877, Seth was appointed by Governor Pennington as the Lawrence County sheriff. In 1884, while on a mission to bring a horse thief back to Deadwood, he met Theodore Roosevelt, who at the time was a deputy sheriff from Medora, North Dakota. When Roosevelt was elected president, Seth organized a group of fifty cowboys, including Tom Mix, to ride in the president's inaugural parade in 1905. The Bullock Hotel, constructed by Seth in 1896 in Deadwood, South Dakota, stands today as a historic building.

Agnes's youngest sister, Alma, married George Wheeler Schofield. George had an outstanding military career, reaching the rank of brigadier general. Alma's brother-in-law was John McAllister Schofield. Schofield Barracks is a US Army installation located in Honolulu, Hawaii. It is named after Lieutenant General John

McAllister Schofield. He was sent to Hawaii in 1872 as secretary of war for President Andrew Johnson. So while Frederick Kislingbury did not come from a family of elite members, he certainly married into such a family. I'm sure that these people were models for him to follow.

Frederick and Agnes had their first child, Harry Howard Grant Kislingbury, who was born at Detroit, Michigan on June 18, 1867. Frederick's enlistment expired on June 3, 1868, and he reenlisted one month later, on July 3, 1868. He was assigned duty with Company K, Fourth US Infantry, and six months later was transferred to General Services, serving as a sergeant at Omaha, Nebraska. His mother, Maria Kislingbury, died during this period at her home in Rochester. Frederick was discharged on June 9, 1869, and he went back to Detroit just in time for the birth of his second son, Walter Frederick Kislingbury, born on August 13, 1869.

On February 2, 1870, Frederick reenlisted in the army and was again assigned to General Services, likely at Detroit. His next two sons, both named Louis Pelouze Kislingbury, were born at Detroit. The first Louis was born on December 25, 1870, his father's birthday, and the second Louis was born on October 2, 1872. I assume the first Louis died prior to the birth of the second Louis. Neither of them was living by 1880. Frederick had been appointed to the command of a company of scouts.

After some time he was returned to Detroit. Frederick was discharged on February 1, 1873, at Detroit with the rank of sergeant. Here he applied for a commission in the army. He passed the examination with great credit, and in October 1873, he was appointed second lieutenant.

Lieutenant Kislingbury was called to duty at Fort Jay, Fort Columbus, New York Harbor. He waited there for assignment, which came in December, when he was assigned duty at Fort Concho, Texas. His duty there was to assist in building a telegraph network across the southern plains. He moved his family there, and it was there that he met Lieutenant Greely. Kislingbury provided guard support while Greely supervised the installation the telegraph system.

During his assignment at Fort Concho, his youngest two sons were born at the fort. Douglass Ebstein Lohman Kislingbury was born on March 2, 1874, and Wheeler Schofield Kislingbury was born on June 21, 1876. Wheeler Schofield obviously was named in respect to Agnes's brother-in-law George Wheeler Schofield.

Shortly after the birth of his son Wheeler, Frederick was transferred to Dakota Territory, where he first had responsibility for procuring lumber for building purposes. Soon, however, he was assigned duty negotiating with the Indians in an attempt to promote peace. During the period from 1877 to 1880, Frederick had duty at Fort Yates, Fort Custer, Fort Big Horn, and Fort Buford, all in Dakota Territory. His home station during this period was Standing Rock, Dakota Territory.

A newspaper article published in the *Bismarck Tri-Weekly Tribune* on November 16, 1877, probably best describes the type of duty in which Kislingbury was involved:

> Standing Rock, D. T., Nov. 12th, 1877.—Lieut. Kislingbury, of the 11th infantry, who, with a small party from this post, has been scouting in the neighborhood of the Black Hills since the middle of last month, returned yesterday morning. On their way home the whole party narrowly escaped destruction by a large party of Indians on the north fork of the Cheyenne river, supposed to belong to the Brule Agency. A few straggling Indians—not over a dozen—had been met, and, in accordance with instruction, disarmed. From some of these information of the neighborhood of an Indian camp was gathered.
>
> The camp, when found, numbered about one hundred Indians, who met Lieut. Kislingbury's party, uninvited, armed and stripped to the breech-cloth, and as the saying is, took the little scouting party in. In the language of a member of our post trader's establishment, who was an interested spectator, "he was never more scared in his life. He didn't consider his top-knot worth a red." The amount of it was Lieut. Kislingbury's little party escaped by giving up the arms and releasing the captured Indians. There is no

doubt the party were fortunate in escaping on so reasonable terms.

Ten days later, on November 26, the following article appeared in the Bismarck Tribune:

> Standing Rock, D.T., Nov.19, via Bismarck, Nov. 22.—The special dispatch from Bismarck in your issue of the 16th, headed "Scared by Savages," does great injustice to Lieut. Kislingberry and his party. Lieut. Kislingberry did not surrender the arms of his party. He had captured twelve Indians with arms on the 5th inst., and in trying to find their camp, was surrounded by about fifty more, who were within less than one hundred yards of him, and numerous enough to have killed his party at the first volley. Observing hostile demonstrations on the part of the Indians, he parleyed with their chief, invited him to come unto the agency and feigned to treat them as friendly Indians. Finding that they were not disposed to come in and were posted and prepared to attack him, he voluntarily released his prisoners and restored them their arms. His party consisted of only seven white men, including himself, seven Indian scouts and two volunteer Indians. It was very mortifying to Lieut. Kislingberry to release his prisoners and restore their arms, but a different course would have been foolhardiness. When he found that a fight would result so disasterously, he displayed high moral courage and good sense in avoiding it. None of his friends would have escaped alive if a fight had taken place.
>
> Very respectfully, W. P. Carlin, Lieut. Col. 17th Infantry, Com. Post

Lieutenant Colonel Carlin must have had great respect for Lieutenant Kislingbury. He was his commander for nearly two years.

While Frederick seemed to cope with the death of two of his sons, the death of his mother, and being vilified for his actions toward the Indians, something happened in April 1878 that was extremely difficult for him: his wife, Agnes, died. Frederick went to Michigan to ensure that she had a proper burial. She was buried in the churchyard of St. John's Anglican Church in Windsor, Canada, across the river from Detroit. Agnes's sister, Jessie, accompanied him back to Standing Rock to care for Frederick's four sons.

The relationship between Frederick and his sister-in-law, Jessie, became closer, and in the middle of 1880, they married. Now stationed at Fort Custer, Montana Territory, Kislingbury left the fort for days at a time, sometimes weeks, checking on Indian movements and picking up information. In December 1880, when he was 150 miles from the fort, he received a dispatch from the fort informing him that his wife had contracted mountain fever. He traveled back to the fort on horseback as rapidly as he could, through the deep snow and bitter cold. By the time he got back to the fort, she had lapsed into a coma. She died soon after his arrival. The children were again without a mother.

Kislingbury was now in a desperate condition. In the midst of all of this, Greely contacted Kislingbury concerning the planned Arctic expedition. After some discussion between Greely and Kislingbury, it was determined that Kislingbury would join the expedition as second-in-command.

Greely and Kislingbury had different concepts as leaders. Greely was of the order that discipline must be maintained at any cost. This, in his opinion, was the only way that he could maintain control over his troops. Kislingbury moved more to negotiation strategy. This would be a problem between them later on.

Since Kislingbury was going on the expedition, he needed to find someone who would care for his children. Douglass, now seven years old, was put on a stagecoach and sent to Deadwood to live with his Uncle Seth and Aunt Martha Bullock. Seth and Martha had three children of their own. Wheeler, the youngest of Kislingbury's children, now five years old, went to live with his Uncle George Wheeler and Aunt Emelia Alma (Bullock) Schofield. Walter, soon to be twelve years old, went to live with his Uncle John P. Kislingbury, in Rochester, New York. Harry, the oldest at fourteen years old, probably went to live with the Charles Clark family in Detroit, Michigan. Clark had grown up in Rochester, New York, and was a schoolmate there of Kislingbury's. They had been friends for the past twenty-five years.

Kislingbury arrived on June 2 at Washington, DC, where he met with a few of the party members and they departed on June 6, 1881, for St. John's, Newfoundland, on the *Proteus*, the ship that would take them on to Lady Franklin Bay. Upon their arrival at St. John's, Kislingbury supervised the loading of the materials that would be taken with them to Lady Franklin Bay. They departed St. John's on July 7. On the way to Lady Franklin Bay, Kislingbury wrote letters indicating how much he missed his boys:

> Poor little men! When I stop to think how I have torn myself from them I almost give way. I can hardly realize that I am now separated from them, everything from Fort Custer to here was done with such a rush and now it is much like a dream.

He wrote home telling his family not to worry about him, an indication that he realized that there was danger ahead. He seemed to be dreading the decision he had made to go to the Arctic region and leave his children behind.

After stopping at Greenland to pick up Doctor Pavy, the two Eskimos, the dogs, the material for the quarters, and supplies, they pushed through the ice to Fort Conger at Lady Franklin Bay.

A few days before reaching Lady Franklin Bay, Kislingbury wrote a letter to his children. Part of the letter described the journey and the activities at Greenland. Some of the letter was of a more personal nature, and it tells how he misses his children and recognizes the perils that may follow. He assures them, however, that he expects to return:

> The Governor of Disco has your addresses, and his wife is to make and send you something for Christmas, and I think it altogether likely that you will find something else turn up then to show you that I have not altogether forgotten you—that is, provided certain instructions I sent from St. John's are attended to. But just think what a long time poor papa

has to wait before he can hear from his pets again. Please God, however, that it may only be for a year, and that the ship may come or get through to us next year. Imagine, my boys, what a treat news will be to us. You must not worry about me should the ship not be able to reach us. In case the ship doesn't get to us the second year, we will get back all right someway. You must pray for papa—ask God to give him strength of will to go through manfully the long night, that he may be able to endure his hardships, and that he may be successful. I pray for all my darlings morning and night and many times when I'm lost in thought, and if my mind could be read it would be found that papa is always thinking of his boys. I am certain my little men are striving hard in their studies. I feel that you will both bend your energies to become everything you know papa desires in you. Above all things be truthful, and never, oh never, my darlings, stoop to anything dishonorable, no matter how small may be the act. Among your comrades be charitable, friendly, and benevolent. Let these traits be distinguishable in all your acts through life. I wish you both to visit your mamma's grave at Sandwich as often as you can do so, and see that everything is in order. The flowers should be taken up in the Winter and kept until the following Spring. You must also call on Father O'Connor whenever you pass the school. He wrote me a very kind letter and said that he would be pleased to see you frequently.

After they unloaded the supplies and constructed the quarters, the *Proteus* was ready to return to St. John's. The ice in the bay was not cooperating, however, and the ship was stuck in the bay, possibly to be there for the entire winter.

Greely and Kislingbury appeared to disagree on what type of military discipline was required of not only the enlisted men but also the officers. This necessity for discipline would be demonstrated several times in the future. It appears that Kislingbury thought it unnecessary to arise in the mornings as early as Greely felt. This resulted in a verbal reprimand by Greely to Kislingbury. As evidenced by his earlier letters, Kislingbury really wanted to get back home, which was an additional incentive for him to write the following letter to Greely:

> Fort Conger, Lady Franklin Bay, Aug 26, 1881.
> 1st Lieut A. W. Greely,
> 5th Cavalry, Acting Signal Officer
> and Assistant/Commanding
> International Polar Expedition.
>
> Sir: In conversation at breakfast this morning you said in effect that if I could not agree to certain ideas of yours I "had better go." This I take that my services are no longer desirable to you as a member of this expedition.
>
> After receiving such a suggestion or invitation to go from my commanding officer, because, possibly, I expressed myself too freely, the only thing I feel left for me to do is to be relieved from duty as a member of the Expedition and ordered to report to the Chief Signal Officer of the Army. On other occasions you have seen fit to find fault with me over matters in which I may have been lacking, or which might have been annoying to you, but of no practical importance, and from your final request of this morning, already stated, it will doubtless be better that I go.
>
> You and I disagreed this morning because I differed from you in the matter of early breakfasting. I objected to being compelled or required to breakfast so early. You would have me breakfast when the men do at 7 a.m. I would not agree that the officers should be required to rise at the same time and breakfast at the same time with the men. You then said that I "had better go" unless I saw fit to do as you required in such matters. If I had been accused of anything of a serious nature warranting you in telling me this or anything tending to a necessity for a severance of my connection with the Expedition I would act differently in this matter—would doubtless resist being relieved—but if such a trivial matter as this morning causes you to express such a wish as you

did—so readily—I cannot but feel that the comfort, peace and harmony, & even success of the Expedition, may be jeopardized if I remain. It is possible that I'm at fault but, if so, it can be only because I've been too candid.

The sacrifices I make in parting from the Expedition will be in every way of a serious nature. Pecuniarily, I place myself in a very embarrassing position. The years pay and allowances paid me in advance by the government has been nearly all absorbed in the liquidation of my liabilities which would have been settled from month to month had I not come on this Expedition but which were paid by me before I left—knowing of course that there would be no opportunity to negotiate many matters during my absence.

But the many personal sacrifices I make are too numerous to particularize. I have also been put to no inconsiderate expense in the matter of personal outfit for clothing suitable for this climate, and incidentals occasioned by changing station such a distance—which was not by any means covered by allowances received from the Government. I shall therefore expect the Government to be at least lenient to me, or thoughtful, considering my pecuniary matters, in some manner that may suggest itself during the ensuing nine months—until I have reimbursed my advance pay and allowances and can commence again to draw my regular monthly pay.

It is hardly necessary to say anything further. Yet I shall leave the Expedition in sorrow. I am become fond of Arctic life. I see many bright hopes ahead. Physically I feel myself competent to endure the privations, hardships and depressing influences incidental to life here, and contemplated working hard for the success of the Expedition.

But I must be in the way or you could not have told me what you did this morning and rather than be the slightest bar to the present or future success of the Expedition, I abandon all my bright expectations; and feel that it would be better that I go before it becomes too late for me to do so.

The *Proteus* is still within reaching distance. With the assistance of enough men to help me take my things off to ship I can reach her over the ice. As there is a probability of the vessel being obliged to winter in the Arctic, I would ask that enough subsistence and antiscorbutics sufficient to last me until next season be furnished me.

I would also ask that you furnish me a letter to hand to the Chief Signal Officer of the Army explaining this matter and the state of my pecuniary affairs.

I am, Sir, very respectfully, Your obt servant, Fred F. Kislingbury, 2d Lt 11 Inf.

Greely responded the same day with an order relieving Kislingbury and allowing him to return to St. John's with the *Proteus*:

Fort Conger, Grinnell Land.
August 26, 1881.

Orders No. 5. 2d Lieut F. F. Kislingbury, 11th Infty, A. S. O. is at his own request relieved from duty as a member of this Expedition, and, returning by the Steamer "*Proteus*" to Saint Johns, Newfoundland, will report in person without delay to the Chief Signal Officer of the Army at Washington, D.C.

A. W. Greely
1st Lieut. 5th Cav. A. S. O. and Asst. Comdg. The L.F.B. Expedition.

Kislingbury packed his belongings and headed out the half mile to the shoreline. But alas, the *Proteus* had managed to get through the ice and now was on her way southbound. She was within sight, but Kislingbury had no means to communicate that the ship should come back to get him. He was stuck with the expedition until another ship returned, hopefully, in the summer of 1882, the next year. Since Kislingbury missed the boat, Greely needed to amend order number five, which he had just issued:

Fort Conger, Grinnell Land.
August 27, 1881.

Orders No. 6. The execution of order No. 5 current series from these Headquarters being rendered impracticable by the departure of the Steamship "*Proteus*" its provisions are so far modified as to direct 2d Lieut. F. F. Kislingbury, 11th Infty, A.S.O. to proceed from this place to Saint Johns Newfoundland, by the first visiting Steamship. In the mean time Lieut. Kislingbury will be considered as on waiting orders at this place.

1st Lieut. 5th Cav. A. S. O. and Asst. Comdg. The L.F.B. Expedition.

With this order, Kislingbury was no longer a part of the expedition. His position as second-in-command no longer applied. This position was given to Lockwood, and Kislingbury was just along for the ride, waiting for the ship to arrive the following summer. Much of his time was spent hunting, probably, with Long, the best hunter on the expedition. He also helped cache supplies that would be used along the way for the farthest north trip during the summer of 1882.

Kislingbury liked taking strolls. In one particular case it caused quit a panic among the members of the expedition. He checked out from the fort, but seven hours later he had not returned. The temperature had dipped to fifty-four degrees below zero. A relief party was sent out to look for him and found that he was all right. He had misjudged the time for the trip that he was taking.

By July 1882, Kislingbury became quit anxious over the ship returning. He continually checked for open water to see if the conditions were favorable for a ship to get through. By the end of August, all hope of a ship arriving in 1882 ended. When the spring of 1883 came and there was no sign of the relief ship, Kislingbury did not appear nearly as anxious. He continued to hunt and help with other duties, although he still was not officially a member of the expedition.

On August 8, 1884, as no relief ship had arrived, the party

departed Fort Conger with the *Lady Greely* launch, with three boats filled with personnel and supplies tied behind. A week later, on August 15, facing problems with the ice in the sound, some of the members of the expedition felt that they should try to return to Fort Conger. Kislingbury had made recommendations to Greely concerning staying near the land or guiding the launch toward the center of the sound. In every instance, Greely would not accept his advice. Kislingbury was among those who thought that it would be best to turn around. Greely disagreed. Doctor Pavy came up with the idea that he would announce, as his professional opinion, that Lt. Greely was too ill to continue the leadership of the expedition, and that Lt. Kislingbury, by virtue of his rank, would assume command. Kislingbury and Sergeant Rice agreed to the plan, but one more person had to agree for it to be implemented. That was the leader of the enlisted men, Sergeant Brainard. Brainard promptly declined to take part in any such plan, and as a result the plan was scuttled.

On August 18 Greely fell off the launch. Kislingbury and Lockwood pulled him back to safety. But two weeks later Greely reprimanded Kislingbury for discussing their position with the men, even though, according to Greely, Kislingbury was not part of the expedition and, as such, should not come under his authority. Greely felt that it encouraged discontentment.

According to Lockwood's journal entry of October 7, 1883, Sergeant Connell was reduced in rank for using intemperate language. Greely informed Lockwood that if they returned to America, he would prefer charges against Connell for mutiny. He further stated that he would prefer the same charges against Doctor Pavy and Kislingbury when they returned to America.

Near the end of October, Kislingbury ruptured himself while on a sledging journey. He suffered from this injury for nearly eight weeks before it was healed. At times the pain was so excruciating that he fainted.

It wasn't until April 1884, after Lockwood had died, that Greely made the following entry in his journal concerning Kislingbury:

> On Lockwood's death I felt it obligatory to order Lt. Kislingbury to duty with the expedition; a step which had

> not been taken, first, because Lt. Kislingbury had never requested it, and secondly, in case of my death his return would have thrown the command on him to the detriment of Lt. Lockwood, who had labored hard and successfully on all occasions. I complimented Lieutenant Kislingbury highly on his labors the preceding autumn, when he had spared neither strength nor exposure to collect our scattered supplies, and had overworked and seriously strained himself.

This entry certainly affirms the belief that Kislingbury had been relieved of duty with the expedition and, as such, was not obligated to follow Greely's orders. But just five days after making this declaration, Greely made the following entry in his journal:

> Lt. Kislingbury shows very decided mental derangement, and the doctor informs me that my heart is in a very dangerous condition. The death of Lieutenant Lockwood and the mental incapacity of Lt. Kislingbury materially changed the condition of affairs when my death seemed imminent. If I should die, Sergeant Brainard would be my legal successor.

It appears that Greely was using the same argument that was used against him by Pavy, Rice, and Kislingbury in August the year before to wrestle control away from him. Now he was using it to wrestle control away from Kislingbury. Yet it does appear that the mental capacity of Kislingbury had diminished. Brainard states the following in his journal on May 1:

> Lt. Kislingbury's mind is almost gone. Only a few days ago he talked so hopefully of the future and the happy meeting with his young sons. Yesterday he threw himself on the small sledge outside and, weeping like a child, he said, it is hopeless. I cannot fight longer!

According to entries made in Jacob Bender's journal on May 11 and 12, Greely did restore Kislingbury's status as part of the expedition but denied it the next day. On May 11 Bender wrote the following:

> Lt. Greely acted the man for once in his life and spoke to Lt. Kislingbury, and asked his, Lt. Kislingbury to forgive him for not putting him on duty sooner.

On May 12 Bender recorded the following entry:

> Lt. G. and Lt. K. on the war path. Lt. Kislingbury asked Lt. Greely to give Lt. Kislingbury an order publishing his being put on duty, and a letter in which Lt. G. would state what he said the day before, the latter denying of having said or came to Lt. Kislingbury, and called Lt. Kislingbury a liar. This all in front of enlisted men.

Kislingbury continued to weaken until, on June 1, he passed away. His death is chronicled by Brainard:

> Lt. Kislingbury became unconscious at 8 a.m. and breathed his last at 3 p.m. The last thing he did was to sing the Doxology in a clear but weak voice and, falling back in his sleeping bag, was soon in the embrace of Death."

A newspaper reported that while sinking into a peaceful slumber he whispered these last words: "Aggie! Aggie! Aggie!" meaning his first wife. Greely read the burial service that afternoon, and Kislingbury's body was moved to the ice field the next morning.

Three weeks later the rescue ship arrived. Kislingbury's body was taken from the ice field and placed in a vat containing an alcoholic preservative. When the rescue ship arrived at St. John's, Kislingbury's body was placed on the ship, the *Bear*, in a metallic container and sealed shut. The *Bear* then traveled to Governor's Island in New York, arriving on August 8. A funeral salute was given, with shots fired, and the bodies were unloaded. Secretary Lincoln and generals Sheridan and Hancock were present. Kislingbury's remains were placed on a barge and then taken to Rochester, New York, for burial. He was buried in the Mount Hope Cemetery on August 10, 1884.

The New York Times had spent at least months, if not years, searching for a chance to write a story about cannibalism. The New York Times reporter suggested to the family that the coffin be removed from the grave and opened, as it might not contain a body. The family could ill afford to pay for such a procedure, and the county coroner would not. The New York Times paid an undertaker and a doctor to do the task. When the casket was opened, the body was found to be in a very dilapidated condition. It had now been two and a half months since Kislingbury's death, and his body had lain out on the ice field for three weeks, was placed in an alcoholic solution for another three weeks, and then had been relocated to the sealed casket for four more weeks. The body was identified as that of Kislingbury by his brother, John, who noticed the false teeth and the marks on the body's right toe, which had been injured earlier in Kislingbury's career when a horse stepped on it. The doctor concluded that the openings between two of his ribs had been caused by a knife. John stated that he was "perfectly satisfied with the result and was glad that it had been done."

Lieutenant Frederick F. Kislingbury was, without doubt, a very brave man. Serving in the Indian Wars, his motive was to encourage peace, even though he put his life in danger at times to achieve it. While it may not have been in his best interest to join the Arctic expedition, his motives were just, and he knew the perils of such a mission. His willingness to risk his life cost him his life.

Probate court was held in Rochester, New York, to determine guardianship of Kislingbury's four sons. The court ruled that three of the children, namely Harry, Douglass, and Wheeler, should be placed in the guardianship of Charles L. Clark of Detroit, Michigan. The other son, Walter, was placed under the guardianship of John P. Kislingbury, Frederick's brother, residing in Rochester. Through Mr. Clark's efforts, the United States Congress passed a bill authorizing the monthly payment of ten dollars to each of the sons until each obtained the age of twenty-one years. In a letter written in 1885 to General Hazen, Greely's superior, Clark writes the following: "Harry is still attending the Michigan Military Academy. The other two boys are still with me and are getting along nicely." The other two boys he is referring to are Douglass and Wheeler. In 1887, in a court in Rochester, New York, John P. Kislingbury was appointed temporary guardian of Douglass and general guardian of Walter. Another brother to Frederick Kislingbury, Willaim Kislingbury, was granted temporary guardianship of Wheeler.

The oldest son, Harry, became a railroad engineer. He traveled throughout the southwest. He first was married to Anna Hawks. They had a daughter, born on July 16, 1896, in Coconino County, Arizona. He married Catherine Christman in El Paso, Texas, on April 14, 1910. In 1920 he was living in Winslow, Arizona. He spent some of his train engineering life in Mexico, where he nearly escaped death when the train he was engineering went off the end of a bridge that had been blown up. The inscription "Harry Kislingbury '89" is written on the wall above the Dripping Springs trail in the Grand Canyon, apparently written by Harry. His wife died in Holbrook, Arizona, on April 18, 1939. Harry died on March 1, 1943, and is buried in the Pioneer cemetery in Prescott, Arizona.

Walter lived in Rochester through 1889; however, in 1890 he joined the army at Fort Sherman, Idaho. He was assigned duty with Company E of the Fourth Infantry. He was discharged in 1894 after serving a little over three years. He apparently moved to Arizona after his discharge. He married Laura Coburn, and they had three sons: Francis, born in 1894, who died in infancy; Walter John Lind, born in 1895; and Henry Dadey, born in 1897. All three were born in Coconino County, Arizona. Walter died in El Paso, Texas, on September 3, 1903, at the age of thirty-three.

According to family lore, Douglass married Lillie Mae Kislingbury, the daughter of his uncle, John P. Kislingbury. A birth record of one of their children lists his mother's maiden name as Lillie M. Dickson. The marriage took place in New York sometime prior to 1897. They lived in various states. In 1900 they were living in New York, in 1903 in South Dakota, and in 1905 and 1910 they were back in New York; in 1916 they lived in Missouri and in 1920 in Lincoln, Nebraska. They had several children including Marion, Fuller, Elizabeth, Graham, and Enid. At some point they moved to San Mateo, California, where Douglas died on November 20,

1946. His wife, Lillie, died in San Mateo, California, on December 10, 1965.

Wheeler married Catherine Wahl on October 20, 1896, in Rochester. They had three children: Wheeler, born about 1898 in New York; Dorthey, born in 1899, also in New York; and Agnes, born in 1902 in California. Wheeler became a brakeman for the railroad and traveled the southwest United States. On August 14, 1913, Wheeler married Eda Agatha Furrer in San Francisco, California. Wheeler and Eda (Edith) had at least one child, Harry, born in 1920. Wheeler died in San Francisco on March 10, 1952. Eda died in 1955, and his first wife, Catherine, died in 1965.

5

Octave Pierre Pavy

(1844–1884)

OCTAVE PIERRE PAVY, also spelled Pavie, was born in New Orleans, Louisiana, on June 22, 1844. He was the youngest of three children born to Pierre Joseph Pavy and Caroline Pavy. His father, Pierre Joseph, known as PJ, was born in France about 1811. PJ was the son of the elder Pierre Joseph Pavie and Marie Magdaleane Pardou. Octave's mother, Caroline Henri Rentrop, was born in St. Mary's Parish, Louisiana, on December 11, 1815. She was the daughter of Peter Henri Rentrop and Marguerite Bertrand. Peter was born about 1789 in Germany, and Marguerite was a native of Louisiana, born there about 1793. Pierre Joseph Pavy and Caroline Henri Rentrop were married in St. Martinville, Louisiana on January 16, 1838.

Octave's older brother, Alfred Henry Pavy, was born in New Orleans on January 18, 1841. Octave's sister, Louise, was born in New Orleans in 1842. After a short illness, Louise died at the residence of her grandmother Marquerite Bertrand Rentrop in Berwick Bay, Louisiana, on July 22, 1852. She was only ten years old.

Little is known of the early life of the Pavy family. The family moved to France when Octave was a child, probably around 1855. Octave's brother, Alfred, returned to Louisiana in 1865. Octave received most of his education in France, and after study in the sciences and the arts, he graduated from the University of Paris in 1866. Octave became interested in the medical field and studied medicine at the Medical Faculty of Paris. As a student in Paris he attracted the notice of eminent surgeons by his dexterity with the scalpel. Before his course was completed, his wanderlust nature became manifest, and he soon forced himself upon the attention of the French government by a series of daring expeditions in Africa, Australia, New Zealand, and Iceland. His mother, Caroline, died in New Orleans on October 29, 1867, a year after Octave's graduation. Octave's father, Pierre Joseph Pavy, was back in France, but he returned to New Orleans in 1868. He and a partner, Joseph A. Hincks, as cotton merchants, operated a business in New Orleans called P. J. Pavy & Co.

It was during this time that Octave became involved with Therese Loiseau, possibly a relative of his, with whom he had a daughter, Berte Pavy, born in Paris on July 6, 1869.

Octave Pavy met and became acquainted with Gustave Lambert. Lambert had ambitions of reaching the North Pole using a hot-air balloon as transportation. He had had extensive exposure to the northern climate, as he had traveled on a whaler through the Bering Strait in 1865 and 1866. He had an intense desire to explore the North Pole region. He felt that reaching the pole via balloon travel was the way to go. A plan was decided upon and on June 27, 1869, the monster balloon *Le Pole Nord* made its maiden flight in Paris, France. The "car" that the passengers rode was attached to the balloon with sixty-four ropes. There were nine persons in the car on that first voyage, including Gaston Tissandier and Wilfrid de Fonvielle, the organizers of the expedition.

The test flight proved successful, lasting three or four hours and landing some distance from Paris. Octave Pavy was one of two doctors and one of twelve people who were selected to go on the balloon *Le Pole Nord* on its journey toward the North Pole. Pavy shared Lambert's enthusiasm for polar exploration and acted as his secretary in planning the expedition to the polar region. According to the Blairsville (Pennsylvania) Press, published in January 1869, the vessel was originally named *Faith in Science*, to the "great scandal of the religious world." This name, however, must have been replaced by the name *Le Pole Nord*, as it was referred to by that name on its maiden flight in June 1869.

Lambert's plan to reach the North Pole via balloon was postponed in 1870 with the onset of the Franco-Prussian War. In the French effort, Octave Pavy organized and equipped a body of infantryman and cavalry, consisting of veteran soldiers and sailors of French parentage who had been residing in North America. He served as leader of the group known as the Black Guerrillas. Phillips Beauregard, nephew of the noted American Confederate general P. T. Beauregard, served with him. Pavy's friend Gustave Lambert was killed in this war. As a result, the balloon expedition had to be canceled, thus putting aside Octave's dreams of polar exploration.

Octave Pavy's dreams were reignited when he found a new opportunity for polar exploration. He, along with Phillips Beauregard, returned to the United States in May 1871. Pavy had drafted a plan to attempt to reach the North Pole by way of the Bering Strait. Octave Pavy, Captain Mikes (first name unknown), Doctor George Chismore, and three others were to make the journey. Mikes had had experience in traveling by raft in the Atlantic Ocean in 1867. Chismore, who had already sailed on the Arctic Ocean, was a famous doctor from California. He had experience in Alaska while in the US Army and with the Western Union Extension Telegraph. The plan was to charter a ship that would sail from San Francisco to Siberian settlements. At the settlements they would take on board dogs for sledge purposes, dried salmon for food, and reindeer skins for clothing. This trip was to be scheduled so that they would reach the Bering Strait by the first of August in 1872. The plan called for having Pavy's party and stores deposited on Wrangell Island. If that became impossible because of ice hindering their way, they would land in the neighborhood of Cape Jakan or Herald Island. After landing and unloading the party and stores, the chartered boat would return to San Francisco.

They planned to bring over ten thousand pounds of materials, to be transported over eight hundred miles across Wrangell Island to the open polar sea to the north. There they would launch a raft that would carry the party and their supplies northward to the pole. After having reached the pole, they would return by way of Smith Sound, expecting to get to either Etah or Cape York. Arrangements would be made to have a ship take them to St. John's, Newfoundland, and back to the United States.

According to the Overland Monthly and Out West Magazine published in June 1872, Octave Pavy "from his own resources, equipped an expedition, which started from San Francisco in May, 1872." And according to an article in the New York Herald dated July 29, 1872, "Mr. Pavy, the gallant American explorer, who left San Francisco in the spring, will attempt a course northwest of Bering Strait." Both articles suggest that the expedition had already begun, and the former article states that Pavy paid for it from his own resources. Other articles state that the death of "a financial associate of Pavy's in San Francisco" caused the expedition to be canceled upon the eve of its departure.

In an article by Lilla May Pavy (who would become Octave Pavy's widow) in the North American Review in March 1886, she states, "The Arctic project for which Dr. Pavy had matured all plans, until within a few hours of departure from San Francisco, was suddenly brought to a close in June, 1872, by the death of his financial associate." None of the articles name the financial associate except for an article appearing in the Missouri State Genealogical Association Journal, which states, "Mr. Ralston, his American backer, suffered financial setback so the expedition was called off."

If "Mr. Ralston" was indeed the financier of the expedition, it would have been William Chapman Ralston, from San Francisco. Ralston, who was born in Ohio, began his career in New Orleans as a clerk. It is possible that Octave Pavy's father knew Ralston as a result of his father's business in New Orleans. Ralston moved to San Francisco in 1851. He had a desire to create a financial institution. He became a major investor in the Comstock Lode, a silver mine that was discovered in 1859. In 1864, through the resources he had accumulated, he created the Bank of California. He solicited assets to provide capital funds. Using funds from the bank, he invested in woolen mills, cigar factories, and the Alaska fur trade. He constructed an elaborate building for the bank. He also built expensive hotels and many other major buildings in San Francisco. Ralston dreamed so expansively, so expensively. His funds were often stretched by the breadth of his interests. He seemed always to skirt the edge of calamity. One of his desires was to harvest the seal herds in the Bering Sea. If in fact he agreed, with Octave Pavy, to finance the expedition to the North Pole via the Bering Strait, it is likely that the Alaska fur trade was his motivation.

The later part of 1871 and the spring of 1872 were spent preparing for the expedition. In 1873 the Comstock Lode closed, along with many banks. Ralston's kingdom began to close in on him. The Bank of California operated for two more years before examiners found out that the bank had fifteen million dollars' worth of debt but only five million dollars in assets. The bank was closed down. A day or two later Ralston died, apparently drowned in a nearby body of water; his death may have been due to a severe stroke, rather than drowning.

Whether financing for the expedition came from Pavy's own resources, from Ralston's resources, or from other resources cannot be confirmed. What is known is that Octave Pavy was disappointed in having again missed an opportunity at polar exploration.

There are many accounts of the activities of Octave Pavy during the years following his failure to execute the expedition of 1872. One report says, "For the next four years, sunk in despondency, the thwarted explorer became a vagabond living along the banks of the Missouri River, working at a series of menial jobs." But the report that is most interesting is that which appeared in the Kansas City Star (undated).

The article, titled, "WHEN DR. PAVY WAS A MISSOURI WINE MAKER," is centered around a winemaker living in Liberty, Missouri. Pavy, it seemed, would knock on doors asking for food and shelter. One evening he knocked on the door of James M. Jones. Jones was once a wealthy man, being the president of a bank in Liberty. The bank, however, had been robbed of about eighty thousand dollars by the James Gang. Jones sold all of his property except his residence to make up for the loss. He became engaged in the modest and not especially lucrative occupation of growing grapes on a hillside near his habitation and making wine from the grapes. Jones invited Pavy in and fed him and served him wine. Pavy praised him for the fine food but criticized the wine. He convinced Jones that he was an expert on winemaking and that the conditions were not right for making wine where he lived. Pavy suggested instead that he should make brandy, to which Jones agreed. Pavy was willing to show Jones how to make it. Pavy would peddle the brandy on the streets, and Jones would provide him with food and shelter.

One day Doctor Joseph M. Wood, a celebrated surgeon of the early days in Western Missouri, recognized Pavy and was surprised to see him peddling brandy on the streets. Pavy had shown up at the doctor's home in Kansas City some weeks earlier in a similar destitute condition as when he showed up at the Jones house, made his name known, and asked for aid. Doctor Wood gave him help, but no sooner had Doctor Wood begun to interest his friends on Pavy's behalf than the eccentric disappeared. Doctor Woods asked Doctor Pavy to assist him in an operation the afternoon of the day they met in Liberty, and Doctor Pavy accommodated him.

Some time later, Marsena Stone, a minister, found him wondering aimlessly along the Missouri River. Reverend Stone helped him get on his feet. He also trusted him sufficiently that he allowed his daughter, Lilla May Stone, to be courted by Octave Pavy. Octave and Lilla May went to New Orleans, where they were married on February 28, 1878. He returned to Missouri, where he enrolled at the Missouri Medical College in St. Louis. He graduated from the college in 1879.

This man Pavy, a man who sunk to the lowest of levels and a man who often reached for the top, remained in the area of Liberty until 1879. Manifesting at all times the keenest interest in accounts of exploring expeditions, especially those directed toward the far north, he finally entered into a correspondence on the subject with James Gordon Bennett, owner of the New York Herald and the ship *Jeannette*. Bennett, an Arctic enthusiast, obtained the cooperation and assistance of the United States government in fitting out an expedition to the pole through the Bering Strait. The expedition planned by Bennett was very similar to that which Pavy had planned in 1872. Pavy was engaged as surgeon on the expedition. Even though privately owned, the *Jeannette* was to sail under the orders of the United States Navy and subject to naval laws. As a result of these laws and regulations, which excluded a civilian surgeon from service on the *Jeannette*, Dr. Pavy was released. He had lost another chance of polar exploration.

The *Jeannette* departed from San Francisco on July 8, 1879 with thirty-one people aboard. She pushed northward to Alaska's Norton Sound, searching for a long overdue ship, the *Vega*. The last communication with the *Jeannette* was on August 27, 1879, before she started north toward Siberia. In September the ship was caught in an ice pack and drifted with it for the next twenty-one months. In June 1882 the pressure of the ice finally began to crush the *Jeannette*. Taking boats and supplies from the ship, the men headed back toward Siberia. Some of the expedition members survived; however, many died, including the famous explorer George Washington DeLong.

But Octave Pavy wasn't giving up on going to the polar region. Captain Henry W. Howgate, an officer with the United States Signal Corps, planned an expedition to Lady Franklin Bay pending financial approval by Congress. Northern exploration was not new to Howgate, as he had had prior experience in 1877 and 1878 aboard the ship *Florence*, going to the Cumberland Gulf and Disko Bay. Octave Pavy was accepted as surgeon and naturalist for this expedition. Octave traveled to Washington, DC, early in 1880. Once again Octave was hoping to get to explore the Arctic. The expedition would sail in June aboard the *Gulnare*, a ship of questionable quality for making such a journey. The United States government refused to finance the mission because of the vulnerability of the *Gulnare*. Captain Howgate decided to fund the mission using private funds; however, it appears that Captain Howgate was not using private funding, but instead was spending government funds to which he had access, in equipping for the mission. He later was indicted for spending over two hundred thousand dollars of government funds without authorization. The expedition originally was to be under the command of Lt. Greely; however, Greely declined to take the command when it was determined that it was not under the direct control of the United States government. One wonders if Lt. Greely was aware of the funding fiasco and refused to be a part of it for that reason. Command of the expedition was given to Lt. Gustavus Cheyney Doane and Lt. George Howe. Lt. Doane would ensure the arrival of the expedition at Lady Franklin Bay with all necessities. Then Lt. Howe would take command of the expedition and remain at the expedition site while Lt. Doane returned with the *Gulnare* to St. John's. Octave Pavy would be the expedition doctor.

The *Gulnare* arrived in St. John's, Newfoundland, around the end of June 1880. July was spent loading supplies and preparing for the trip to Lady Franklin Bay.

While at St. John's, Octave Pavy prepared a will. It reads as follows:

> I, Octave Pavy, being in good health and of sound and disposing mind and memory, do, on the eve of my departure on a long and Perilous journey, make and publish this my last will and testament, hereby revoking all former wills by me at any time heretoforemade.
>
> I give, bequeath and devise all my property, real, personal and mixed, both in France and America, to my wife Lilla May Pavy, to her and her heirs forever.
>
> Witness my hand, at St. Johns New Foundland, this 26th day of July 1880.
>
> (signed) Octave Pavy M.D.
>
> Signed, executed, and declared by the above named testator to be his last will and Testament, in the presence of us who hereunto subscribe our names in the presence of the said testator and of each other.
>
> (signed) W. S. Jewell
>
> (signed) H. Clay

It should be noted that in the event of his death, all of Octave's resources would be given to his wife, and no mention is made of his daughter residing in France.

The ship departed the next day, July 27, 1880, for Lady Franklin Bay. The expedition members included Henry Clay, whose fellow Kentucky countrymen deemed it foolish of him to risk his life on such a venture; Sergeant George W. Rice, the official photographer for the expedition; and Sergeant Winfred S. Jewell. Those who said the *Gulnare* was not suitable for the trip through the ice in Smith Sound on the way to Lady Franklin Bay were correct. The ship was damaged in its attempt, and after unloading its cargo at Disco, Greenland, it had to return to St. John's. Sergeant Rice and Sergeant Jewell returned with the ship. Octave Pavy and Henry Clay stayed in Greenland, with the understanding that they would be picked up the following year.

During the year that followed, Octave Pavy accomplished much while in Greenland. He traveled with Krarup Smith, the royal inspector of North Greenland, along the coast of Greenland as far north as Upernavik and into the interior of Greenland. He acquired the Eskimo language, familiarized himself with the habits of the natives, made climatic studies, and investigated the most effective mode of treating the diseases peculiar to the region. He familiarized himself with the Eskimo sledge. He engaged two Eskimos, Jens Edwards and Frederick Christensen, who would accompany the expedition to Lady Franklin Bay. He took great care in selection of food that could be purchased for the expedition. He located sledges and dogs, which were vital for the expedition.

The following is a letter he received from Smith at the end of his Greenland sojourn:

> Godhavn, July 13, 1881.
>
> My Dear Sir:
>
> Before we part, I wish by this to acknowledge the great and never tired attention, which you during your stay in North-greenland always and everywhere have paid us here, be it the Danes or be it the natives, in medical respects. Not a few of us will ever be you very much obliged for your kind and—as the results show—most successful treatment.
>
> As your experiences about our ailments here in this region now will be numerous, our obligations toward you certainly would be still greater, if you, dear Sir, before leaving us in a short resume would give your experience and opinions in regard to our common diseases and the best way of behavior in respect to them from the side of our administration.
>
> Without doubt also my government would be much pleased, if time would allow you to furnish me with such a valuable communication. Certainly our medical arrangements here will have to be reformed before long, and every

contribution to information about our hygienic and medical conditions, when derived from personal experience, will then be of use to the administration in the mother-country.

Last, dear Sir, our best wishes for your further progress towards the North! I am now assured, that very few men are so well fit for travelling in polar regions as you are, but you know, that it is my opinion, that you Americans commonly underrate the difficulties and obstacles in the real polar, paleocrystic sea and along its coasts.

May your hopes not be disappointed!

I am, Sir, Yours
Most gratefully and respectfully
(signed) Krarup Smith,
Inspector in North-greenland

Dr. Octave Pavy, Surgeon
of the Howgate-expedition from 1880

On July 20, 1881, one week after he received the letter from the Greenland inspector, Octave Pavy joined the Greely expedition at Godhavn, Greenland, and boarded the ship *Proteus*. He was sworn in as the expedition's doctor for one year and was to receive one hundred dollars per month for this service. He was contracted as "Surgeon of the rank of first lieutenant." Precut lumber for the living quarters, food, dogs, sledges, and other supplies were loaded. The Eskimos selected by Pavy, Jens Edwards and Thorlip Frederick Christensen, were also picked up. This completed the uniting of all of the expedition members.

Octave was not only the doctor on the journey, but he also had charge of the dogs. In a journal entry dated July 30, 1881, he writes, "Mr. Norman wakes me at 5:30—took a cup of coffee—at 6 gave walrus meat to the dogs to eat." On August 1, 1881, he writes, "At 1 a.m. I am to write my report, when Mr. Norman comes and tells me that the dogs are on deck. I find them over the steaks of walrus meat, work till 2 o'clock to put them back." On August 3 Pavy writes, "One of the dogs died this morning, the others begin to get poor. I will give them a little more to eat—the close confinement and the dampness is perhaps the cause of the trouble. I will let them out a little today." And on August 5 he writes, "Today I had thrown overboard one of the dogs, which was sick. This makes the third. The others are better. I hope to save them." Pertaining to his duties as doctor, Pavy writes, "Just as we were to have a chat with Kislingbury and Lockwood, I was called to see Frederick. He has cramps of the stomach. I take care of him—he is very sick and retire at one o'clock."

Doctor Pavy had apparently brought with him much medical equipment and supplies, which he kept in his charge. On August 4 he wrote in his journal, "My bed is so crowded with things and I am so much in agitation that I lay myself upon the bench in the cabin. At 6 a.m. I wake and go to see Frederick. Since I departed from Upernavik, I have not laid once upon my bed, the bench in the cabin is my bed."

From his journal we notice hints that he does not necessarily agree with some of Greely's commands. The first hint of this comes out in his journal entry of July 31. He writes, "A spirit of indiscipline begins to show itself among some of the men. There are 2 or 3 that I would send back if I was the commander." In an undated entry in his journal, probably referring to Cape Sabine, Pavy writes, "If I had been commander, I would have taken a boat and would have examined the surroundings for good winter quarters. I would have been immediately decided, but at the first difficulty he hesitates." Pavy, who had had an interest in polar exploration for the past twelve or fourteen years, certainly was better schooled in this area than Lieutenant Greely. His command in the Franco-Prussian War certainly had given him the experience and confidence to lead. His education was greater than that of his commander. This would certainly lead Pavy to believe that the decisions, if he were to make them, would at least be on a par with Greely's, if not superior. He expected his opinions to be respected by the commander, and that the commander would act according to Pavy's opinions. He would be disappointed to learn that not only would the commander not value his opinions, Pavy would be treated as a subordinate by the commander and sometimes even be disciplined by him.

After stopping at several points on the way to Lady Franklin

Bay, including some where Octave Pavy disembarked to examine or explore and to gather plant specimens, the *Proteus* arrived at Lady Franklin Bay on August 11, 1881.

The next few days were spent unloading the *Proteus* and assembling the quarters. The expedition members maintained their quarters aboard the *Proteus* during this time. After about a week, the unloading of the ship was complete and the permanent quarters had been constructed to the point where the men could move in. Pavy shared a semiprivate area with the officers, separated from the enlisted personnel and the Eskimos.

Pavy had already used his medical skills caring for the dogs as they made the trip up to Lady Franklin Bay, as well as caring for the men who had illnesses while aboard the *Proteus*. Although he was with the expedition primarily to provide medical care, this was not about to stop him from Arctic exploration, which was dear to his heart. These expedition trips would take two forms: scouting the area around Lady Franklin Bay and establishing camps for travel farther away from the expedition's quarters. Octave Pavy was to be involved with both of these efforts.

Doctor Pavy's first exploration effort at Fort Conger was a trip he and Sergeant George Rice took, commencing on August 29, 1881, and returning September 8. The purpose of the trip was to check for traces of the *Jeannette*, the ship that was to sail to the polar region by way of the Bering Sea and had not been heard from, and to check on caches left from earlier expeditions. They were to head toward Lincoln Bay, a distance of about forty miles to the northeast of Fort Conger, where they expected to find the caches. Then they were to proceed northward toward Cape Joseph Henry, about another hundred miles.

They proceeded to Lincoln Bay and found some of the caches; however, Sergeant Rice broke through some thin ice and as a result was disabled by an attack of acute rheumatism. The party started back toward Fort Conger. They managed to get back as far as St. Patrick Bay, some ten miles northeast of the fort, when Rice could go no farther. Pavy erected a tent for Rice and returned to the fort. Three separate parties were sent out to reach Sergeant Rice and bring him back to Conger. No sign was seen of the *Jeannette*. Following is the report of this exploration journey as reported by Octave Pavy upon his return. Changes in sentence structure and punctuation have been made for ease of reading:

Fort Conger, Grinnell Land
Morning of September 14, 1881

I have the honor to enclose the report of my overland journey between the dates of the 29th August and the morning of September 8th.

I left Fort Conger, Discovery Harbor, accompanied by Sergeant Rice, on August 29, 1881 at 7 p.m. Our provisions, including two backpacks, two blankets and a shelter tent, were strapped on our shoulders. We caught up with the party sent ahead of us at 8 p.m. We then went in a northwest direction. We camped on the top of the cliffs that form the south side of St. Patrick Bay at 1:30 a.m. At 10:30 p.m., during the march, we met up with Lt. Lockwood and his party.

At 11:30 a.m. on August 30th, we cooked breakfast. Sergeants Ralston and Linn were sent back with the empty wagon at 1 p.m. Accompanied by Sergeant Rice, I followed the high cliffs of St. Patrick Bay in a westerly direction at a height of 1500 feet. The walk was very tiresome. At 4 p.m. we saw a [illegible] to the north. From 4 p.m. to 5:30 p. m. we followed the valley towards the north, finding numerous fresh tracks of musk oxen on the snow. From 7 p. m. to 11:30 p.m. we ascended a mountain over 2000 feet high bearing southwest from Mt. Buford. From its summit the view extended to the south over the snowy peaks of the U.S. Range and at our feet to the north over an extensive valley.

To the northeast we could see the summits only of the mountains of Polaris Promentory, the sea in that direction being covered by fog. We descended until 12 p.m., when we camped in the expectation that the fog would raise in the morning.

August 31st. I awoke at 8 a.m. The fog was still very thick, but at 11 a.m. it raised. At 11:30 a.m. we started. The descent was very steep. At 1 p.m. we reached the valley leading north; however, it was southwest of Cape Beechey. We walked until 3 p.m. We saw numerous traces of musk oxen and foxes. The weather was beautiful. We ascended a small hill and halted. The first cache was left there for the return journey. We saw nine musk oxen while building a small cairn for provision. Rice went in pursuit of the musk oxen and fired two shots at them with the revolver without success. From this point ascended several hills in a northeast direction. We arrived at the lake at 11:30 p.m. When breaking the ice for water, Rice saw a small fish six or eight inches long. From the lake, we reached the coast and followed it on the ice foot to a point south of the black cliffs. Finding it impossible to pass on account of the absence of ice foot and the almost perpendicular cliffs, we returned to a point south where at 1:30 a.m. on September 1st, we struck camp. We broke camp at 11:30. We climbed by a very steep ravine on the plateau of a mountain 1500 feet, and followed its ascending grade in a northward direction. The wind was blowing a strong gale, with drifting snow. This day's walk was very disagreeable.

We reached Wrangell Bay at 12 p.m. and struck camp close to a watercourse 200 feet above the level of the sea. We found many traces of musk oxen and seal. We broke camp at 11 a.m. on September 2nd. The weather was very fine. We followed the west and north shore of the bay on the ice foot. Then we took the coast northward from the ice foot which, in places, is formed by very heavy ice. Here and there pools of fresh water prove that this ice has not melted this year. Have seen very few pieces that I would call Paleocrystic; none at all in the straits. The ice was in motion under the influence of the tide. Reached Cape Frederick at 9 p.m. Here the pressure of the ice upon the coast is great. We found traces of coal at the head of the bay. We crossed on the ice to the northeast shore and ascended its very steep grade. We saw a lake about a mile and a half in extent and mistook it for a bay. We were obliged to ascend the hill once more. We then walked towards a bold cape that I took to be Cape

Constitution. We then returned to the southwest where we had left our sacks. We followed the coast and at 10 a.m. on August 3rd we found the depot of 1000 ration left by Sir George Nares in 1875.

On August 3rd at 1:00 p.m. we put up our tent. We had walked 22 hours on a few biscuits and a cup of chocolate. Rice complained of his feet paining him considerably. At our farthest north I have seen no traces of the Jeanette expedition. We are now 1000 feet above the level of the sea, with an horizon as clear as it can be possible to find. I can follow the line of the Greenland coast to the northeast from Cape Brevort to Cape Bryant! Then an indentation, and another point that I take to be the land of Cape May. Further north, two other spots of land separated by two lines of horizon and of different shade, can be clearly seen. The farthest of these I believe to be Beaumont Island, the other, more to the east, Cape Britannia or Stevenson Island.

To the south, on the Grinnell Land coast, Cape Frederick the seventh bars all view of land. On the Greenland coast I can see as far as Kennedy Channel, to the east the ice is closely packed on the coast. To the north, the sea is as far as the view extends, as a white sheet, dark only in a few places by pools of water. On the Grinnell Land side, from south of Cape Frederick the seventh, as far north as I can see, there is a broad channel of open water extending at my feet about two miles from the coast.

On September 4th at 8 a.m., I called Rice. He suffers extremely from his swollen feet; and can scarcely put on his boots. We descend from the summit of the hill to the depot of provisions which were placed about 75 feet above the level of the sea. The weather is beautiful.

We worked all day in opening and closing barrels! It is difficult work for men that are not coopers. Of the provisions, as I have before stated to you, 1200 pounds of canned meat are still good! All of the bread is spoiled; the chocolate, stearin and rum are good; part of the tea, potatoes and tobacco is spoiled.

At 6 p.m. we broke camp. One mile from camp, Rice, with a revolver, killed a white hare. I added its weight to my own! The skin and skeleton is worth its carrying. We crossed the bay on the ice 2 miles from its head. Followed the same route as the day before! And after 16 hours of walk struck Wrangel Bay at 10 a.m. Sept. 5th. Rice is exceedingly tired. Broke camp at 6 p.m. and following again our old track in the fog, on top of the plateau, we reached the most northeasterly lake of Beechey valley at 3 p.m. on September 6th. Rice is exhausted and he cannot eat. His left knee is considerably swollen as well as both wrists. His pulse beat is 112. He told me that several times he has been affected with acute rheumatism. I admire his endurance and pluck. It would be difficult to find a better man to travel with. At 7 p.m, I woke up Rice. We started 9 p.m. Rice can scarcely walk.

At 9 a.m. on September 7th we arrived at our first depot on the journey and put up our tent! We ate roast-beef and chocolate, but Rice had no appetite. His articulation seems to be swollen. The situation is critical! He wants me to leave him there and return to Fort Conger for a relief party; but before I leave him we must reach the other side of St. Patrick Bay! It is impossible of thinking of leaving him here.

At 8 o'clock on September 8th we broke camp and followed slowly the valley to the west of Mt. Buford! We ascended the mountain on top of which we had camped on August 30th. We partly lost our way in the fog and came down in St. Patrick Bay valley, following a cliff formed by rockslide, which I think I would be afraid now to climb. The energy and endurance of Rice is wonderful. At 9 p.m. we arrived in the valley of the end of St. Patrick Bay. We put up the tent! I left Rice at 10 p.m. and reached Ft. Conger at 4 a.m.

Very respectfully,
Your obedient servant
Octave Pavy
Acting Assistant Surgeon
U.S. Army

Pavy was not at the fort very long before he was off on another trip. This time he, along with the Eskimo Jens, was sent by Lieutenant Greely to take seven hundred pounds of provisions to Cape Murchison, where they would be cached. In October, he, along with others of the expedition, was gone for a week again, searching for any indication of the *Jeannette*. Pavy made trips in November, January, February, and March 1882, as well as some shorter trips during the same year.

On one of these trips, in which the purpose was to supply forward bases with the necessary food and equipment for future treks farther from Fort Conger, Pavy made a suggestion to his fellow teammates. He suggested that they should not wait for some other group of people to explore points farther away; instead they should use the supplies and go on. None of the team went along with Pavy's suggestion, because as military men, they felt a compulsion to be obedient to their commander.

No supply ship had arrived in 1882. There was the possibility that none would arrive in 1883. Octave Pavy was concerned about the men's health in the event that the relief ship planned for arrival in the summer of 1883 did not make it through the ice to Fort Conger. If such were the case, the expedition would need to retreat on their own facilities, and the men had to be in the best shape for the retreat. Because of his concern for the health of the expedition members, Pavy wrote the following letter of recommendations to Lieutenant Greely:

Fort Conger, Grinnell Land
March 8th, 1883

To the Commanding Officer,
Sir:

I have the honor to respectfully submit to you a few considerations that I value of high importance as concerning the future health of, at least, a part of the command, and therefore liable to influence the chances of success in a retreat that you consider inevitable.

As exposure and labor, at an early period of the season of 1883 may result in grave impairment of the health; as also, in case of accident of a serious nature, the patients would probably not have recuperated in August, becoming then an encumbrance, threatening to compromise the safety of all, by rendering the departure impracticable (as in the case of Dr. Kane), I should earnestly recommend that no work entailing exposure of more than a night or two in the field should be undertaken during the month of March.

My personal experience, and the risks run last year by our early parties, with the examples of Dr. Kane and Sir George Nares, satisfy my mind as to the dangers to be apprehended from sledging during the month of March.

As medical adviser of the expedition, I consider it my duty to state that although the health of the command has been better this winter than the previous, it will nevertheless not be submitted with impunity to as much hardship as in 1882. If temporarily, it withstood, it would certainly be at the expense of vital energies that I think of the highest importance, perhaps of necessity to husband, in view of the future work of the fall, in which we will have to contend with contingencies that defeated the efforts of Sir John Ross and the detached party of Dr. Kane's expedition.

I will also, respectfully call your attention, while it is still time to the important question of coal; as it would be probably injurious to the general health of the command, that we should be left without fuel during the three months previous to our departure.

As to the very important question of foot gear, I should earnestly recommend (considering the insecure state of the moccasins and Labrador Esquimaux boots) that each man employed in any work entailing exposure for several consecutive days should be provided with an extra pair of boots or moccasins, the only appropriate foot gear at our disposal.

I have the honor to be very respectfully
your obt. servant
act. ass. surgeon
Octave Pavy

Lieutenant Greely did not take favor with the letter and immediately shot back a reply. This reply stated that the objective of the expedition was to "gather knowledge of the Arctic regions," and that seemed to be of more importance to Greely than the welfare of the expedition members. This exchange seems to be the beginning of the friction between Greely and Pavy. That reply follows:

Fort Conger, Grinnell Land
March 9th 1883
Actg. Asst. Surg. O. Pavy
U.S. Army

Sir: I have the honor to acknowledge the receipt, this day, of a communication from you regarding the future operations of this command.

The letter was undoubtedly called forth by the prospective departure, on March 10th, of a party of six, with dog sledges, to establish depots on which depends the success of our geographical work in North Greenland.

You recommend therein that the energies of this party be devoted to ensuring such conditions as would facilitate a retreat by boats, a possible contingency but not inevitable as you state it.

The grounds upon which you make this remarkable recommendation are but in part medical, and depend largely on future contingencies, i.e. "the future of War", which may disable some member of the party and so encumber our possible retreat.

You admit that the health of the party has been better this winter than in 1881–1882.

This expedition was planned and fitted out solely for the purpose of increasing our knowledge of the Arctic regions. While I have the honor to command it, and as long as I am fit for duty, I shall continue to pursue the object in view.

In assuming charge of this work I considered it important and dangerous. As an American Soldier I have yet to learn that any prospective dangers or accident, should deter a man from pursuing to his utmost any end which is in the line of one's duty, and instead prepare for a prospective retreat.

To practically abandon it and think only of personal safety, especially at a time when there seem possible discoveries which would be valued by the world and creditable to my country, would be difficult for me even under the most adverse circumstances, but now—under favorable circumstances—would appear dishonorable and unmanly. Could I for a moment listen to such a recommendation your mention of Kane's name evokes to my memory such an example of perseverance under trying and adverse circumstances as would render such actions impossible.

Your recommendations will not be followed in this respect.

I am Sir,
Respectfully Yours,
A.W. Greely,
1st Lt. 5th Cav. A.S.O. and Asst.,
Commanding

In April 1883, Pavy made a suggestion to Lieutenant Greely that, had it been enacted, might have changed the outcome of the expedition. He suggested that he and Lieutenant Kislingbury, along with one of the Eskimos, take a sledge team to Cape Sabine in order to leave a message. The message would be to the effect that in the event the 1883 ship could not reach them at Lady Franklin Bay, rescue crew were to leave caches there at Cape Sabine. The trip would be over a thousand miles long and would take two months. Lieutenant Greely decided not to let them go.

By the first of June, as the expedition members were becoming more concerned about the possibility of a relief ship not arriving, their edginess became more apparent. The contract made in Greenland between Greely and Pavy, when Pavy joined the expedition, was for Pavy to serve one year as the expedition's naturalist and surgeon. He was to be paid one hundred dollars per month and serve with the grade of second lieutenant. Interestingly, I see no mention, in any correspondence, of Pavy referred to by his military rank. This contract was renewed in the summer of 1882 for another year. Doctor Pavy had more and more wanted to be removed from the control of Lieutenant Greely, and Greely felt it his duty to maintain Pavy under his control. Pavy had said to Greely that he would not renew his contract. Greely decided to relieve Pavy of his duties as naturalist. He wrote the following order:

Fort Conger, Grinnell Land,
June 1, 1883.

Orders No. 2.

2nd Lieut. James B. Lockwood, 23d Infty., A. S. O., will relieve A. A. Surgeon O. Pavy, U.S. Army, of the duties of Naturalist of this Expedition. A. A. Surgeon O. Pavy on receipt of this order will transfer to Lieut. Lockwood all collection and specimens in his charge. An inventory [illegible]. He will also furnish as far as practicable such data as will enable Lt. Lockwood to make the written reports required by communications from the Commanding Officer to Dr. Pavy under date of May 2d 1883. Lieut. Lockwood will make the report required by the above mentioned communications within five days from the completion of the inventory of specimens.

You are advised that at least six hours daily will be given to this work until the completion of this transfer.

The portion of the collections made by Dr. Pavy which he may desire to keep as personal, and which are not needed to perfect the official collections, can be retained by him, awaiting final approval by the Chief Signal Officer of the Army.

A.W. Greely,
1st Lieut., 5th Cav., A. S. O. and Asst.,
Commanding the L.F.B. Expedition.

Lieutenant Lockwood filed his report to Lieutenant Greely nine days later. He complained about the manner in which Doctor Pavy had organized the specimens. There was also a disagreement over which of the items were of a personal nature and should not be included in the inventory.

June 10, 1883
1st Lieut. A. W. Greely, 5th Cav,
A.S.O. and Asst., Commanding.

Sir:—In reply to your communication of the 8th inst. I have the honor to transmit herewith a copy of the "List of specimens", turned over to me by Dr. Pavy, which is the only written data received from him pertaining to the transfer or to the reports required by you and is substantially the only information elicited either written or verbal. My efforts to obtain anything more have been unsuccessful.

The "condition of the specimens" I can best state in detail, though as there was no complete itemized list of any portion, it was difficult to know what was of the collection and what not. All the mounted plants were in your possession; the others in vials with alcohol, in small boxes or bags or in the large tank with birds etc. The stuffed birds were, with a few exceptions, wrapped in paper and packed in boxes. Those not stuffed were in vials with alcohol or in the tank referred to. The insects (all much covered with dust) were on cork in two small boxes, one open and the other nailed up; also in many small match boxes, vials, etc. The two ermines and hares were in the box with the birds; most of the other animals in vials with alcohol as were also the various water organisms, fishes etc. The Eskimo relics were mostly packed in one large box together with most of the fossils, shells etc. Most of the deer antlers were in a box together. The musk-ox skins were on the roof of the house and the "skeletons" on the tripod or under the ice in the water. None of the skeletons are yet "prepared". The only specimens regularly packed in boxes were the stuffed birds and animals (with perhaps a few exceptions), some of the insects and most of the Eskimo relics, fossils, deer-antlers etc. The appended list embraces, with a few exceptions, all of the specimens labeled, but many were found without any descriptive data attached and few or none with such data complete. The Eskimo relics almost wholly wanted any data by which they could be identified. The specimens were found in and outside of three wall tents occupied also by medical stores and the personal effects of Dr. Pavy.

The collection generally was very much confused and no attempt at arrangement according to classes, numbers or otherwise or at keeping it separate and distinct, was apparent.

Very respectfully,
Your obdt servt.
J. B. Lockwood,
Second Lieut., 23d Inf.
A.S.O.
1 enclosure

In the first part of July Lieutenant Greely issued an order requiring Doctor Pavy not only to turn over all medical stores, but also all notes and observations. That order is listed below:

Fort Conger, Grinnell Land,
July 9th, 1883

Order No. 3

Acting Assistant Surgeon O. Pavy, having officially declared his unwillingness to renew his contract with this expedition, will transfer to 2d Lieut. James B. Lockwood, A.S.O., the medical stores and supplies for which he is responsible. He will also turn over to that officer not later than July 19, 1883, in a sealed package his diary. By diary will be understood all notes and observations made during this Expedition as well as memoranda of current events. Similar action will be taken regarding all collections of any kind, made since July 20th, 1881, which will be packed, boxed and addressed to the Chief Signal Officer. Clerical and other assistance will be furnished as needed.

A.W. Greely,
1st Lt., 5th Cav., A.S.O. and Asst.,
Comdg. the Expedition
A.A. Surgeon O. Pavy,
U.S. Army

Pavy responded with a request for assistance in the inventory of the medical supplies:

Fort Conger, Grinnell Land,
July 9, 1883

To the Commanding Officer.

Sir: I have the honor to respectfully request that for a week beginning the 10th of July, the help of my hospital steward—(or of the man that since the beginning of the Expedition has been chosen to perform that duty)—should be allowed to me, for the complete and detailed inventory of my medical stores.

I will also respectfully request to be officially informed if it is or not the privilege of a surgeon serving with a military command to be, on his demand, furnished with the assistance of his hospital steward or of the enlisted man detailed for that duty.

I am sir,
Respectfully yours,
Octave Pavy
Actg. Asst. Surgeon,
U.S. Army

Lieutenant Greely seems put out by the tone of Pavy's response. He informed Doctor Pavy that he could have assistance for a shorter period of time than requested:

Fort Conger, Grinnell Land,
July 9, 1883

Actg. Asst. Surgeon O. Pavy,
U.S. Army

Sir: I have the honor to acknowledge the receipt of your letter of this date asking the undivided services of Pvt. Biederbick for a week from July 10th to make an inventory of your medical stores.

You are advised as you have already been verbally, that Pvt. Biederbick is under orders for two days field service, and that he will be at you command from the 12th instant.

The inventory of your stores cannot possibly require more than two days labor if they have been properly cared for, and I cannot see that your interest will suffer by the postponement.

As you are to officially abandon this Expedition within ten days, I see no reason why your question should be answered, particularly as it bears, and improperly, on my action in this matter.

I have only to invite your attention to the fact that there is no hospital steward connected with this expedition, nor have you ever requested one. Pvt. Biederbick has assisted you in that capacity for two years without interfering with his other duties, and the interests of the service. Do not demand a change.

I am, Sir:
Respectfully yours,
A.W. Greely,
1st Lieut., 5th Cav., A.S.O. and Asst.,
Comdg. the Expedition

On July 19, Octave Pavy formally submitted his notice to Lieutenant Greely that he desired not to renew his contract:

Fort Conger, Grinnell Land,
July 19, 1883

To the Commanding Officer.

Sir: My second contract expiring on the 20th of this month, I wish to respectfully express my desire not to have it renewed.

As I do not intend to remain in the service and as (according to your view) our work will in the short space of a month or two be virtually ended by the arrival of a ship in Discovery Harbor, or by our reaching her in Kennedy Channel, my action is of minor importance.

As a matter of course I offer my services to the Expedition, and declare myself willing and ready to perform the same duties as in the past; still devoting myself entirely to this welfare and success of our undertaking.

It will be well understood by me, that I shall not consider the Department as being indebted for any remuneration, and that all expenses incurred by my living will remain to my charge.

I am Sir,
Your Obt. servant
Octave Pavy,
Actg. Asst. Surgeon,
U.S. Army

Lieutenant Greely did not respond very favorably to Doctor Pavy's letter of resignation. He responded with a lecture on Pavy's moral duty and ended by telling him that he, Greely, was willing to renew his contract at any time:

Fort Conger, Grinnell Land,
July 19, 1883
Actg. Asst. Surgeon O. Pavy
U.S. Army

Sir: I have the honor to acknowledge the receipt of your communication of July 18th wherein you reiterate you unwillingness to renew your contract as Actg. Asst. Surgeon, U.S. Army. I cannot concur in your opinion that such action is of minor importance.

Whether this Expedition remains a month or a year without an official medical adviser, time is unimportant, the moral aspects important. Ship or no ship, retreat or no, you joined this expedition under a moral obligation to serve during its continuance, and you will know that the Surgeon General never would have sanctioned your contract had he surmised even the possibility of your quitting, under any circumstance, a command situated without the confines of the civilized world.

I have the honor to advise you that should you at any time consent, I should deem it my duty to renew your contract as before.

I am Sir,
Very Respectfully Yours,
A.W. Greely

Doctor Pavy responded with a letter stating that his notes were of a personal nature and that he saw no reason to turn them over to Lieutenant Greely. He offered to assist the chief signal officer with any data he had when they returned to the United States:

Fort Conger, Grinnell Land,
July 19, 1883
To the Commanding Officer.

Sir: In conformity with the order of July 9th, I have transferred my medical property and the specimens of natural history gathered by myself and addressed to the Chief Signal Officer.

As you are aware, all my private gathering (except the flowers) were in the first days of June turned over with the general collections.

As to the question of diary etc., I will say that to the best of my ability I have furnished you with all my personal views and official opinions, by reports when desired.

My journal, destitute of any official value, is a mere record of events, hypothesis and reminiscences closely mingled with personal and intimate thoughts synthesized from detached notes and reduced into letters of an entirely private character, for the only use of my family, but on our return to the United States, if my personal opinion concerning events, or even my appreciation of physical, natural, medical geographical etc. etc. phenomena are of any interest to the Chief Signal Officer, I will consider myself honored to be allowed to put at his disposal any extracts of my polar journal and Greenland notes, as well as any of the general arctic information collected by myself during sixteen years of continual arctic studies.

Octave Pavy
I am, Sir,
Respectfully Yours.

This letter really upset Lieutenant Greely and he responded with charges against Pavy that would keep him in the army while awaiting trial by a court-martial. Greely's response and charges of disobedience follow:

Fort Conger, Grinnell Land,
July 19, 1883
Actg. Asst. Surgeon O. Pavy,
U.S. Army

Sir: I have to herewith transmit to you copy of charge and specifications this day preferred against you and to inform you that the originals have been forwarded to the Adjutant General of the Army.

The legal results of this action, prevent the termination of your terms of service with this day, as contemplated by you, but retains you in the Army awaiting trial by a General Court Martial.

I am,
Respectfully Yours,
A.W. Greely,
1st Lt., 5th Cav., A.S.O. and Asst.,
Comdg. L.F.B. Expedition.

Charge and Specifications against Actg. Asst. Surgeon O. Pavy, U.S. Army.

Charge.Disobedience of orders.

Specification 1st. In this that he, Actg. Asst. Surgeon O. Pavy, U.S. Army, having been directed by orders No 3, dated Ft. Conger, Grinnell Land, July 9, 1883, to turn over to 2d Lt. James B. Lockwood 23d Inft., A.S.O., his diary, did fail and refuse to obey such order.

This at Ft. Conger, Gr. Land July 19, 1883.

Specification 2d. In this that he, Actg. Asst. Surg. O. Pavy, U.S.A., having been verbally ordered by 1st Lt. A.W. Greely, 5th Cav., A.S.O. and Asst. Commanding, to turn over within two hours his diary to 2d Lt. Jas. B. Lockwood, 23d Inft., A.S.O., did positively refuse to obey said order.

This at Ft. Conger, Gr. Land July 19, 1883.

Specification 3d. In this that he, Actg. Asst. Surg. O. Pavy, U.S.A., having been ordered in arrest by 1st Lt. A.W. Greely, 5th Cav., A.S.O. and Asst., commanding, did refuse to obey said order, and so refused until Lt. Greely called for a guard to enforce it. When he, Actg. Asst. Surgeon O. Pavy, said. "I accept the arrest physically but not morally".

This at Ft. Conger, Gr. Land July 19, 1883.

A.W. Greely,
1st Lt. 5th Cav., A.S.O. and Asst.,
Comdg. L.F.B. Expedition

Witnesses:
1st Lt. A.W. Greely
5th Cav., A.S.O. and Asst.,
2d Lt. Jas. B. Lockwood,
23d Inft., A.S.O

The phrase "originals have been forwarded to the Adjutant General of the army" is completely false, as they obviously had no means to send them. With the refusal of Pavy to turn over all of his notes, Lieutenant Greely placed him in an order of arrest and confinement to limits:

Fort Conger, Gr. Land,
July 19, 1883
Actg. Asst. Surgeon O. Pavy,
U.S. Army

Sir: Your order of arrest this day made will confine you to your private quarters, except the times needful for meals, personal offices and such exercise as you judge requisite for health. Exercise will be taken within one mile of the astronomical observatory.

Very Respectfully Yours,
A.W. Greely,
1st Lieut., 5th Cav., A.S.O. and Asst.,
Comdg. the Expedition.

Doctor Pavy responded, "I accept the arrest physically but not morally."

August came, and no relief ship arrived. The expedition abandoned Fort Conger and headed south on the twenty-seven-foot launch *Lady Greely*, towing three other small boats, toward Littleton Island. An entry from Doctor Pavy's diary dated August 23, 1883, about fifteen days after they departed from Fort Conger, says, "Israel takes observation, we are at 79 50 [latitude 79° 50' north]." This would place them about one hundred and fifty miles south of Fort Conger. He further states, "Since 9 o'clock we are yet attached to the ice-foot. We have left our socks on the beach to dry them. The sun shines since two hours. The ice is as thick as it can be, the fog in the offing is thick, we cannot see open water far."

Eventually there was a lane of open water, and the boats carrying the expedition drifted away from shore. Later that day Pavy wrote in his diary, "At 9 o'clock p.m. the men retire. I remain awake with the two sentinels. There is some fog, which lets us see only a faint line of the coast. We are half a mile from the coast, drifting toward the east north east." Pavy's entries for August 24 are much like those of the day before.

The next entry in Pavy's log is dated September 21, 1883. By this time the expedition had abandoned the *Lady Greely* and had been on an ice floe for about a week:

> Awoke. It is impossible to say where we are. During the night a terrible storm of snow. The ice in the pack seems to be moving south. Really, this is terrible to float in this manner, in the fog, in the dark. This seems to me like a nightmare in one of the stories of Edgar Poe. The party of Rice has constructed a house of ice to shelter them. Connell and Ralston—Diarrhea. Brainard and Henry—Eczema. Cross—the palm of the foot abandoned.

Even in this perilous condition, Pavy was thinking of the welfare of his fellow expedition members. This was the last legible entry in Pavy's journal until the party was at Camp Clay on Cape Sabine. After the extended period living on an ice floe, they finally reached Cape Sabine on September 29, 1883.

The winter was extremely tough on the expedition members. Pavy, besides assisting with some of the other tasks, was frequently involved in giving medical treatment, even including amputations. On April 25, 1884, he submitted his evaluation of the condition of the party members, along with ration recommendations, to Lieutenant Greely:

Camp Clay, Ellismere Land,
April 25th, 1884
To the Comdg. Officer of
U.S. Arctic Exp't'n

Sir: The health of the command at this time at the morning inspection is as follows: Very weak and even shows no improvement in the condition of parties under increased rations. I have respectfully recommended in my oral report, 1st that Schneider should be relieved for the present of the duties of shrimper, and allowed a few days to recuperate, having since a month greatly exerted himself. 2nd that the rations of the two hunters, to be as equal as possible to the work accomplished, should be re-established at what they were after the killing of the last game, one pound, and the extra of 8 oz. 3rd that contrary to my previous recommendation, that one shrimp catcher should be put again to the increase of 4 oz. daily. 4th that Israel and Gardiner should for the present be kept under the 4 oz. increase.
I am, respectfully, your obdt svt,
Octave Pavy, M.D.

Doctor Pavy followed up the report of April 25 with an update on April 27:

Camp Clay, Ellsmere Land,
April 25th, 1884

To the Comdg officer of the U.S. Arctic Exp'd.

Sir: Since my report of the 25th inst. I have found no improvement in the general condition of the party, but a constant decrease in its general strength. A slight improvement is perceptible in the cases of Gardiner and Israel, but not great enough to allow the stopping of increased rations. Ellis is rather better, but Biederbick was, and is fastly getting weaker. The general atonic state of the bowels, and the constant increasing obstinate constipation compel me to call to your attention a few recommendations, hoping for the welfare, perhaps even for the safety of the majority of the party, that they will be received favorably. 1st that as the state of our bowels is critical and the general weakness fastly increasing, the following change of diet for the next ten days is necessary: 4 oz. of bacon alternating with pemmican in the morning (raw in the plate) with one pint of tea and one of stew consisting of shrimps, and 1 oz. of blubber and 1 oz. of fresh meat and the usual amount of bread until exhausted. In the evening one pot of tea and two of stew with shrimps, the ordinary amount of bread and 7 oz. of meat

This proposed plan of diet would call but for an increase of 1 oz. only of blubber and the daily use of bacon and pemmican which would now be of the highest necessity in the present state of the party. I have detected this morning a decrease in the strength of the two hunters and a change unfavorable in their health. I could renew my recommendation of the 25th for an increase of ration, and that in pemmican and bacon. Earnestly hoping that these important, perhaps necessary recommendations should be favorably received for the safety of the remaining members of the command.

I am, very respect, your obdt. svt.,
Octave Pavy, M.D.

On May 14, 1884, only twenty-three days before Octave Pavy's death, Pavy asked Greely to write a letter to the commander of the Signal Service attesting to Pavy's service. The following memo was drafted by Lieutenant Greely, and a copy given to Octave Pavy:

May 14, 1884

General Hazen:

Dr. Pavy wishes for the satisfaction of his wife that I should write you as to his performance of professional duties during the past terrible winter. His medical skill has contributed to a very great degree in preserving the lives of the party as now constituted and he has spared himself no physical pains or trouble in carrying out his arduous and trying duties. This notwithstanding his opinion that he was not legally bound to perform these duties.

A.W.G.

On May 19, 1884, after eight of the twenty-five members of the expedition had already perished, Pavy drafted the following letter, which all remaining expedition members signed except Lieutenant Greely:

Camp Clay, May 19th, 1884.

To whom it may concern:

We, the undersigned, members of the Lady Franklin Bay Polar Expedition, desire to take this means of Expressing our acknowledgment of the devoted zeal and professional skill displayed by Dr. Octave Pavy in discharge of his medical duty during the full length of the Expedition. During the past winter, 1883–4, his medical skill has contributed in preserving the lives of the party to the present day.

Fred F. Kislingbury
C. B. Henry
Jacob Bender
E. Israel
Roderick R. Schneider, Chemnitz, Saxony
Nicholas Salor
D. L. Brainard
J. R. Frederick
Francis Long
Maurice Connell
Henry Biederbick

H. S. Gardiner
D. C. Ralston

When Lieutenant Greely became aware of the letter, he was livid. He drafted the following letter to his commander, General Hazen, chastising Octave Pavy and making accusations of theft, of which he claimed he had witnesses. Lieutenant Greely never offered any proof of his accusation:

May 21, 1884

> Gen Hazen: Learn today that Dr Pavy has drawn up and had copied by Sgt. Israel a statement as to his skill, [illegible] this winter. Every man is now on the verge of the grave & under the hands of Dr Pavy who is the strongest of us all & we are all at his mercy so to say. The value of such a certificate is evident. I have sworn evidence of five men that Dr Pavy has stolen at various times bread from his crippled patient Sgt. Ellison & also evidence that he has stolen extract of beef from Medical Stores. He will probably survive. I have no hopes for myself. I close this book today to try & secure it to you. Good bye General.
> A.W. Greely,
> Lt. Comdg.

Octave Pavy passed away eighteen days later, on June 6, 1884. Lieutenant Greely ascribed his death to starvation hastened by narcotics. The latter part of this cause of death, "hastened by narcotics," is Lieutenant Greely's opinion, and apparently there was no evidence to support it.

While Greely was frequently critical of Doctor Pavy, he expressed this view as a eulogy:

> Dr. Pavy was a man of fine education, polished manners, and great Arctic ambition. To his credit at Camp Clay must be recorded the restless energy which marked his physical exertions in behalf of the party the last month of his life. His

> medical skill was great, and contributed much to the general welfare of the party the last winter. His defects and shortcomings have been lightly touched on in my diary. It should be added that his uncertain and changeable moods, and the habits arising from his previous Bohemian life, unfitted him for duty where his actions were subject of restriction or limitation from others.

Twelve days after Octave Pavy's death, the rescue ship arrived. The seven survivors and all of the bodies (except for six, which could not be located) were placed aboard the ship. Octave Pavy's body was one of the six bodies not recovered. The New York Times on July 21, 1884, inaccurately reported that Pavy's body was recovered and aboard the *Bear*, one of the two rescue ships. This report would cause confusion for Pavy's wife and members of her family.

A religious memorial service for Octave Pavy was held in mid-August 1884 at Christ Church in St. Louis, with an address by Reverend Sylvester. A civic memorial was held at the Mercantile Library Hall in St. Louis. Taking part in this ceremony were the acting mayor, his secretary, the French consul, members of the faculty and alumni of the Missouri Medical School, and members of the Historical Society. Besides Pavy's widow, Lilla Mae Pavy, others attending were his brother, Alfred Pavy; Lilla's father, Rev. Marsena Stone; her brother, Dr. Robert Stone; Reverend Morris Cole, who performed the marriage of Octave and Lilla; and Lieutenant George Doane, who was with Pavy on the ship that took him to Greenland on the Howgate expedition.

Much correspondence followed over the next two years between Lilla Mae Pavy, her father, and her uncle and Lieutenant Greely, General Hazen, congressmen, the secretary of war, and diplomats. The subject was the letters, journals, and other effects left by Octave Pavy as well as the funds due the estate from his duty on the expedition. Lilla Mae was greatly upset with Lieutenant Greely, who to her seemed to be dragging his feet and unwilling to accommodate her requests. Lieutenant Greely became irritated over the correspondence and eventually didn't want anything to do with Lilla Mae Pavy.

The spat reached its worst when Lieutenant Greely published his book Three Years of Arctic Service, in which he seemed to berate Octave Pavy over and over. It had become quite clear that Pavy's interest was Arctic exploration and Greely's interest was military discipline and ensuring that he maintained control. Greely gave credit to Pavy for his accomplishments during the early part of the expedition; however, that changed as time went on. From the time they left Fort Conger, it seemed that Greely felt Pavy represented a risk to him as far as the control of his men was concerned. He found fault in nearly everything Pavy said or did. Lilla Mae Pavy reacted by drafting a document describing the accomplishments of Octave Pavy, his background, and his role in the expedition, which was published in the North American Review. She followed this up with an article, "An Arctic Journal," in which she defends her late husband against the slanderous comments of Lieutenant Greely in his book.

It is clear from the document signed by the members of the expedition, as well as the one signed by Lieutenant Greely, that Dr. Octave Pavy performed well in his medical field. It is equally clear that Dr. Octave Pavy made every effort to explore the area where his heart lay. Notwithstanding the language barrier he had to cross, as his primary language was French, and the differences in ethnic background from most of the expedition members, Octave Pavy contributed immensely to the members of the expedition as well as to the United States in supporting the expedition, which reached the farthest point north ever reached at that time. While he seemed to ignore his obligation to care for his child in France, he was still a very brave man.

Lilla Mae's father, Reverend Marsena Stone, moved from New Orleans to Omaha in about 1887. That is probably why we find Lilla Mae living in Omaha and getting married there on July 2, 1891, to Homer W. Case. Eight years later, in April 1899, Lilla Mae and Homer Case were divorced. In 1899 she was involved with selling tickets for excursion trips to Europe. Nothing more is known of Lilla Mae.

Octave Pavy's brother, Alfred Pavy, married Leperle Guidry at Saint Landry Parish, Louisiana, on May 10, 1870. Leperle was the daughter of Alexis Onesime Guidry and Palmire Dupre Guidry.

Alfred, who had been involved with his father's business, was discharged in 1872. The business, P. J. Pavy & Co., had not been doing well financially. It is possible that some of the company's resources had been invested with William Ralston and the Bank of California. Octave's father, P. J. Pavy, closed shop in 1876 and left Louisiana for Paris. He died in Paris the following year.

After leaving his father's business, Alfred became a deputy clerk of court in 1888 and remained in that position until elected clerk of court in St. Landry Parish, Louisiana. Alfred remained in that position until his death in 1910. Alfred and Leperle had ten children, including Felix Octave Pavy, who was likely named after his uncle, Octave Pierre Pavy. Felix Octave Pavy was a medical doctor like his uncle.

Edward Israel

(1859–1884)

THE LEADER OF the Lady Franklin Bay expedition, Lieutenant Adolphus Washington Greely, wanted the best available scientist to accompany him on the expedition. He needed accurate data on tides, ice formations, precipitation, water and air temperatures, barometric readings, cloud formation, wind velocity and direction, magnetic declination, and other observations. The US Army wrote to several universities attempting to fill this vacancy. Princeton University knew of no one willing to risk hazards such as might be encountered on this expedition. The University of Wisconsin declined. Finally, the University of Michigan wrote that they had an unusually bright man, Edward Israel, a member of the senior class who had signified his willingness to go.

Edward Israel was born in Kalamazoo, Michigan, on July 1, 1859, to Mannes T. Israel and Tillie Israel. He had an older adopted sister, Anna; an older brother, Joseph; two younger sisters, Lillie and Mollie; and a younger brother, Gotwalt.

Mannes Israel and his wife, Tillie, were believed to be first cousins. They were married in Kalamazoo on August 26, 1856. Mannes was born on November 22, 1819, in Pyrmont, Waldeck, Germany. Tillie was born in 1830, also in Pyrmont. Mannes emigrated to New York in 1841 at the age of twenty-two. He made a living by purchasing merchandise and peddling it around the country. While traveling across the country in 1843, he became ill and unable to move on and consequently settled in Kalamazoo, Michigan, where he opened a dry goods and carpet store. Mannes was the first Jewish settler in Kalamazoo. While Mannes did not serve in the Civil War, he contributed to a fund that helped equip the Michigan regiments. Mannes died of liver cancer on October 22, 1868. He was only forty-eight years old. After his death, his wife and his son Joseph ran the store named M. Israel & Co., located at 129 Main Street in Kalamazoo.

Edward attended grammar school and high school in Kalamazoo. He entered the University of Michigan at Ann Arbor in 1877. While relatively tall for the time, with his five-foot, ten-inch frame, his forte was not physical activity. Although he did participate in athletics while at the university, his real interests were mathematics, meteorology, and astronomy. He had not graduated when the offer for him to join the expedition came; however, because of his outstanding grades, they agreed to grant him his degree in absentee. His widowed mother, now the head of the family, had grave fears about him traveling to the Arctic, but she finally gave her blessings. He would be the youngest person of the expedition and the only enlisted member of the expedition with a college degree.

Edward Israel left Kalamazoo for Washington, DC on April 28, 1881. On May 2, Edward Israel was officially enlisted in the United States Army Signal Corps with the rank of sergeant. As a meteorologist, it was necessary for him to have the equipment he needed in order to perform his duties. He left Washington and traveled to Baltimore, Maryland, where he met up with Harvard professor Charles S. Pierce. Professor Pierce, the son of Benjamin Pierce of astronomy fame, had produced a pendulum that would record magnetic and meteorology readings in the polar regions. He spent some time instructing Sergeant Israel on the use and care of it. Then the pendulum was crated up to accompany Sergeant Israel on the expedition. He joined Lieutenant James B. Lockwood and several other members of the expedition in Baltimore and then sailed to meet the rest of the expedition at St. John's, Newfoundland. The party arrived at St. John's on June 22, 1881. Before the departure for Lady Franklin Bay, Sergeant Israel conferred with Lieutenant Greely on the equipment he would have on the expedition in order to perform his duties.

They departed from St. John's on July 7, 1881, with all the equipment and supplies aboard the *Proteus*, heading north toward Lady Franklin Bay. After making stops on the west coast of Greenland to pick up Doctor Octave Pavy and the two Eskimos, Jens Edward and Thorlip Frederick Christiansen, as well as dogs and sledges, they sailed into Smith Sound and reached Lady Franklin Bay on August 12, 1881. About five days were spent unloading the vessel. They constructed the living quarters, and each person was assigned to a bunk. Sergeant Israel shared an area with Sergeant Jewell and Sergeant Rice.

The magnetic observatory was erected about two hundred yards from the main building. It was a wooden structure about eight by fourteen feet in size, secured and fastened by wooden pegs in lieu of copper nails. This building housed the pendulum, thermometers, and other instruments used in the measurements of gravity, magnetic readings, etc., in which Sergeant Israel was greatly involved. He had responsibility for all the astronomical work and the observations of magnetic intensity to attend to, and he was also in general charge of the magnetic work. During the month of January 1882, while taking readings on the pendulum in the open observatory, in which the temperatures dropped below minus fifty degrees, he superficially froze one of his feet.

On May 25, 1883, Sergeant Israel led a mission on a four-day excursion. The party consisted of Israel, Private Connell, the Eskimo Jens, and a dog team. The purpose of the excursion was to determine whether Lake Hazen was a practical route through the Bellows. They discovered that the valley they were following terminated, and it was determined that it was not a practical route. They shot several musk oxen while on the journey and brought them back to camp.

On August 7, 1883, a party, including Sergeant Israel, accompanied Lieutenant Greely on an excursion in the launch to see if any sight of the relief vessel could be spotted. None was seen.

Sergeant Israel was responsible for many observations that provided data for locating and mapping areas. On the retreat from Fort Conger, his observations provided precise locations that allowed the expedition party to determine the best course of action at any given time, as related to which way to go and how far it was to a map location.

On December 31, 1883, some three months after setting up the tent camp at Cape Sabine, Sergeant Israel led a discussion concerning Michigan. He must have had a love for his state.

Israel shared a sleeping bag in the shelter with Lieutenant Greely and Sergeant Ralston. He begin to show signs of illness during the middle of January. He declined to take extra rations for his condition, because of his concern for the others. On April 18, Dr. Pavy made an evaluation of the members of the expedition and stated that Israel was one of them who was in a very bad state.

Most of the entries made by Sergeant Israel in his journal expressed his concern for the condition of others. Nowhere does he complain or mention any woes of his own. He made his last entry in his journal on the same day that Dr. Pavy reported that Israel was in a bad state, a month and nine days prior to his death:

Friday, April 18th 1884. Stormy day. Brainard brought in 18 lbs of shrimps. Biederbick quite low, also Ellis.

On May 6 Israel wrote a letter to his mother:

Dearest Mother,

Although our condition is not altogether desperate as yet, I take this opportunity of addressing a farewell note to you, still hoping that I may destroy it in the near future. It will not be necessary for me to detail the history of the expedition, our work, or the retreat of last fall. Will only say that the time spent at Ft. Conger was a very pleasant and profitable one to me, and as you so well know, all happiness is relative. Our winter experience here was not nearly so terrible an ordeal as it must appear to you. Seven of our party have already succumbed; we have on hand about 12 days very short rations, which we supplement with shrimps and seaweed. Our hunters have been so very unsuccessful this season, that the chances appear altogether against our pulling through as a party. Therefore this short note. I don't know how much longer I shall be able to write. In case I perish here, don't take my loss too seriously. My death will be an easy one and I shall make arrangements to have a companion of mine visit you if any of us should return.

Please do forgive me for all the sorrow and worry I may have caused you in the past. If I had returned you would have found me a changed man.

Still hoping that things may take a more favorable turn, than I anticipate, believe me.

Yours,
Edward Israel

On May 18, Greely wrote, "Israel is quite broken down and the whole party is in bad spirits."

On May 23 Ralston died. Israel left the sleeping bag a few hours before Ralston died. On May 26 Greely wrote the following:

Israel is now in a exceedingly weak condition, and unable even to sit up in his bag. I am compelled to raise him and feed him, which is a tremendous drain on my physical strength. He talks much of his home and younger days, and seems thoroughly reconciled to go. I gave him a spoonful of rum this morning; he begged for it so exceedingly hard. It was perhaps not fair to the rest to have given it to him, as it was evident it could not benefit him, as he was so near his end. However it was a great comfort and relief to him, and I did by him as I should like to have been done by in such a time. Nobody objected to my action openly, as Israel has always been a great favorite.

Edward Israel died at about three o'clock on the morning of May 27, 1884. Lieutenant Greely wrote the following:

Sergeant Israel was a young man of some fortune, a graduate of Ann Arbor University, a promising astronomer, with a future before him. His death affected me seriously, as his cheerful and hopeful words during the long months he was

> my bag-companion did much to hold up my hands and relieve my overtaxed brain. He had always endeared himself to all by his kindness, consideration, and unvarying equanimity, and was often called at Sabine our Benjamin. His services were very valuable in our scientific work, and despite his weak physique he had sought field service. In reading the burial service I was mindful of him and his people, and omitted every portion which could be distasteful to his co-religionists.

On a sad day in 1884, August 11, Kalamazoo's flags were at half-mast. Every business was closed. More than three thousand stood reverently at the depot with bowed heads when the body of Edward Israel was brought home. An American flag covered Israel's casket. Mayor Pratt, council members, police and fire detachments, civil groups including the local Bnai Brith Lodge, and an honor guard of former university classmates formed a procession to the Israel residence. The services were conducted at the Israel home by Rabbi Ignatz Mueller of Cincinnati, according to the ritual of the Hebrew faith. Israel's remains were taken to the Mountain Home Cemetery, where the mayor announced a municipal resolution of tribute and delivered a moving eulogy. That the funeral was conducted so quietly and without any bands or music was in deference to wishes of Edward's mother, who was loved by all classes of the community. Edward was buried in the Jewish section of Mountain Home Cemetery in Kalamazoo. A historical marker was erected near his grave in 1972 in memory of the youth who gave his life in the name of science.

The forecasting system advanced by Greely, Israel, and the others led to the US Weather Bureau. Israel's death helped, through pioneer research on that non-obscure Arctic venture, to open the way to a new frontier. Truly, Edward Israel was a brave and courageous man.

Edward Israel's family continued to operate the family business in Kalamazoo for some years. Eventually most of the family moved to Manhattan in New York City.

Anna, the adopted sister, remained in Kalamazoo. She married Sigismund Speyer, an immigrant from Germany, sometime around

1884. Sigismund died sometime between 1900 and 1910, so she was left as a widow. They had two children, Alfred and Elsie.

Tillie, Edward's mother, passed away in 1908.

Joseph, the older brother, who was born about 1857, moved to Manhattan in about 1891, where he was engaged in a business. He married Clara Merchant, and they had two children, Edna and Magnon. The marriage ended in divorce. Joseph's health deteriorated, and he became an invalid in 1906, requiring the constant care of a trained nurse. He resided on the eight floor of a hotel, and on April 14, 1909, one year after his mother's death, when the nurse had left his room, he either fell or jumped to his death out a nearby window to the ground below. He was brought back to Kalamazoo for burial. One of his children, Edna, died four years later, in 1913 at the age of eighteen.

Gotwalt, known as "Goddy," who was born in February 1864, never married. He died in New York in 1911, two years after his brother's fatal fall. He was living at the home of his sister, Lillie.

Edward's sister Lillie was born in December 1861. She married Solomon Charles Lowenstein. They had a son, Edward, who was born in May 1886, and a daughter, born in May 1888.

The youngest sibling of Edward was Mollie. She was born in Kalamazoo on September 22, 1867. She married Arthur J. Mack. They moved to Manhattan in about 1899. They had two children, Emlen and Smithie.

7

Winfield Scott Jewell

(1850–1884)

WINFIELD SCOTT JEWELL was born in Lisbon, New Hampshire, on September 20, 1850. He was the son of Ebenezer and Mary (Young) Jewell. Ebenezer, was born in Exeter, Maine, on June 23, 1819. Ebenezer was the son of Ebenezer and Patience (Quinley) Jewell. Winfield's mother was born in Lisbon on September 18, 1830. She was the daughter of Ithiel and Nancy (Wells) Young.

Winfield's father had been married previously before marrying Winfield's mother. His first wife was Ann Eliza Wells, whom he married on September 11, 1845. Eben and Ann Eliza had a daughter, Mary Rosette, born in July 1846. Ann Eliza, died on September 27, 1847. Eben married Mary Young on February 20, 1848, a few months after his first wife's death. Eben and Mary had four children. Herman was born in Lisbon on February 12, 1849. Next was Winfield, and then Ann Eliza, who was born on January 12, 1853, and was named after Eben's first wife. Ammi was born in 1857.

Ebenezer, also known as Eben, farmed near Sugar Hill, a village a few miles east of Lisbon. He also had some connection to the US Patent Office. When the call came for him to serve in the military, he enlisted in the US Army at Lisbon on November 16, 1861, serving in Company H in the Eighth Infantry of the New Hampshire Volunteers. His daughter Mary Rosette died on September 23, 1862, while he was on duty in Louisiana. She had been attending school at Sugar Hill. Ebenezer died just five days later, on September 28, 1862, from a disease that he had contracted at Camp Parapet, Carrolton, Louisiana.

Winfield's mother, Mary, now had to raise the surviving four children without a husband. Herman was now thirteen years old, Winfield had just turned twelve, Ann Eliza was nine years old, and Ammi was about five. A little over three months later, on January 2, 1863, the number of children had dwindled to three, as Winfield's younger brother, Ammi, died from diphtheria.

Nearly six years later, on October 3, 1868, Winfield's mother married Philemon P. Oakes. Winfield's mother and stepfather were living in Lisbon in 1870, along with Winfield and Ann Eliza. Ann Eliza was attending school and Winfield had attended school and was now listed as a "day laborer." Some reports say that he taught school in Lisbon. Herman was now married to Lizzie Sanders and had a two-year-old son, Seaman. They also lived in Lisbon.

Winfield began his military career on October 20, 1871, by enlisting in the Army Signal Corps at Washington, D.C. He was assigned duty as a clerk. His mother, Mary, died shortly afterward, on December 8, 1872, from malarial fever.

Winfield was discharged from the Army Signal Corps four years later, on October 20, 1875, again at Washington, DC, with the rank of private. It would be a little over a year before Winfield again enlisted in the army, on January 5, 1877. Again he was listed as a clerk. Some records suggest that Winfield was a schoolteacher in the Lisbon area. If so, it must have been between when he was discharged from the army in October 1875 and when he reenlisted in January 1877.

Winfield's career and fate were now beginning to take shape. He was sent to be part of a team to observe and record the weather on Mount Washington, New Hampshire. Sergeant Cone, who had been the chief observer in the weather station from 1877, suffered from an accident while descending the mountain in January 1878. Private Murphy, who had been on his support staff, replaced Cone as chief observer. On August 16, 1878, Winfield Jewell replaced Murphy as chief observer; Murphy was promoted to corporal, and Jewell was promoted to sergeant. Jewell held this position until May 16, 1880, when he was relieved to report back in Washington DC to act as the meteorologist for the expedition to Lady Franklin Bay. He must have done an excellent job, as he was made chief observer, promoted to sergeant, and eventually had a major trail on the mountain named Jewell Trail in his honor.

While Lieutenant Adolphus Greely was scheduled to lead this expedition, funding for it was not authorized by Congress. Captain Howgate, who was the chief disbursing officer of the Signal Corps, said that he would fund the expedition using his own private funds. Without government funding, the army and navy backed out of the expedition. A ship, the *Gulnare*, was contracted for this voyage. It was not as well suited for ice as the *Proteus*, which was to be used the following year. Two lieutenants took leaves of absence from the army to lead the expedition. Jewell apparently wanted to go on the expedition badly enough that he accepted an early discharge from the army so that he could go as a civilian. He was one of fourteen civilians that would be on the expedition. Others included George Rice, the photographer, who would be on the expedition the following year, as well as Doctor Octave Pavy and Henry Clay, the grandson of the Henry Clay of fame.

On June 21, 1880, Winfield received his discharge from the Army Signal Service in Washington, DC. Three days later, on June 24, he left with the expedition team for Lady Franklin Bay. On the way they would pick up needed supplies, including the lumber for their quarters, dog teams, and drivers for the teams. They stopped at St. John's, Newfoundland, loaded supplies, and were still there on July 26 when Pavy made his will, which was witnessed by W. S. Jewell and H. Clay.

The expedition departed St. John's on July 30. On August 9 they encountered a gale, and as a result, ice smashed a hole in the stern of the ship. The *Gulnare* returned to Disko, and from September 8 through 21, repairs were made to the ship. From Disko, the *Gulnare* went to the mines at Ritter Bank, Greenland, to replenish its coal supply; however, the ship obtained only a short supply due to non-anchorage and ice. Supplies, including the lumber for the quarters, were left at Ritter Bank, along with Doctor Pavy and Henry Clay. Besides doing research in Greenland, they would find dog teams and drivers for the expected expedition of the next year. The *Gulnare* returned to St. John's, mostly under sail, arriving near the end of September. From there she proceeded to Washington, DC.

We must assume that Winfield went back to Lisbon, where he probably taught school. But by spring, the Lady Franklin Bay expedition was getting ready for another try. Winfield went to Washington, where he enlisted on April 23, 1881, for a period of five years. He was given the rank of sergeant. The party would leave Washington no later than May 15 and be at St. John's by June 15. According to an entry made in Rice's journal on March 6, 1883, Rice and Jewell left Washington twenty-one months before this date, so that would make their departure date from Washington June 6, 1881. Rice and Jewell seemed to have developed a comradeship from the time they spent together on the Howgate expedition. After assembling in St. John's, Newfoundland, they departed for Greenland on July 7. They picked up Pavy and Clay, the lumber for the quarters, the dog teams, the dog team drivers, and supplies and headed toward Lady Franklin Bay. They reached Lady Franklin Bay on August 10, 1881. Rice, Jewell, and Israel shared a tent while waiting for the quarters to be assembled. Jewell and Israel could relate to each other, as both were in the meteorology field. On August 25, the three of them moved into the quarters. The three of them had quarters together next to the chronometers, chronograph, and anemometer, all used to record climate information.

As early as August 28, Jewell was involved with hunting and exploration of the area around them. On September 9, Jewell was part of a party that was sent out to rescue Rice, as he had been out exploring and ended up with rheumatism and could not return home on his own. On November 29, Jewell was on the sick list, but he recovered by December 3. During the following months Jewell was involved in his primary duties, which included placing and reading meters, measuring the water temperature and the thickness of the ice, testing sound signals, and making magnetic observations.

In March 1882, Jewell was part of a team that included Lockwood, Brainard, and Fredericks, who was the dog team driver, with the mission of caching supplies for an expedition north later in the year. They were gone for ten days. In the later part of March, Jewell was part of another, similar mission. On this trip Jewell traveled about one hundred and sixty miles, with temperatures dipping to minus thirty-five degrees.

In April, Jewell headed a support team for the group that would reach a point farther north than any person had been. During the last part of May and into June 1882, Jewell was involved with many more excursions. Jewell also accompanied Rice to various points where Rice would take photographs. Throughout the fall and winter of 1882–83 Jewell was involved with making and recording instrument readouts. Beginning in March 1883, Jewell was involved with providing support for exploratory teams, much as he had done the year before.

On October 8, the expedition departed from Cape Sabine in the steam launch *Lady Greely*, with three boats in tow. The hope was to get to a place where they would be rescued before the winter set in. After losing the *Lady Greely* in the ice, they reached land on foot two months after they departed from Cape Sabine. The supplies they had expected to be cached there did not exist. Now winter was setting in, and they had very little to keep them alive for the next few months. By the end of 1883, the party was very weak, including Jewell.

On April 7, 1884, Lockwood reported in his journal, "Jewell is much weaker this morning." Five days later, on April 12, 1884, Jewell died. Pertaining to Jewell, Greely made the following statement in his journal:

> Jewell failed after Lockwood's death, and, despite extra food, four ounces daily, died on the 12th, becoming unconscious in my arms. I fed him for several days before his death, and labored assiduously to inspire him with new courage and vigor. He was an excellent man, and had been a most efficient and conscientious observer. He had also performed extraordinary field service considering his slight physique.

Jewell's body was recovered from the ice field at Camp Clay during the rescue and brought back to New York aboard the *Bear*. His remains were taken from there to Lisbon, New Hampshire. Services were held for him on August 7, 1884. He was buried in the Grove Hill cemetery in Lisbon.

After enduring the winter weather on Mount Washington and acquiring the necessary skills to be part of an Arctic expedition team,

Winfield Scott Jewell devoted himself to the work that was set out for him. He knew the perils of serving of the Arctic, yet he bravely performed his duties. Winfield Scott Jewell was truly a brave man.

Winfield's sister, Ann Eliza Jewell, married George Myron Trickey in East Corinth, Maine, on December 29, 1878. Ann Eliza had probably moved to Maine to live with an aunt after her mother's death, until she married. George Trickey was a farmer, farming near Corinth, Maine. George and Ann Eliza had four children: Winfield, born November 19, 1880; Carl, born September 22, 1882; Walter, born July 5, 1885; and Cedric, born January 5, 1890. Their four sons all married: Winfield to Florence Marcella Buck, Carl to Edith Jones, Walter to Sara Salley, and Cedric to Lois Eaton. Ann Eliza died on February 25, 1914, in Corinth, Maine. George Myron Trickey died on May 12, 1937. They are buried in the Corinthian Cemetery in Corinth, Maine, along with others in the family.

Winfield's brother, Herman Eugene, was a worker as well as a foreman in a pulp mill. Herman and Elizabeth Sanders had a son, Seaman Jewell, born in 1868. In 1871, Herman and Elizabeth had another child, Lucien, who died on March 31, 1873, in Lisbon when she was only two years old. On June 22, 1878, Herman and Elizabeth were married in St. Johnsbury, Vermont. Two years later, when the 1880 census was taken, Herman and Elizabeth were living apart in Lisbon. The census record lists Elizabeth as being widowed; however, Herman is listed as still being married. On April 30, 1881, Herman's wife, Elizabeth, married Henry S. Wheeler, the marriage taking place in Lisbon. The following year, on March 23, 1882, Herman married Emma Mullikin Gammell in Barnet, Vermont. Sixteen years later, Herman married for the third time, this time to Mary A. Moore on December 1, 1898, at Somersworth, New Hampshire. Herman died three years later, on September 24, 1901. His son, Seaman Jewell, died on March 18, 1942, in Claremont, New Hampshire.

George W. Rice

(1855–1884)

GEORGE WALTER RICE was born in Little Bras d'Or, Cape Breton, Nova Scotia on June 29, 1855. He was the oldest of eight children of Joseph Frederick Rice and Mary Ann (Munn) Rice. His siblings were Roswell Henry Rice, Robert Rice, Lewis Rice, Amy J. Rice, Alice L. Rice, Eliza G. Rice, and John Munn Rice.

He moved with his family to Baddeck, Victoria County, Nova Scotia, at a young age, and he spent his childhood there. Sometime prior to 1875 he moved to Washington, DC.

George had an uncle, Moses P. Rice, who came to Washington, DC in the very early 1860s. Moses became involved in photography and photographed many of the political figures around Washington, including President Lincoln in 1863. George became an active worker in his uncle's photography business and was drawn to the photography trade, which he chose as his profession.

George studied law at Columbian College in 1877 and 1878, an institution that another Rice, Reverend Luther Rice, was instrumental in founding. The college is currently a part of George Washington University.

George was a very dedicated person. He did not seem fixed on getting married. He visited his hometown of Baddeck in the summer of 1875; upon returning to Washington, DC, he received several letters from a schoolmate of his that seemed to hint that they should have a closer relationship. In the letter the classmate scolded George for not seeing her when he was home. Later she was upset because he had not answered one of her letters. In 1877 George received personal letters from a lady in Brooklyn, New York, who apparently had been a customer of his uncle's photographic shop. In this letter the lady spilled out all her personal laundry and hinted that she wanted to be a good friend of George's. My perception was that he did not reciprocate the desire to become personal with either of these ladies.

In 1880 George W. Rice was offered a chance to accompany the expedition heading toward Lady Franklin Bay that year. He accepted the offer to go as the photographer. He departed Washington aboard the *Gulnare* on June 21, 1880. The ship was damaged while attempting to get through the ice in Smith Sound, only a couple of hundred miles from their destination, Lady Franklin Bay, and was forced to return, bringing back all of the expedition members except Doctor Pavy and Henry Clay, who stayed in Greenland.

When a follow-up expedition to Lady Franklin Bay was planned to depart in 1881 on the *Proteus*, George was again invited to be the photographer for the expedition. He was offered the rank of sergeant and was enlisted in the army at Washington, DC, on May 2, 1881, for a period of five years. His enlistment record revealed that George was five feet, seven inches tall and had gray eyes and brown hair. He had a tattoo on his arm that identified him with his English heritage.

George departed Washington on the sixth of June under the charge of Lt. Frederick Kislingbury, one of the three officers of the expedition. All of the expedition members united in St. John's, Newfoundland. The following excerpts from George Rice's journal best describe the departure from St. John's toward Greenland aboard the ship *Proteus*:

> July 7, 1881
>
> This morning the freight for the expedition that arrived per *Hiberian* was hoisted on board the *Proteus* and every preparation made for a start. At noon Capt. Pike gave the order to "get under weigh". At about 12:30 we moved from the anchorage and amid cheers and the waving of handkerchiefs from the shore, steam slowly through the narrows. Considerable interest is taken in our departure and it is with

feelings of regret we gaze, for the last time for many days, upon that most interesting feature of society and civilized life represented by a group of gaily dressed ladies who stand on Signal Hill and kindly waved us goodbye.

Bleak and cold as Newfoundland gets with its drapery of fog hanging over its high cliffs, we shall exchange it for the desolate land of eternal snow with regret. Our start is a formable one and we go coasting along the bold shore. Under full sail and steam at a splendid rate. The wind is a pleasant land breeze and we are soon carried by the entrance to the great bays, Conception and Trinity. The ship's crew are busily engaged cleaning up the decks and putting things in their proper places, "making things ship shape", as the mate says.

Our party occupy their time in locating and [sic] doffing their city costumes and donning clothes more substantial and better adapted to ship life. Some are evidently meditating on the future of our arduous undertaking towards which we have taken our initial step today and which has probably, in many cases, never been so seriously considered as at this moment to realize that we have left behind our relatives, friends, society, civilization and when any that makes life pleasant, in this terrene sphere, for the long space of two years is enough to furnish ample food for reflection even to the most thoughtless and then it is impossible to avoid looking forward with something like apprehension to the future sojourn in those regions of perpetual snow and ice under a hostile sky. No matter how much forethought may be exercised, these thoughts have never so strongly infested themselves as at this time when we find ourselves in the mid Atlantic, with our ship's prow pointed to the north star and every revolution of the propeller speeding us nearer our inhospitable destination and further from home and friends. We retire at a late hour to be lulled to sleep by the motion of the ship, which does not yet become unpleasant and dream of icebergs and polar bears.

July 8, 1881

We are moving along at a splendid rate. The weather is fair but the temperature is growing much cooler. Now that we are all together a roll call to make acquaintance is not amiss. We are members of an Arctic Exploring Expedition sent out under the auspice of the War Department, United States America (or more immediately of the Chief Signal Office, USA) "for scientific observation in the arctic regions." The plan of the expedition is to establish a station at Lady Franklin Bay, Latitude 81 degrees 40 minutes North and spend two years in observation and exploration making sledge journeys to the north at such times and seasons as are practicable and formable. The Expedition is under the command of Lieut. A. W. Greely.

For our transportation to Lady Franklin Bay the United States government has chartered the sealing steamer *Proteus* owned and sailing from St. John's Newfoundland. She is commanded by Capt. Pike who has for his first officer Mr. Norman, second, Mr. White. Mr. McPherson is first engineer and Mr. Carmicheal second. The crew is composed of sturdy Newfoundland sailors. Capt. Pike and his mates have all had long experience in ice navigation and our ship is specially adapted for her mission, as she was built for the seal fishing and every thing that experience could suggest was done to make her capable of resisting the action of the ice.

Five days after departing St. John's, George Rice wrote this in his journal:

Tuesday, July 12, 1881

The wind is still adverse. The temperature has fallen very low and indicates the presence of ice. At 8 P.M. we fell in with the ice. A long narrow strip of field ice bergs, which we carefully steam at half speed, following the tortuous channel, which the openings in the ice affords. The crow's nest has been hoisted up to the fore-top gallant mast head and in it the second mate stands and directs the movement of the ship.

The presence of the ice has calmed the sea and we are surrounded with a most beautiful scene. The beautiful blue-green edges of the ice blending with the dark blue ocean and lighted up by the oblique rays of the setting sun, presents a panorama of rare beauty resembling some rare mosaic on a grand scale.

In the fore ground can be seen several seals of the Harp species. Lt. Kislingbury hazards several shots at them without effect, as the distance is too great. Occasionally a mammoth whale can be seen emerging like some miniature island among the ice. It blows, sending a spurt of water, which dyed with the same tints of the setting sun presents all the colors of the rainbow.

Our position can only be ascertained by dead reckoning as no meridian observations have been made. We place this flow of ice in Latitude 61 degrees North.

They had moved north two degrees, about one hundred and thirty-five miles, in one day. George Rice seemed confident that the ship would get through the ice to Lady Franklin Bay after the failure of the *Gulnare* the year before.

Wednesday, July 13, 1881

Our party, or those who have been so unfortunate as to be seasick, are now renewing their spirits in the water kept smooth by the ice. This Mal De Mer has visited our party pretty generally without regards to age or status. I am so fortunate as always to enjoy an immunity from it. Lt. Greely has experienced its unpleasant effects in a large degree.

We fall in with another ice pack. Latitude about 63 degrees. It presents the same appearance as the former pack we met. The wind coming off it makes the temperature very cold, making us realize that we must expect the whale "Boreas" chilly breath earlier than we anticipated. During our passage the prevailing winds have been from the north, which argues well for our success as the ice will be driven out of Smith Sound admitting of our passage through it. We sighted land for the first time today.

A couple of days later they had moved north about another 250 miles. George Rice enters a description of the surroundings in his journal:

Friday, July 15, 1881

We can occasionally see the land when the fog lifts. The Capt. and Mr. Israel both were successful in getting a meridian operation. Our latitude is 66 degrees 42 minutes North. Land well in sight. I recognize the land very readily from my remembrance of last year's cruise. To a stranger from the south the weird appearance of these latitudes is most remarkable and fascinating. A dark bold striking coastline icy and which the snow clad mountains ascending to dizzy altitudes can be seen as the gauzy curtain of fog lifts. The sea is dotted with bergs presents no other obstruction of the eye and as we again turn our eyes to land we are impressed with the silent and desolate appearance of everything. No sign of animal or vegetable life disturbs or beautifies the scene. Silence reigns supreme.

On July 16 they reached Godhaven, Greenland. Rice writes the following:

I instantly recognized the conformation of the land from my recollection of my trip in the *Gulnare* last year and was able to direct the way to the harbor of Godhaven, which we soon reached and dropped anchor at about 10 P.M. The sun was still up and the little basin like harbor looked very peaceful and inviting as we steamed into it. It was calm and still as a duck pond and in the glassy water which was clear as crystal was reflected the towering frowning cliffs which surround it. The picturesque Esquimaux in their furry costumes were soon gliding over the water towards us in their peaceful and fairy like kayaks and the pantalooned maidens tripped down to the rocks to get a nearer view of us. It is all so novel and charming that those of us who have not been here before cannot repress the greatest interest and curiosity in surroundings so strange and unlike the civilization we have left.

Dr. Pavy and Henry Clay, who we expected to join us here are at Ritenbenk, a distance about 70 miles. We will leave here in a few days for Ritenbenk and will then proceed to Upernivik, our last stopping place until our destination is reached. From information Inspector Smith gives us never to infer that our chances for getting through the ice this year are very good. The winter in Greenland has been a very mild one and reports from the northern stations state navigation clear of ice.

A ship would travel from Godhaven to Copenhagen, on the way carrying mail to the United States. This is the first time we find out that Rice is gathering material for the Herald, a New York City-based newspaper.

Sunday, July 17, 1881

This morning we are informed that a boat leaves here for Egedesminde where a Danish ship is lying about ready to start for Copenhagen and will carry our mail matter which can be sent to us, via Denmark. We are all therefore very busily engaged writing to friends and relatives. I send communication to the Inf. Herald reporting our arrival and stating our chances for getting through to Lady Franklin Bay as well as I can judge from the latitude here.

At this time of the year, at this latitude, the sun is above the horizon for all but two hours each day. George writes the following:

July 18, 1881—Monday

It is difficult for one not noting the time to distinguish night and day here. The sun does not set till about 11 P.M. and is up again at 1 A.M. The morning and evening nightfall blend into one, casting a silvery musty light over everything. I am writing this in the cabin at midnight without the aid of artificial light.

On July 19 he did his first photographic work of the expedition. He writes the following:

Tuesday, July 19, 1881

I make several negatives today. Photograph the *Proteus* and Godhavn harbor. I also made a group of the Governor's family and Miss Smith and her Governess. They are very much pleased to have the opportunity of being photographed and dress themselves for the occasion with great care. Miss Smith and her companion looked particularly charming in the bright lively colors of the Danish peasant girl. At least they look very charming to us who do not expect to see another female in a civilized costume for two years.

The ship sailed to Ritenbenk, Greenland, on July 21 and toward Upernivik the next day. Rice writes the following:

Thursday, July 21, 1881

Left Disco this morning at 2 a.m. and after a run of about 60 miles along the coast of Disco Island arrived in Ritenbenk.

Friday, July 22, 1881

Left Ritenbenk this p.m. for Upernivik. Will pass through the Waigat Strait separating Disco Islands from the mainland.

The expedition arrived at Upernavik on July 24. They were now over seven hundred miles north of St. John's with nearly that distance remaining to Lady Franklin Bay. George Rice describes the settlement:

Sunday, July 24, 1881

Arrived at Upernavik this morning at 5:30. The latitude of the place is 72 degrees, 48 minutes North. It resembles the other Danish settlement we have visited. Consists of the residence of the Governor, the storehouse, cooper shop, smithy and the turf huts of the Esquimaux population.

Rice was part of a party that went from Upernavik to Proven to procure the two Eskimos that accompanied them on the expedition. George Rice relates an unusual incident that occurred while he was at this outpost. They returned to Upernavik with the two Eskimos on July 28.

A party (Lt. Lockwood, Gov. Elberg of Upernavik, Cross, Lynn and myself) started this morning for Proven to procure two Esquimaux to accompany the expedition as dog drivers and hunters. This distance is about fifty miles. We took the inside passage through the islands as the sea was too rough to go outside. Our conveyance was the little steam launch '*Lady Greely*'. We arrived at Proven at 9:30.

At Proven a better opportunity for study of the habits of the primitive aborigines is afforded than at any other place we have visited. The whalers and exploring parties seldom get there, so the influence of the white man is less perceptible. They retain their habits of life as practiced before the Dane inspired their condition to a greater extent than in other parts of Greenland.

I spent at least three hours in one of the most uninviting igloos or huts I saw. The manufacture of a cap of eider down, for which I was waiting, gave me a pretext from so long a stay. The hut was built of turf rocks and moss and was entered by a long tunnel, so low that I was compelled to crawl on my hands and feet to affect an entrance, a most disagreeable and humiliating proceeding, as the dogs and natives (not much better than the former in point of cleanliness) enter in the same way.

On reaching the small interior hole, which is at once their living, eating and sleeping room, I was surprised to see the mistress of the house in a state of almost complete nudity sitting on the shelf or platform on which they sleep. I turned aside to give her an opportunity of donning a more complete costume but a furtive backward glance soon showed me that she appeared to prefer being dressed as nearly a la Venus as possible. I at once faced the music and had soon made a satisfactory arrangement by which I was to receive a cap in exchange for a neckerchief I wore. The former however, was not in esse so the contract remained executory until it was completed.

The maker measured the time of my interests with precision and was soon busily engaged in cutting up eider skins and fitting them into a cap. Her scantiness of clothes appeared to give her an advantage, as she seemed to get along more expeditiously by holding the skin between her feet while sewing.

The room was very low and the atmosphere stifling and nauseating from the odors exhaled by the skins and oil. No glass in the window, as a substitute they used the membranous tissue of the stomach of the seal which when oiled is almost transparent. There was not stove or fireplace, instead they used a hollow stone for a lamp with fuel of oil and moss for a wick. The floor was of lime and earth. The sleeping arrangements were very simple, a platform about two feet high extending from the wall six feet occupying one side of the room. This is the receptacle of skins and furs during the day and when the natives retire they make it a funeral couch, each deciple of Morphaes drawing over him or herself so many of the skins as are necessary to comfort.

The costume of the Esquimaux women is so nearly like that of the men that at first sight it is not easy to distinguish the sexes although the females make theirs up in a much more elaborate manner festooning more ornamentation upon it. The feet are encased in a pair of dainty socks reaching above the knee. Next come the pants or trunks which, however, are very short, coming down not more than half way of the thigh. The socks are pulled up to meet them. The upper part of the body is covered by a cassock of sealskin devoid of buttons and is pulled in over the head. An attached hood can be drawn over the head or allowed to fall back on the shoulders at pleasure.

My cap being complete, I was glad to get away from the nauseating surroundings and breathe the fresh air again. Many of the natives however occupy much better dwellings than the one I have described. Such a one represents the habitations of the poorer class who have not intermixed with the Danes. In the evening I entered a larger dwelling occupied by a half breed and finding an old violin on the wall, I soon had a number of the fair sex dancing enthusiastically to my rather imperfect music. I became very popular with them at once and in leaving Proven, which we did at 10:30 p.m., a bevy of dark maidens were at the shore to bid me good bye or their Esquimaux equivalent. Through the efforts of Gov. Elberg the two Esquimaux, Christiansen and Edwards, were induced to accompany us. They exhibited considerable emotion pining themselves very unlike their stoical Inuit American relatives. On parting with their friends they shed bitter tears that fell indeed until their homes were out of sight. We had a very pleasant passage returning. The midnight sun making it light as day.

The ship departed from Upernivik in the afternoon of July 29, 1881, and on August 2, after stopping at Littleton Island to examine stores left there by the British and taking some photographs, they continued northward toward Lady Franklin Bay. Ten days later they managed to break through the ice, and after determining that the harbor near the coal mine was inaccessible, they docked at Discovery Harbor, repeatedly charging the ice until the ship reached the shore.

While Sergeant Rice helped unload the cargo, he also was involved with making numerous photographs and assisting the commander with meteorology reports to be sent back with the ship.

After about a week of discharging all their cargo, the *Proteus* was released to return to St. John's. The construction of the quarters had begun, and during this time Sergeant Rice was kept busy writing letters and preparing the photographs he had taken to be sent back on the *Proteus*. The weather and the ice prevented the *Proteus* from departing Lady Franklin Bay until August 22. Sergeant Rice believed that the odds of a ship getting through the ice into this harbor in the future to resupply or rescue them were slim. He writes the following:

> Many letters to write, as no other opportunity may be offered for years, at least one year, and our experience of this season rather shakes my belief in the ability of a ship to reach this latitude every season. It is a mere chance.

Sergeant Rice was assigned quarters near the center of the building, which he shared with Sergeant Jewell and Sergeant Israel. The three of them shared a tent while awaiting the quarters to be prepared for occupancy. On August 25 Jewell and Israel moved into the quarters; however, Rice continued to occupy the tent for the solace it provided.

Rice's first trek from the quarters was a trip of about fifty miles each way with Doctor Pavy to Lincoln Bay. The purpose of the trek was to examine the depot of provisions left by the English expedition of 1875–1876 as well as to check for any signs of the *Jeannette*, a ship that had vanished a year or two before. They departed Fort Conger on the evening of August 29, 1881, taking with them a small tent, blankets, spare clothing, cooking apparatus, alcohol, and rations. Ralston and Lynn accompanied them as far as St. Patrick Bay, taking rations to that point in order to provide for the return trip of Pavy and Rice. They arrived at St. Patrick Bay at one o'clock the next morning, having traveled six hours in temperatures down to zero.

They started traveling again near noon on August 31. They reached the cairn at Cape Beechy after making a difficult descent. A cache of food was made at this point for use on their return trip. Sergeant Rice took a shot at a musk ox; however, he missed. Their next attempt to reach Wrangel Bay was by the ice foot; however, it was washed away at Black Cliffs, where the cliffs descended almost perpendicularly to the water. They had to retrace their footsteps, and they camped at the foot of a ravine just after midnight on September 1, where they stayed until about noon.

In order to travel farther north they had to ascend to the top of a mountain with an elevation of twenty-five hundred feet. A strong breeze was blowing. Their progress was difficult and slow with the snow blinding them and with a temperature below zero. After over twelve hours of traveling they finally reached Wrangel Bay and had their first warm meal. They had eaten only two biscuits each all day. They managed to cut through the ice at Wrangel Bay and get some badly needed water.

They left the camp just after midnight on September 2. The temperature during the night had been very low, and their boots were frozen stiff. When Sergeant Rice placed his canteen of rum to his mouth to take a drink, the canteen stuck to his lips, removing some of the skin.

While attempting to cross on some fairly recently formed ice, Sergeant Rice fell through and got wet up to his waist. His boots were filled with water. He emptied the boots; however, the wet socks retained so much of the water that he had wet feet all day. They reached Cape Frederick VII at nine o'clock that evening and were forced by the high cliffs to follow the shoreline, arriving at the north side of where the depot rations were placed; however, due to an error, they passed by them. Then, instead of camping and waiting until the next day, they decided to continue on to Cape Union. It was farther than they had supposed, and they did not reach Cape Union until ten o'clock the next morning. They had been walking for over twenty-two hours continuously. They were pleased indeed to find the cache of provisions at that site.

They spent the day examining the one thousand rations, which were left by the English six years before. The provisions were generally in good condition. While the bread was spoiled, the chocolate, preserved meat, stearine, etc. were all in good condition. Some of the tobacco, tea, and sugar was spoiled; however, most of it was usable.

Rice's feet and legs were badly swollen, and he was lame all day. He assumed that the cause was the long walk and the exposure to the weather; however, it was caused by acute rheumatism. They started out traveling again at six o'clock that evening. The progress was very slow, as he suffered excruciatingly at every step. They traveled for sixteen hours before reaching Wrangel Bay on the morning of September 5. The brook that they had gotten their water from on the way out had now dried up, so they had to melt snow for drinking water. After eight hours of rest, and with Rice suffering from the effects of the painful rheumatic attacks, they departed toward home. They reached Cape Beechy at 3:00 pm on September 6. The rheumatism was now so severe that Rice's breathing was difficult and painful. They begin again at 9:00 pm after a six-hour rest. Sergeant Rice's pulse was up to 114, and he asked the doctor to leave him, saying he would catch up, as he was in such pain. Dr. Pavy opted to carry nearly all the load that Rice was carrying. After a short distance they abandoned some of the unneeded supplies. Only with the greatest of willpower was Rice able to travel that day due to the rheumatism. His limbs and chest pained him so much that he groaned with every step.

The next morning they reached a small cache of provisions that they had left on the way out between Cape Beechy and St. Patrick Bay. They prepared their meal and erected their shelter tent. Rice tried to rest; however, the pain was so great that sleep was impossible.

That evening they attempted to start toward St. Patrick Bay; however, it was impossible for Rice to walk. Finally it was decided that Doctor Pavy should go on ahead to home camp to get assistance for Rice, and Rice would proceed toward St. Patrick Bay, where the relief party would meet him. Rice and the doctor moved ahead for another fifteen hours before it was determined that Rice could go no further. Pavy then left him and headed back toward Fort Conger for help.

Dr. Pavy reached the home camp, and while many volunteered to assist in bringing back Rice, five, headed by Sergeant Brainard, were selected. They brought along a ladder, which was used as a means of carrying Rice. They placed a tent over the ladder to try to keep him warm in the below-zero weather. They reached a hill that the men could not traverse carrying Rice. Private Bender was sent back to the fort to get additional help. Five more people came to assist and managed to move Rice up the hill and get him on a sledge to move him to the home station. They arrived there just after midnight on September 10, about twelve days after they had left on the journey. Two of the rescue party had badly frozen feet.

Rice's condition began to improve immediately after he was given warm food and shelter. Six days later, on September 16, 1881, his condition improved enough that he was able to leave camp to help Private Henry place poisoned meat for the wolves in the valley near Mount Cartmel.

Rice was appointed the editor of a newspaper, the Arctic Moon. The first issue was published on November 24, 1881. The newspaper was short-lived.

Rice participated in many treks while at Fort Conger. Some of them were to cache provisions for journeys away from camp, some were to take photographs, others were to hunt or bring in provisions, such as musk oxen that had been killed.

Another long trek that Sergeant Rice made was in the early spring of 1882. This trek was to be made to the north toward Cape Joseph Henry, as was the trek in September of the year before. Again the party would consist of Rice and Doctor Pavy, accompanied by Jens the Eskimo dog-sledge driver. The purpose of the trip was to check again for signs of the *Jeannette* and to determine if there was an open sea to the north of Cape Joseph Henry. Cape Joseph Henry was about ninety-five miles due north of Fort Conger. The route that they would take made it no less than one hundred and fifty miles each way. They would need to backtrack several times in order to maintain all the needed supplies for the trip.

Preparations for the trip began on March 15, 1882. They packed clothing, cooking gear, and a whole list of other things that would be needed for the long trip. By March 18 the preparations were completed, and they departed camp on the morning of March 19. It was extremely cold, the temperatures ranging from twenty-five to forty-five degrees below zero.

Jewell and Fredericks, the other Eskimo driver, went along as a support team as far north as Lincoln Bay, a distance of about forty miles. At Depot B, some ten miles out, they met up with a party of seven of their comrades who were returning from a trek to the Greenland shore. They had experienced temperatures as low as sixty-one degrees below zero. Rice's party departed at about ten o'clock on the morning of March 20 and stopped about six o'clock that evening, when it began snowing and blowing so much that they could not see to continue. They were somewhere between Cape Beechy and Wrangel Bay, some thirty miles north of the fort. Rice and Jewell dug a snow house for shelter while the doctor and the Eskimos fed the dogs.

The next day they got started at about noon. The temperature was a mild ten degrees below zero. They traveled along the ice foot on the edge of Robeson Channel, the channel separating Grinnell Land from Greenland. Water from the channel had blown onto the shore of Grinnell Land and frozen, creating rubble ice and making the traveling difficult. Steering and pushing their sledges over and around these mounds of ice, with over six hundred pounds on each sledge, was a difficult task. The sledges were upset a couple of times, damaging the runner on one of the sledges. They managed to reach Wrangel Bay at about seven-thirty that evening, probably progressing northward no more than ten miles.

They erected the tent, but it could not accommodate the entire party, so Rice and Jewell burrowed into the snow and spent an uncomfortable night in which the temperature dropped to twenty-four degrees below zero. Rice's knees were swollen and rather stiff, which made him fear a recurrence of the acute rheumatism he had experienced the previous September. By morning his condition had improved. They continued their northerly trek, reaching Mount Parry, where they had stored some provisions on the September trip. Most of the provisions had been destroyed by a polar bear. They gathered up the remnants and continued traveling. They managed to get to the ice floes that covered Robeson Channel and found the traveling much better as they crossed over a snow bridge from one floe to the next. At fifty-thirty in the evening of March 22, they reached Lincoln Bay and set up camp; the temperature was thirty-five degrees below zero. They attempted to sleep in a snow hut; however, they had no way of closing the entrance, and the cold air entered, at forty degrees below zero.

The next morning Jewell, with his team of dogs and the driver Fredericks, started back toward Fort Conger. This left Doctor Pavy, Rice, the Eskimo Jens, and their dog team to continue on the journey. In order to cut down the weight they had to carry, only two one-man sleeping bags were brought along. One of them was used by Pavy, while Rice and Jens shared the other bag. They could fit into the bag only by "spooning," which did not make for a very comfortable sleep, as neither could turn without the other person turning too.

They continued their journey on the morning of March 24 with an outside temperature of forty-two degrees below zero; it had been down to fifty-six below during the night. All three of the men had been frostbitten, Rice on his fingers. On the evening of March 25 they reached Black Cape. They cached their load and started back to get more stores. They got back to the snow house at Lincoln Bay at four-thrity in the evening of the next day.

They started out again the next morning and reached the tent at Cape Union at four o'clock that afternoon. The temperature was considered quite warm at eleven degrees below zero; however, the wind was blowing hard. After spending a miserable night in the tent with the snow blowing in, temperature down to twenty-five degrees below zero, and the dogs howling piteously, they started back toward Black Cape to add some more provisions. Their load was heavy, so they had to stop repeatedly. They reached Black Cape late that afternoon, melted some ice, ate lunch, and started back toward False Cape, where they arrived at eight o'clock that night, the twenty-eighth.

In the morning they again began traveling south toward their snow house at Lincoln Bay to get one last load to cache. The temperature during the night had been down to forty-three degrees below zero. Rice was suffering with pains in his legs and discovered that one of his knees was swollen to twice the size of the other. They got back to the snow house at Lincoln Bay after traveling four hours. The temperature during the night was down to fifty-two degrees below zero; however, by midnight it was back up to fifteen degrees below zero. With the drifting snow and high winds they were unable to travel the next day, March 30.

At eight-thirty the following morning, they dug out from the snow, and with a load of nearly four hundred pounds they again headed north toward their tent at False Cape. They reached the tent a little after noon and returned to Lincoln Bay for their last load. They arrived back at their tent at four o'clock that afternoon.

It was now April 1, and because of theglare on the eyes of the sun shining on the snow, they decided to travel at night instead of during the day. They started traveling a little after six that evening, not expecting to visit Lincoln Bay again until their return homeward; however, the sledge bounded awkwardly from the ice foot to a lower level and split one of the runners. They unloaded and carried their sleeping bags and cooking gear back to the snow house, arriving about midnight.

Rice volunteered to go back to Fort Conger and return on foot in five days to have a sledge runner made. Doctor Pavy was at first quite averse to the idea, as it appeared too hazardous. Pavy finally approved of Rice going back, with the Eskimo Jens accompanying him. After some difficult traveling they arrived back at the fort on April 3. The sledge runner was repaired that night, and Rice and the Eskimo Jens started back to rejoin Doctor Pavy. They arrived at Lincoln Bay at six o'clock the morning of April 6. They rested throughout the day.

At seven o'clock that evening they again took off heading northward. For several days they were engaged in hauling stores from Cape Union to Black Cape. The traveling was very difficult, the ice foot inclining at a sharp angle from the cliff to the sea and presenting an inclined plane above which the dogs crawled, the sledge following on one runner most of the time and always in imminent danger of toppling over.

On April 11 they reached Floeberg Beach, the winter quarters of HMS *Alert* in 1875–76. Floeberg Beach is at latitude 82 ° 27 ' north, the point farthest north that a ship had ever attained.

They continued northward and reached Cape Joseph Henry on April 18, 1882. As they looked out over the great frozen sea to the north and east of Cape Joseph Henry, Rice commented in his journal:

> It seems to say to the terrible sea that faces the immense fragments of ice in chaotic piles at its base "so far shalt thou come and no further".

On the nineteenth and twentieth they remained near Cape Joseph Henry, as the weather was so stormy that they could not travel. Rice describes the scene:

> It is impossible to convey any idea of the roughness of its character for we have nothing to which it can be compared. The floes were of great thickness as could be seen as an occasional abutment of the uniform thickness of the floe was joined by new ice on which we stood and found the level of the palaeocrystic floe two feet above our heads. This would indicate, with its 7/8 submerged, a frozen sea of ice 50 feet thick. I think Markham puts it at 75 feet. Of course the only exception to this thickness would be the forming ice connecting the pack after its disruption, but of such forming ice we saw nothing to the north, east, or west of Cape Joseph Henry, yet the above conveys no idea of the character of the surfaces a palaeocrystic floe of any extent furnishes excellent traveling, rolling and undulating like prairie land. Such floes we had met with in Robeson channel but nothing like them could be seen from our present outlook. At some seasons, this immense ice field, under the influence of the sun of endless summer days and the tides and currents, has became disrupted, and the immense pieces of the disintegrated pack hurled and jostled off against each other by the mighty force of storms and currents. The collision of these gigantic bodies has resulted in breaking the edges of each and forcing the immense fragments upon the surface until the edge of each and every floe, great and small, is fringed with an irregular chaotic rampart of ice, bristling with pyramids heaped in rounded masses, and piled in confused heaps. Around this nucleus of ice the eddying sun has lodged and alternately pressed and melted by winter's storms and summer's sun adds its layer after layer to the bluing mass till the ice

> become almost mountains. The winter, again fettering together the pack with icy [illegible]. This new ice, unless allowed to acquire sufficient strength during calm weather is evidently broken up again and again before the severity of the winter holds the floes in its mighty grasp. This adds to the ice wall additional fragments of rubble ice that makes it more forbidding and angular.

They were at a latitude nearly as far north as anyone had ever been. After a few days of exploring the area, they began their retreat to Fort Conger. They again experienced many hardships on the way back, including low temperatures and strong winds, and they retreated sometimes, as they could not pass through many areas. They arrived back at Fort Conger on May 2, 1882.

Throughout the stay at Fort Conger, Rice was assigned the duty of taking measurements of the depth of the ice at various points. On June 29, 1882, his birthday, he reminisces and thinks about the position he has put himself in:

> I passed another milestone in my journey of life today. At seven and twenty, one begins to look at birthdays with a jealous eye; especially when one finds them slipping by under such circumstance as I am now placed. One cannot help reflecting that my present is a time of life not to be passed in the inaction, however, enforced that this arctic existence, shutting us off from the world imposes. I now think that I see very clearly, I have made a great mistake in leaving civilization. Nothing can recompense me for the time lost.

By mid-August 1882 no resupply ship had arrived. The commander decided then that if the ship scheduled for the following summer did not arrive by August 12, the fort would be abandoned and they would make their way in the launch, the *Lady Greely*, to either Littleton Island or Cape Sabine. Sergeant Rice did not concur with this decision, as he believed now that a ship would arrive. In his journal he states the following:

> We think the ship is due now and cannot imagine why she does not put in an appearance. The Doctor and a few of the men think that she has not been sent. I cannot think that, for even if the Government are unfavorably placed towards us the only result would be an order recalling us. I cannot imagine why Lt. Greely should decide to leave us on the 12th of August next year simply because the ship has not arrived this year [sic]. He thinks that because the ship did not arrive under such apparently favorable circumstances that we cannot expect to see her next but will have to retreat. The causes for the non-arrival of the ship may be outside of the circumstances of which we are able to judge. We may have open water here while the entrance to Smith Sound is choked up or the north water impassible. The successful navigation of Smith Sound depends upon many conditions. We were quit willing to admit that the ship might fail to reach here one of the two seasons on which the attempt will be made, yet no sooner does she fail than we judge other seasons by this. And again how can it positively be said that we will start by August 12th. We know that there may be conditions of the ice in Lady Franklin Bay under which Cape Leiber cannot be reached from here by boat or sledge.

Rice never again made a journal entry in opposition to Greely's opinion on this matter.

The events concerning Rice during their remaining year at Fort Conger were, for the most part, routine. Rice was active in taking ice depth measurements, hunting, and gathering equipment for the planned exit in the fall of 1883.

After the departure from Fort Conger in 1883, Rice assisted in the steering and navigation of the *Lady Greely* and went on excursions to check for paths to take on the way south from the fort.

During the time at Cape Sabine he was involved in hunting, gathering shrimp, and making trips to search for caches that might contain food. It was on one of these trips that he met his fate.

The account of Rice's death is chronicled in Greely's book, Three Years of Arctic Service:

Early April brought no relief, and game again failed. Christensen's death decided me. I no longer hesitated, but gave the final orders. The orders were verbal. Detailed instructions to such men on such an errand would have been unwise, if not culpable. Rice was regarded naturally as the leader of the forlorn hope, and to him the orders were given simply to go and do the best he could. I, however, cautioned him particularly against over-exertion, knowing his great ambition and fearing for his strength. He had not been well on Thursday, and I had asked him to be fair and candid, so that I might not send a sick and unfit man on so trying and dangerous a journey. I told him that Sergeant Brainard, ever willing and anxious to serve us all, had expressed more than willingness to go in his stead. He on Sunday noon came into my sleeping bag, and had a long talk over the situation. Rice declared that he had recovered entirely from his indisposition, insisted that he was as strong as Brainard, and that the duty should come to him, not only as the originator, but on account of his knowledge of the locality and his familiarity with the appearance of the ice as gained from two trips to Isabella.

About midnight on April 6, 1884, Sergeant Rice and Private Frederick took off toward Baird Inlet to try to recover one hundred pounds of meat that had been abandoned the previous November when Sergeant Ellison became so badly frostbitten that they had to return to camp without it. Rice had been along on that trek, so he felt he knew how to locate the meat. Both Rice and Frederick asked that no special ration be provided to them for this trip, other than what the rest of the party received. Besides rations they took with them a sledge that they would use to haul back the meat, a two-man sleeping bag, a rifle, an ax, an alcohol lamp, and a small cooking pot.

The temperature was eight degrees below zero when they departed. They frequently ran into deep snow banks, which exhausted the men. They were compelled by the weather to camp at eight o'clock on the seventh. They laid their sleeping bag on the snow and had to stay in it for twenty-two hours because of a violent storm. They crawled out of the sleeping bag at about six o'clock on the morning of the eighth. They were so cold that they had to travel for about an hour before they could stop and heat up their food and drink for a hot meal. They had gone almost thirty-six hours without a drink.

On the morning of April 9, the weather had calmed. They were about six miles from where the meat was cached. They decided to drop their sleeping bag and a portion of their rations, planning to return there to rest upon retrieving the meat. Because of frequent open pools of water, they had to make many detours. At times the tidal overflow wet their feet. Late in the morning, the wind picked up, which tended to chill and exhaust them. At three in the afternoon they finally reached the place where the meat had been stashed. After a careful search they found no sign of the meat. Frederick suggested that they return to their sleeping bag and come back the next day for another search. Rice favored searching a little longer, hoping to find the meat.

At about this time, Rice showed signs of exhaustion. They stopped so Rice could rest. They had some warm food and drink, after which Frederick suggested they move to avoid freezing. But Rice was too weak to move. He began talking to Frederick about his personal effects. In order to comfort Rice, Frederick took off his jumper and wrapped Rice's feet in it. Frederick held Rice in his arms until he passed away shortly thereafter. Although he was extremely weak, Frederick managed to get back to the camp.

The rescue ship arrived two months later. Aboard this ship were two of George Rice's brothers, probably Roswell and Robert. The distance from the camp where George Rice died and the months that had passed made it impracticable for the crew to try to find and recover the body. It was left in the Arctic ice.

A memorial service was held for George Rice upon the return of the rescue ships to St. John's, where his family lived. It was held on July 20, 1884, at the Queen's Road Congregation Chapel with Reverend Beaton presiding. In Beaton's presentation, he identifies the members of the Greely expedition with earlier explorers to the north such as Cabot, Frobisher, Davis, Hudson, Bylot, Baffin, and Fox. He also lists Melville, Parry, and Sir John Franklin. About the Greely party he states the following:

I am doing no disparagement to the rest of that brave band, when, in the words of its leader, I say that there was one man who conspicuously manifested this noblest trait of character. George W. Rice, whose family resides among us, was one of the strongest and most cheerful in that little company of brave men. He had one of the best chances of surviving the privations of that awful winter; but when their scanty stores began to diminish he, along with a companion, volunteered to seek some food that was believed to be at some distance from the camp. He found that food after much labor, but the severe cold disabled his companion and the precious stores had to be abandoned. After some time, when certain death began to stare them in the face, as a forlorn hope, he again volunteered to go in search of the much needed food, but he never returned. He perished on the ice-floe, and the memory of his heroism, his self-sacrifice and noble character was all that remained to cheer his companions under their great loss. We are left in no uncertainty, as Christian men, about the nature of such an action. Jesus Christ himself has named it for us; Greater love has no man that this that a man lay down his life for his friends.

George Walter Rice was indeed a noble and brave man. He produced dozens of photographs, including those contained in this book. He assisted in every aspect of the expedition besides that of taking photographs. When it came to perilous journeys or activity, he was willing to say, “Send me.” He represented the best of the best.

David Columbus Ralston

(1848–1884)

DAVID COLUMBUS RALSTON was born on October 3, 1848, at Bloomfield (now called Bloomingdale), Jefferson County, Ohio. He was the oldest of eight children born to Lewis Waltemyer Ralston and Nancy Shotwell Sayers (Sears) Ralston.

His great-grandfather, Andrew Ralston, was born in Scotland on February 25, 1753. Andrew emigrated with his family to the United States as a young child. In 1762, when Andrew was nine years old, Indians massacred his family and burned their home. Andrew and one brother, possibly Joseph, ran into the Pennsylvania woods and avoided death.

Andrew enlisted in the army in 1776 and served honorably in the Revolutionary War. He was wounded in the Battle of Brandywine. He was discharged in 1783, holding the rank of sergeant. Two years later, on December 19, 1785, in York County, Pennsylvania, he married Sophia Waltemyer. They had twelve children, including David Ralston's grandfather, Andrew Ralston II, all born in York County. The family migrated to Bloomfield, Ohio, in 1812.

Andrew Ralston II, was born in York County on February 7, 1797. He married Francis Ann Hesser. They had nine children, including David Ralston's father, Lewis Waltemyer Ralston.

Lewis Waltemyer Ralston was born on September 12, 1825, near Bloomfield, Jefferson County, Ohio. Lewis married Nancy Sears at Cadiz, Harrison County, Ohio, on December 30, 1847. Cadiz is about twelve miles southwest of Bloomfield.

In March 1849, when David Ralston was only five months old, the family moved to Iowa. They boarded a steamship at Steubenville, Ohio, just a few miles east of Bloomfield, and steamed down the Ohio River, meeting up with the Wabash River in Illinois, following the Wabash River to the Mississippi River, and ending up at Keokuk, Iowa, a distance of about a thousand miles. The last eighty miles of the journey were by wagon, terminating at Unionville, Appanoose County, Iowa. A cousin of David's father had settled in Appanoose County some time ahead of their arrival.

The next year, in 1850, the family relocated to a location about five miles east of Centerville, Iowa. They lived there about seven years, moving to Columbia, Marion County, Iowa, some forty miles north, in 1857. At Columbia, David's father was appointed postmaster, and he continued to serve in this capacity until the last year of the War of the Rebellion (Civil War). David Ralston went to the common schools here and received the rudiments of his education. David's family greatly increased; his sister Charlotte Ann was born in 1850; his brother Andrew Jerome was born in 1852; another brother, John Shotwell, who died in infancy, was born in 1855. David's brother William Henry Arrison was born in 1857; another sister, Rose Amanda, was born in 1860; and his youngest sister, Mary Emma, was born in 1861.

In the spring of 1863, when not yet quite sixteen years old, David enlisted as a recruit in the Thirty-Third Regiment of the Iowa Volunteer Infantry. He was first sent to Little Rock, Arkansas, and afterward to New Orleans. From New Orleans his regiment was ordered to Texas. While on his way to Texas, he was taken sick with measles and was sent back to New Orleans. When he recovered he joined his regiment in Texas and remained there for some time, before going back to New Orleans, then later back to Texas. On July 17, 1865, David Ralston was mustered out of the infantry and went to Rock Island, Illinois, where he was discharged in August 1865.

His family, now consisting of his parents, three brothers, (another brother, Lewis Ephraim had been born in early 1864), and three sisters, had moved from Iowa back to Ohio in 1864, settling this time on a farm near St. Louisville in Licking County.

Another brother, George Lincoln, was born in 1865 at about the time of David's discharge. David joined his family in St. Louisville after his discharge.

David worked on his father's farm for a short time, and during the fall and winter of 1866–1867, he attended Kenyon Grammar School at Gambier, Ohio. In 1869, David and his father were operating a general store at Martinsburg, Ohio. During the winter of 1870–1871 he taught a term of district school just south of Martinsburg. In April 1871 he went to Appanoose County, Iowa, where his early home was, and taught a summer and fall term at the district school. In December 1871, he went to St. Louis, Missouri, and attended the Telegraph Institute. While he was there he applied for admission into the US Signal Service. He passed the examination and immediately enlisted. He was sent to Washington, DC, and spent the summer of 1872 there. For a time he was stationed at New Orleans; then he went to Burlington, Vermont, and from there to Boston, Massachusetts.

It was while he was stationed in Boston, either in late 1874 or early 1875, that he met Matilda (McHenry) Fisher, the wife of Eberhard Fisher. Eberhard, a baker by trade, suffered from erysipelas, a disease that developed as a result of a leg wound. Eberhard died from this disease on February 14, 1875, leaving a widow and four children, the oldest, Lizzie, being fifteen years old.

Three months later, on May 18, 1875, David Ralston married Eberhard's widow, Matilda Fisher, in Boston. Matilda gave birth to a daughter, Matilda Amanda Ralston, in Boston on November 30, 1875, nine and a half months after her late husband's death.

David was transferred from Boston to Charleston, South Carolina; then to Milwaukee, Wisconsin; on to Deadwood, Dakota Territory; and finally to Fort Custer, Montana, prior to June 1880. In order to serve at all of these stations before 1880, it seems most likely that David left Boston in late 1875 or early 1876. He may not have seen his daughter before leaving the Boston area.

At any rate, in 1877, a strange series of events occurred in which the location of David and Matilda's young child became a mystery. It was reported that Matilda had a drinking problem and acted strangely at times. Her late husband, Eberhard, had left an estate of forty thousand dollars or more. This was divided between Matilda and their four children. Matilda reportedly went about spending her part of the inheritance wildly and soon found herself destitute. This led to Matilda Amanda, the two-year-old daughter of David and Matilda Ralston, being left in a home for safekeeping and later her mother being unable to locate her. The following affidavit was made by Matilda Ralston:

> Personally came before me, a Justice of the Peace in and for aforesaid County (Suffolk) and State (Massachusetts), Matilda Ralston, claimant, aged 45 years, a resident of East Cambridge, in the County of Middlesex, State of Mass., who being duty sworn, declare, in relation to aforesaid case, as follows:
>
> That in the year 1877 she was in Chicago, Ill. travelling, and being poor and without a home placed her daughter, Matilda Amanda Ralston by the advice of Judge Scully of said Chicago, in the Home for the Friendless No. 1926 Wabash Ave. for safe keeping temporarily. In a few weeks she called for her child. The authorities of the Institution informed her that they had given the child to a family and refused to give her their address. That she applied to Judge Scully who made demand for the child but was informed by the authorities of said Institution that they did not know where the family was who had her child. That her said child was given to said family without her knowledge or consent. That she has made diligent search for said child personally and through others and has been unable to find it. That she is now and always has been ready and willing to take care of and maintain said child. All this she knows of her own knowledge and observations.

It is not known if David knew that he had a child or, if he did know about the child, whether he knew that the child was lost.

Along the path Sergeant Ralston had met and become aquatinted with Lieutenant Greely. Greely knew that Ralston could be useful on an expedition because of his experience as a surveyor.

Greely invited Ralston to join him on the Lady Franklin Bay expedition.

In the spring of 1881, when preparations for the Greely expedition neared completion, Sergeant Ralston left his station at Fort Custer, Montana, for New York. He had planned on visiting his parents in Ohio on the way, but he received a telegram from Lt. Greely stating that if he wished to go on the expedition, he must go east with all possible haste. He continued his journey to the East Coast, meeting up with a party led by Lt. Kislingbury. The party sailed to St. John's, where they met up with Lt. Greely and the other members of the expedition.

They departed from St. John's on the *Proteus* on July 7, 1881, and arrived at Lady Franklin Bay on August 11. The next week was spent unloading the *Proteus* and constructing their quarters. Sergeant Ralston was assigned to a section of the house, which he shared with Sergeant Brainard, Sergeant Frederick, and Private Gardiner.

While Sergeant Ralston's duty was primarily to act as a meteorological observer, he would also be used in exploration. The following extract from Lieutenant Greely's journal details one of the earlier treks, in September 1881, in which Sergeant Ralston participated:

> On September 7th, the harbor-floe being fit for sledge travel, I decided to visit the entrance to the Bellows, a valley which was situated some fifteen miles southwest of the station at the extreme point of Discovery Harbor, which I temporarily named Basil Norris Bay. The Bellows Valley received its name from the officers of the English expedition of 1875, on account of the high and constant winds which were always experienced in it. It is separated from Black Rock Vale to the westward by a high, peculiarly shaped bluff called Bifurcation Cape. I was accompanied by Lieutenant Kislingbury, and Sergeants Brainard and Ralston, with Eskimo Jens as a dog-driver.
>
> Excellent ice for the sledge was fallen in with, and the trip was made in about three hours, notwithstanding some

delay in the centre of Basil Norris Bay, on our discovery of ten eider-ducks in a water-space surrounding a palaeocrystic floe. They were evidently two females, with their full-grown broods, which, incautiously delaying their migration to the southward, the sudden advent of winter had caught and detained. The young ones were killed with pikestaff, but the older ones flew away some distance after being driven from the water, and were killed by Lieutenant Kislingbury with his rifle.

On nearing the shore Sergeant Ralston discovered a herd of fourteen musk-cattle, which were quietly grazing on a low plateau near the entrance to Black Rock Valley, some three miles distant. The party were armed only with one rifle and revolver, so Lieutenant Kislingbury and the sergeants were sent to surround the herd, of which I ordered that eight only should be slaughtered. It seemed then to me, as now, that unless there was immediate necessity for the meat, this interesting species should not be exterminated by indiscriminate slaughter.

The musk-cattle thus killed, with those already obtained in the vicinity of Conger, afforded us a liberal and satisfying diet of fresh meat until the ensuing summer.

Sergeant Ralston was selected as one of the members of the team that would provide support when they reached the farthest point north ever attained at the time. The party consisted of Lieutenant Lockwood, Sergeant Brainard, the Eskimo Fred, and a support crew of ten other men. They left Fort Conger on April 3, 1882. The temperature that morning was twenty-nine degrees below zero. They took the supplies on four sledges, dragging on average seventy-eight pounds per man.

They went to the first depot, Depot B, and picked up additional supplies they had cached there, each man dragging one hundred and thirty pounds and each dog one hundred pounds. Sergeant Ralston had been designated as the cook. While preparing breakfast on April 6, Ralston froze his fingers; it was forty degrees below zero. The temperature fell as low as forty-nine degrees below zero that night. One of the members, suffering from rheumatism, was ordered to return to Fort Conger. Another froze one of his toes and had to turn back. The wind reached an estimated sixty miles per hour at times. The wind was so violent that, while at work, the men were frequently blown over, and one gust lifted the dog sledge, with its load of two hundred pounds, from the ground. The sledge struck Ralston on the forehead, knocking him several yards and injuring him severely. Two more of the support crew were sent back to Fort Conger with lung pains and bladder trouble. This left eight men: the three that would go the farthest north and a five-man support team to move all the supplies to the place where Lieutenant Lockwood, Sergeant Brainard, and the Eskimo Christensen would begin the journey north.

On April 27 the party reached Cape Bryant, the final destination for the support team. Sergeant Ralston and Sergeant Brainard were suffering from snow-blindness after eleven hours of movement in the bright snow that day. The men had been away from home camp for twenty-four days and had traveled about one hundred and sixty miles, pulling the load of supplies. After a day's rest, the support party was ordered to return home to Fort Conger. The exploration team would continue moving north, about ninety miles from Cape Bryant. Sergeant Ralston and the other four men of the support party returned to Fort Conger, now traveling much faster with their lighter loads. They had to wait out some bad weather; however, they all reached the fort intact.

While the expedition party was at Fort Conger, most of the time Ralston was involved with reading meteorological instruments. At times he was required to go quite a distance from the fort for these readings.

In August 1883 they had to abort Fort Conger to move south in an attempt to meet up with their rescue ship. Sergeant Ralston was assigned at times to drive the *Lady Greely,* the steamboat carrying the expedition members.

While at Cape Sabine he did his share of hunting and helping with other chores. He was ill at times, as was most of the party. As the time passed Sergeant Ralston recognized that he might not survive. On May 10 he drew up a will.

Sergeant Ralston died thirteen days later, at one hour past midnight on May 23, 1884. He had been sharing a sleeping bag with Sergeant Israel and Lieutenant Greely. Israel left the bag before Ralston's death; however, Greely stayed in the bag with Ralston's body until five o'clock in the morning. Ralston's body was carried to "Cemetery Hill," where he was placed alongside his fallen comrades. Of Ralston, Greely writes, "Ralston was an excellent observer and an efficient man in the field, with whom I never found a shadow of fault until his last days at Sabine."

Greely is referring to an incident when Ralston was performing the duty of cook and was accused by some of the men of not allocating the food fairly.

The rescue ships arrived on June 22, thirty days after Ralston's death. His body was placed aboard the steamship *Thetis*, which took it to St. John's, where it was placed in a casket and prepared for shipment to New York. The ship carrying Ralston's body arrived off Governor's Island on August 8. Secretary Lincoln and generals Sheridan and Hancock, along with other army and naval officers with troops, received the bodies from the vessels. The forts fired a funeral salute. Sergeant Ralston's body was immediately shipped by rail to Howard, Ohio, arriving the evening of the next day.

On Sunday, August 10, David Ralston was laid to rest in Jelloway Cemetery, two miles northwest of Howard. People came from miles away to observe the procession, which was preceded by hundreds of carriages and many men on foot. The throngs of people present, estimated at two to five thousand, pressed forward eagerly to get a glimpse of the casket and witness the ceremonies. David Ralston was truly a brave man.

Upon learning of the fate of the Lady Franklin Bay expedition, David Ralston's family members exchanged much correspondence with the Signal Service. David's father, Lewis Ralston, and his brother George Ralston wrote letters to the Signal Service. David's widow, Martha Fisher Ralston also corresponded with the Signal Service. All parties claimed ownership of his body and estate. Martha Fisher Ralston, as his widow, wanted his body to be buried in Massachusetts. She wrote the following letter to the Signal Service:

August Friday 8th 1884

Dear Sir

Asking your assistance In regard to the body of my lawfull Husband Sergt D C Ralston also wishing to clame his body papers and stop all persons claming his money I am marrid to Him ten years the 23rd of May last age of his child also nine years

please Inform Direct to Mrs Matilda D C Rolston
Boston Harbor
any further information direct to
Col P Whiteing
Boston Harbor
Deer Island

Obviously it was too late for her to claim the body, as it was buried before the Signal Service could act on her letter. David's father, Lewis Ralston, claimed that David had divorced Matilda, and as such she had no claim to anything concerning David's body or his estate. She was not even mentioned in his will:

Camp Clay, Garlington Island
Ellesmere Land May 10th, 1884.

I, David C. Ralston being of sound mind do declare this my last testament. To my sister Rose A. Ralston I give and bequeath Five hundred (500) dollars. To my sister Mary E. Ralston I give and bequeath Five hundred (500) Dollars. To my two youngest brothers living each I give and bequeath the sum of Two hundred and (fifty) dollars. My Gold watch and pencil I give and bequeath to my brother William H. Ralston. The reward due me for assisting in attaining the highest latitude is to be devoted in the purchase of a ladies gold watch and chain to be presented to my sister Rose A. Ralston. There will be engraved in letters upon each of the above mentioned watches presented to my sisters a suitable inscription such as they may select, from whom they come. My diary and notes after the Chief Signal Officer is through using I desire to be given to my eldest sister Charlotte H. Walkenshaw my flowers I wished disposed of as follows.

1st. To my Sister Charlotte H. Walkenshaw as complete a collection as possible mounted and bound in one album at a cost not to exceed Fifteen (15) Dollars.

2nd. To my sister Rose A. Ralston the next best collection of flowers mounted and bound in the same manner and cost.

3rd. To my Sister Mary E. Ralston the third best collection mounted and bound in the same manner and cost.

To my brother Andrew J. Ralston I give and bequeath Two hundred (200) Dollars.

The balance of my personal property I give and bequeath to my Father and Mother, Lewis W. Ralston & Nancy Ralston. If either not living, I give and bequeath it to my youngest unmarried brother to be used by him in preparing himself for the profession of Civil Engineer, his course of instruction to be taken at the institute of Technology, Boston, Mass. This will, and my papers & notes &c are left in charge of the Commanding officer of this Expedition, Major A. W. Greely. As executor of this will I appoint David L. Brainard, who will personally see that the provisions of it are carried out and will personally present to my relatives at Howard if possible the articles mentioned now in my possession and will remunerate himself accordingly. If D. L. Brainard is deceased I appoint as executor my brother in law Henry Walkenshaw as executor. As the second Executor in case of the first named being deceased I appoint Henry Beiderbick, a member of this Expedition.

(Seal)

David C. Ralston

Witnessed

A. W. Greely, 1 Lt 5 Cav U.S.A.
Fred. F. Kislingbury 2d Lt 11th Inf, A.S.O.
Edward Israel, Kalamazoo, Mich.

The address of the parties named in my will is Howard, Knox Co. Ohio with the exception of Henry Walkenshaw (my brother in law) his address though can be obtained from my parents.

Matilda had not divorced David, yet she may not have received any of David's estate. She did, however, receive a widow's pension. The article appearing in the Chester Times in Chester, Pennsylvania on December 31, 1884, may shed some light concerning her:

IS MRS. RALSTON'S STORY TRUE?
A Denial that She Was Abandoned but that She Squandered Her Fortune.

Boston, Dec. 31.—The publication of the story of Mrs. Matilda Ralston, widow of Sergt. Ralston, of the Greely relief party, in which she represented that she had been heartlessly abandoned by her children and left to die in the almshouse, has brought out a statement from Lawyer Lang, the guardian of the children by the lady's first marriage to Mr. Fisher. Mr. Lang says that the first part of her story is true, but the latter is not. A friend of Mr. Fisher said that a few years after her first marriage Mrs. Fisher left her husband, having become infatuated with Ralston. Soon after Fisher died, leaving $50,000, one-half of which his wife received and the remainder went to the four children. She then left her home with Ralston, to whom she was married, but he left her, after getting possession of nearly all her money, and she never saw him again. Mrs. Ralston and her oldest daughter then traveled all over the country in questionable style,

> spending their money extravagantly, and finally the mother was arrested for drunkenness. The two younger children, whom she charges with having deserted her, say they are willing to provide for her in any home she may select, but they decline to furnish her with money to squander as she did the $20,000 within the past four years.

In 1888, Matilda Ralston's son, Alexander H. Fisher, was appointed guardian of Matilda. She was referred to in the order as "an insane person." On May 28, 1888, she was placed in the Boston Insane Hospital, where she remained until her death on September 10, 1904. She was buried in the Mount Hope Cemetery in Boston, Massachusetts.

Nancy (Sears) Ralston, David's fifty-nine-year-old mother, died on March 19, 1886, less than two years after the death of her son. She was buried in the Jelloway Cemetery next to her son.

David's father, Lewis, died on June 12, 1926, outliving his wife by forty years. He is buried alongside his wife. Lewis Ralston's cousin, Samuel Moffett Ralston, was elected governor of the state of Indiana.

David's oldest sister, Charlotte Ann Ralston, married Hugh Wilson Walkinshaw. She was a schoolteacher, and he was a lawyer. They were the parents of three children: Lewis Clark, David Robinson, and Myrtle Hargrave. David's brother Andrew Jerome Ralston married Sarah Thresia Rice. They had five children: David Lewis, Mary E., Nanna Rose, Georgia Charlotte, and Francis Elma. He worked for the railroad and on a ranch in Arkansas. His brother William Henry Arrison Ralston married twice and had two children, Cora and Ruth. He served as county treasurer for Knox County, Ohio. David's sister Rose Amanda Ralston married Thad Ackley, a jeweler. They lived in Warren, Ohio. His sister Mary Emma Ralston married Henry Charlton Conrad. He was a farmer residing in Tujunga, California. Henry and Emma had seven children: Nancy Laura, John Ralston, George, Cora, Henry Stark, Helen Gould, and Virginia. His brother Lewis Ephraim Ralston married and worked as a secretary in Cleveland. His youngest brother, George Lincoln Ralston, owned a printing press in Los Angeles. He married

Margaret Laubert (Fell). They adopted three children: Carl Ackley, Henry Joyce, and Irene May.

And the mystery of David's long-lost daughter unfolds. It was discovered that she was raised by the family of Lars Johanson. She went by the name of Bessie Christine (Ralston) Johnson. The family relocated to Long Beach, California, where she met and married Captain Charles Reiner, a sea captain from Norway. Charles and Bessie had five children: Bessie Amanda, Ruth Christina, Carl Ralston, Francis Lincoln, and Stanley David. It is evident by the names she gave to her children that Bessie never forgot her heritage.

David Columbus Ralston would have been proud of his child and the grandchildren and great-grandchildren that his short time with Matilda (Fisher) Ralston, produced. While his relationship with his wife may have been prompted by his compassion for what she was going through, the results turned out well. David can surely be consider a brave and honorable man who chose to serve his country and volunteered for an extremely dangerous mission. He lived and gave his life as a hero.

10

Hampden Sidney Gardiner

(1859–1884)

HAMPDEN SIDNEY GARDINER was born on January 19, 1859 in Philadelphia, Pennsylvania. He was the fifth of eight children born to John Hampden Gardiner and Adelaide Masters Gardiner.

Hampden's father was born on December 23, 1822, also in Philadelphia. He was one of the eighth generation of Gardiners, descending from Lion Gardiner, who emigrated to the colonies in the 1600s. His father was Sidney Gardiner, and his mother was Mary Holland Gardiner. His fifth cousin, Julie Gardiner, married John Tyler, president of the United States.

Hampden's mother, Adelaide Masters Gardiner, was the daughter of George Masters. She was born in Philadelphia in 1827. John Hampden Gardiner and Adelaide (also known as Adelene or Adeline) Masters were married at the Chambers Presbyterian Church in Philadelphia on November 9, 1843.

Hampden had two older twin brothers, one of them his namesake, Hampden Sidney, and the other, George. They were born on December 19, 1844, over fourteen years before Hampden was born. The first Hampden Sidney lived only two weeks, dying on January 3, 1845. He also had two older sisters, Adeline, born on February 14, 1848, and Celestine, born on October 22, 1853. He had a younger brother, Lionel, who was born on July 13, 1864, and died on November 22, 1865, when he was about a year and a half old. He also had two younger sisters, Helen Marion, born on March 24, 1861, and Mary (also known as Minnie), who was born on

December 15, 1866. His only living brother, George, died in April 1866 when he was just twenty-one years old.

Hampden's father was a upholsterer by trade. During the Civil War years he volunteered for military service, serving with many different units. In 1863, he fell from a horse, injuring himself so badly that he was to suffer from it for the rest of his life. He was discharged after the war at the grade of colonel and received a pension as a result of his injury. Afterward he obtained a clerkship in the US post office, which he retained until his death.

Little is known of Hampden's childhood. He likely attended the church where his parents were married. It must have been a blow to him losing George, the only brother he knew, when Hampden was only seven years old. But his mother must have been even more sorrowful, having lost three of her four sons.

Hampden became interested in telegraphic technology. This, along with his father's military service, probably prompted Hampden to enter military service. He enlisted in the Signal Corps in Washington, DC, on September 3, 1879. His enlistment record states that he was five feet, eight and a half inches tall and had blue eyes and dark hair. His occupation was listed as "instrument maker." He was sent to Sandy Run, North Carolina, a Signal Service station connecting Wilmington, North Carolina, with New River Station. Here he stayed at the MacMillian home, where the wires for the signals ran nearby. It was also here that he met Minnie Lou MacMillian, the nineteen-year-old daughter of Dugald and Mary MacMillian. Hampden and Minnie obtained a marriage license on April 18, 1881.

Hampden and Minnie Lou were married eighteen days later, on the sixth of May. About a month after that, Hampden was in Washington, DC, where he met Lt. Kislingbury and part of the expedition party. Hampden must have known before he married that he was going to leave on the expedition and that he would be gone for at least a year, and possibly three years. He must have departed North Carolina shortly after they were married in order to get to Washington before the eighteenth of June. His new bride would never see him again. It should be noted that Hampden's military pay and allowances were held for him by the military until his return, and his wife did not receive any living allowance from him.

From Washington the party went to Baltimore and sailed from there to St. John's, where they met up with the rest of the expedition members.

Hampden's skills as an instrument maker must have qualified him for the expedition. Greely's service prior to this expedition was in the Signal Service, supervising the installation of telegraph lines. Hampden likely came in contact with Greely through his work on the telegraph lines, or through someone who knew both of them. At any rate, he volunteered for the Arctic duty, Greely accepted him, and now he was on his way.

Hampden must have been well qualified for his position, having been promoted to sergeant in the short time he had served prior to the expedition.

On July 21 the expedition reached Rittenbenk, Greenland, a stop on the way to Lady Franklin Bay. Gardiner and five others of the party spent the day hunting in the "whale boat," one of the boats they were taking with them to Lady Franklin Bay, and returned with fifty-nine ducks. Twelve days later they arrived at Littleton Island, some two hundred and fifty miles south of their destination. Gardiner was part of a party that searched for a cache left by the English on the island some six years before. After many hours of searching they finally found it. It contained mail left for Captain Nares's expedition. The cache would be returned to St. John's with the *Proteus* so it could be sent to the English admiralty.

Upon reaching their destination, Fort Conger, they constructed their quarters. Gardiner shared a section of the quarters with Brainard, Frederick, and Ralston.

It is difficult to determine just what Gardiner's duties were. In Powell's book *The Long Rescue*, Gardiner is listed as being a meteorologist. Meteorology relates to weather and climate. It seems, since he was identified earlier as an instrument maker, that his primary function while on the expedition would have been to make, read, and repair meteorological instruments. While he was used for these functions, he also was used in a host of other functions, sort of a jack of all trades. We find him helping others in many instances.

Rice states in his journal of September 10, 1881, "Gardiner kindly arranged a cot for me in the quarters." Gardiner also assisted in many other ways. We find him hauling coal, hunting, cooking, supporting exploratory treks, repairing boats, etc.

Gardiner had a gift for music. Rice comments in his journal of October 30, 1881, "Our Sunday evenings are generally spent in singing. Lt. Kislingbury, Gardiner, Ellis, and Schneider, taking prominent parts." On November 30, 1881, he writes, "Some days ago Lt. Greely spoke to me about arranging some exercises for the evening; music, etc. I told him I thought it would be useless to arrange a programme, that the singing was generally spontaneous, but said I would get a good chorus together and get something started. I therefore spoke to Ellis, Schneider, Gardiner and Lt. Kislingbury; good voices and was promised their support."

However, Gardiner's primary reason for being part of the expedition was the scientific work that needed to be accomplished. Lt. Greely states in his book *Three Years of Arctic Service*, "Sergeants Gardiner, Jewell, and Ralston were particularly charged with meteorological and tidal work." In this respect, Gardiner applied himself wholeheartedly. One of his early tasks was to build piers for the pendulum that had been obtained through the efforts of Sergeant Israel. The bricks and cement used to build the piers that held the pendulum had to be precisely preheated and laid in the lean-to built for the instrument. Gardiner also rebuilt a chronograph, an instrument that was loaned to the expedition by the Coast Survey, which was damaged en route and was unserviceable. The instrument was used to register star observations for time in connection with the pendulum.

While these activities were vital to the mission, much of Gardiner's activities were centered around taking tidal observations, the height or depth of the tides in Smith Sound, several times a day. In order to compile these readings, holes were made in the ice in Smith Sound, and the rising or lowering of the depth of the water, as related to the depth of the ice, was recorded. It required Gardiner, or others of the expedition, to continually make treks from the home camp to the location of the ice holes in order to take readings, make new ice holes, or keep the old ice holes open.

In November of the first year of the expedition, Gardiner fell down and broke his leg while making a trip to the ice hole. He was disabled until the middle of December, when the leg finally healed.

Gardiner's work in meteorology was essentially over when the expedition departed from Fort Conger in 1883.

Around the first part of October in 1883, Sergeant Gardiner suffered from a felon, a purulent infection, on one of his fingers. The pain and throbbing were continuous and debilitating. This condition persisted for several months, finally being considered healed in the middle of March 1884. However, even after that, he was able to do very little, as the weakness from lack of nourishment was setting in. In the middle of April, Doctor Pavy reported that Gardiner and six others of the party were "in a very bad way." The journals of a number of expedition members indicate that in May, Gardiner was failing fast. The journal entries from the eighth through the eleventh of June report that Gardiner was unable to do anything, being very weak and in a dangerous condition.

Hampden Sidney Gardiner died on June 12, 1884, only days before the rescue of the expedition. His body was laid out on the ice foot and never was recovered by the rescue crew, which arrived on June 18.

Lt. Greely's journal entry dated the twelfth of June does well to describe Gardiner:

> Gardiner died today of inflammation of the bowels and starvation. He was apparently dead at 11 a.m., and was removed from the tent; but, showing signs of life, later was deposited on an old buffalo robe, where he died about 5 p.m. It will be necessary to bury him in the ice-foot. His death touched us all very dearly. We have become hardened to death by his constant invasion of our party, but Gardiner's death seemed especially trying, as he has appeared to live mainly by will power for the past two months. The doctor predicted in April that Gardiner would be the next one to go, but he has lived until this time, six days later than the doctor himself; and mainly, as I believe, from his intense desire to return home and see again his wife and mother. In the early

morning he was partly out of his sleeping bag, holding in his hands an ambrotype of his wife and mother, which he continually looked at and frequently spoke to. His last words were "Mother! Wife!"

Sergeant Gardiner was a young man of excellent habits, fine mind, and amiable disposition, and had ambition and application. He was a valuable man to the expedition in many ways, and had endeared himself to his comrades. He was more religious than perhaps any other one in the party; although allowed only eight pounds of baggage on the retreat, he denied himself to bring with him his Bible, our only one, though I had a prayer book.

A Philadelphia newspaper further described Gardiner:

Sergeant Gardiner was an attache of the Signal Service of the army, at North Carolina, and from his knowledge of scientific instruments and their practical use he rapidly obtained promotion to the rank which he bore. He married in his Southern home, and his separation from his wife, who still survives him, was a great hardship to her. He was very bright and intelligent, and his stout, robust build well fitted him for a life of danger and peril.

With the death of Hampden Gardiner, his parents had lost all four of their sons. Even though they had their four daughters (Adeline, Celestine, Helen, and Mary), it must have grieved them horribly.

Hampden made a will on April 8, 1884, four days before his death. The following is the text of that will:

Camp Clay, Garlington Island
April 8, 1884

I the undersigned being of sound and disposing mind do hereby declare this to be my last will and testament.

I give and bequeath to my wife, Minnie Lou Mac Millan Gardiner, one half of the value of all my real and personal property, the remaining half to my mother and unmarried sisters jointly. As executor I appoint my father, John H. Gardiner of Philadelphia.

(signed) Hampden Sidney Gardiner
Witness
Henry Biederbick
Nicholas Salor

Hampden did not reveal to the other expedition members that he was married until some time after they had left Fort Conger. Newspaper articles covering the rescue of the surviving expedition members and naming those who had died listed Hampden as being unmarried. Hampden's parents probably knew of his marriage, as it is likely that he saw them on his way from North Carolina to join the expedition party in Washington, DC.

At the time of his death Adeline was the only one of Hampden's sisters who was married. As such she was to receive nothing from Hampden's estate. Half of the estate was to go to Hampden's wife and the other half to be divided among his mother and his three unmarried sisters. His father was to be the executor.

After news of Hampden's death reached his wife and his father, both parties begin corresponding with the chief signal officer in Washington, DC. Both parties were concerned about Hampden's estate and his belongings. His personal belongings were minuscule. They consisted of two journals he had kept while on the expedition, a map, two pocket books, pencil memoranda, tin type, one plain gold ring, one silver pencil, one lead pencil, one eraser, and a bible. However, his estate included money owed to him for his back pay while on the expedition. When all of his back pay was combined, including extra duty pay, quarters, rations, and his basic pay of thirty-three dollars a month, it added up to nearly three thousand dollars. When the commissary stores, which he owed, was taken out, he still had an estate of about twenty-eight hundred dollars. This would equal well over a hundred thousand dollars in today's currency.

A few days after the news broke of his son's death, John Gardiner sent a letter to the chief signal officer asking that the effects of his son be sent to him. Gardiner sent two more letters to the Signal Office in August, again asking that his son's papers, etc., be sent to him and asking if a certified copy of Hampden's marriage to Minnie Lou and a power of attorney from her was all they needed to send his son's belongings to him. In September the Signal Service responded to John Gardiner's letters, stating that the office was waiting for a copy of the marriage record along with a power of attorney from Minnie Lou.

In September the county clerk of Pender County, North Carolina, attested to the validity of the marriage of Hampden and Minnie Lou.

On December 1, 1885, John Gardiner's attorney sent a letter to the Signal Office telling them that the Philadelphia Register of Wills had granted letters of administration to John H. Gardiner and asked them to hold all of his son's estate until he requested it. Soon afterward, Hampden's father received all of the estate to administer.

On December 15, an attorney representing Minnie Lou wrote a letter to the chief signal officer. The attorney asked the signal officer the value of Minnie Lou's husband's estate. Her attorney wrote, "With the view of obtaining precise information as to her interest in her deceased husband's estate, the value of it &c, she wishes a full and detailed account from the proper and most reliable governmental sources, of all wages and money of her husband that were paid by the government of the United States to John H. Gardiner, his father, now of Philadelphia, Pennsylvania. formerly of Red Banks, New Jersey. She wishes this account to be certified or authenticated as to be competent evidence in any legal proceedings she may deem proper to institute."

In June 1885, Minnie Lou Gardiner wrote a letter to the Signal Service asking that her marriage license be returned to her.

In December 1885, fully a year and a half after her husband's death, Minnie Lou's attorney continued to write letters to Washington offices and representatives, trying to determine what funds had been sent to John Gardiner. Finally they got an answer stating that all the funds, over twenty-eight hundred dollars, had been sent to him. No verification could be found that he ever sent to Hampden's widow the fourteen hundred dollars that her husband left her in his will.

Minnie Lou had a job with the post office at Magnolia, North Carolina. In 1886 she received a widow's pension of eight dollars per month, so she could probably support herself. In January 1889, Congress passed a bill to increase her pension to thirty dollars per month. It didn't make that much of a difference, because on June 4, 1889, Minnie Lou McMillian Gardiner died. She was only thirty-one years old. She is buried in the Magnolia Cemetery in Duplin County, North Carolina.

Hampden's oldest sister, Adeline, married Henry K. Clark in about 1875. They had two children, Adeline Bessie Clark, born in May 1878, and Ethel S. Clark, born in March 1883. Ethel married Harvey A. Reed, and they had three children: Marjorie and twins Eleanor and Richard.

His sister Helen Marion married Henry A. Conover in about 1885, and they had children: James and Gardiner. His other two sisters, Celestine and Minnie (Mary), never married.

Hampden's father, John Hampden Gardiner, died in Glenside, Pennsylvania, on September 11, 1895. His widow, Adelene, died on January 21, 1916. Both John and his wife were buried in the Monument Cemetery in Philadelphia, which was founded in 1837 on North Broad Street, across from Temple University. In the 1950s, it fell victim to the school's need for parking lots. Thousands of those interred there were transferred to a mass grave in the suburbs. Their monuments were dumped into the Delaware River, where they are still visible today. It should be noted that some of the bodies were moved to Lawnview Cemetery in Rockledge, Pennsylvania. Because of John Gardiner's Civil War service, he and his wife may have been moved there.

Hampden Sidney Gardiner wanted to follow in the footsteps of his brave father. He recognized the danger of going on such an assignment in the Arctic area. Scores of explorers had died while on journeys to the polar region, but he was willing to risk his life for the mission. He was truly a brave soldier.

11

William H. Cross

(1845–1884)

William H. Cross was born on January 20, 1845, in the District of Columbia. He was the fifth of nine children born to John Washington Cross and Ann Maria Westcoat. His eight siblings were James, Catharine (Kate), Roseana, Thomas, John, George, Mary, and Franklin.

William's father, John Washington Cross, was born in the District of Columbia about 1814. He married Ann Marie Westcoat in Washington, DC on December 21, 1833. William's mother was born about 1815 in the District of Columbia. William's father died on July 1, 1854, when William was just nine years old. He was buried in the Congressional Cemetery in Washington, where many celebrities are buried, including John Philip Sousa and J. Edgar Hoover. William's mother was left to raise the children. She still resided in Washington, DC in 1860, with all nine of her children living with her. Her son John died on February 11, 1872, at the age of twenty-eight years. He was buried in the Congressional Cemetery.

William married Mary Ann McGrath in Washington, DC, on June 3, 1869. Mary Ann was born in New York City on November 2, 1844. Her parents were John and Ann (Dolan) McGrath. Their son, Charles Franklin Cross, was born in Washington, DC on March 28, 1870.

Shortly after Charles was born, on October 4, 1870, William enlisted in the US Navy as a machinist and was discharged a year later, on September 29, 1871. He again served in the navy from July

9, 1875, until his discharge three years later, on July 8, 1878. He reenlisted the next day and served until his discharge on December 27, 1880. He had worked as a machinist for each of his enlistments.

During part of his naval career, he worked for Winfield Scott Schley. Schley was the chief of the Bureau of Equipment and Recruiting for the Navy Department. Schley would be instrumental in the rescue of the survivors that were on the expedition with Greely. It is likely that Schley recommended to Greely that Cross accompany him as a machinist on the expedition in order to maintain the steam launch.

On May 21, 1881, shortly before the expedition members left for St. John's, Newfoundland, to join the expedition, William H. Cross was sworn into the army of the United States at Washington, DC by Lt. Greely. He was assigned duty with Company B of the Signal Corps at Fort Myer, Virginia. By June 14, he had joined Lt. Lockwood at Baltimore, Maryland, for departure for St. John's. They sailed on the steamer *Nova Scotia*, joining with the rest of the party, which was led by Lt. Kislingbury, at St. John's. The entire expedition departed St. John's on July 7 aboard the *Proteus*, headed for Greenland, where they would pick up additional supplies and then continue on to Lady Franklin Bay.

On July 25, while in Greenland, Cross, along with Lockwood, Rice, and Linn, made a trial trip around the harbor in the steam launch that at St. John's had been christened the *Lady Greely*. The next day, Cross, along with Lockwood, Elberg, the governor of Upernavik, Rice, and Linn made a journey in the *Lady Greely* to Proven, a distance of about fifty miles, to pick up the two Eskimo dog sledge drivers, Edwards and Christensen.

By mid-August the expedition had reached Lady Franklin Bay and had set up quarters. On August 21 Cross did some work on the house with Ellison. On the twenty-eighth, Cross went hunting with Jewell and Ellison, and the next day Cross was with Lockwood and Brainard on a trek to St. Patrick Bay. On the last day of August and on September 12 and 13 he made trips with Brainard.

Cross continued making trips, many of them with Brainard or Ellison. He also built a new Hudson Bay sledge and spent time working on the tide gauge. At Thanksgiving time a rifle-shooting contest was held, in which most of the party participated. Cross placed third.

In the latter part of November, the weather getting much colder, Cross badly froze his ear. Just before Christmas the first winter at Fort Conger, Cross had a toothache that gave him a badly swollen cheek. During the following months, Cross was busy working on the sledges, hunting, and doing other odd jobs. Ellison wrote in his journal on March 23, "Cross is doing a little of everything."

In August 1882, a year after their arrival at Fort Conger, Greely reported in his journal on August 28, "The engineer is drunk today. He fell from the launch into the water, where he would have drowned if he had not been rescued by Brainard. I learned from Lieutenant Lockwood that he had stolen a portion of the alcohol which was sent with the launch for fuel on the late trip up Archer Fiord, and was drunk at that time. He evidently avails himself of every opportunity to purloin and conceal a portion of the fuel alcohol sent out with parties." This was the first written mention that Cross had a drinking problem.

Ellison's journal on August 29 states that "Cross fell into the water twice today. Brainard had to get him out." And on August 31 Ellison's journal states that Cross is under arrest. However, the next day, September 1, Cross went to Dutch Island to look after the *Lady Greely*. He found the launch on her side, nearly full of water. He ran back to the station to get help to set the boat upright, which took about an hour.

The remainder of 1882 went by with Cross working mostly with Ellison and sometimes Rice, hunting, building a lean-to, and performing other various duties. On Thanksgiving another shooting match was held, and like the year before, Cross came in third.

On January 7, 1883, Cross went to Dutch Island to check on the *Lady Greely* and came back to the fort with the report that the ice had been forced up around the launch and that, from what he could see, she must be nearly crushed by the pressure. The next day a party led by Lt. Lockwood went to the launch to evaluate the situation and release the boat from the pressure of the ice. They dug a trench about two feet wide around the launch and found that part of her side was crushed in and one of her ribs was broken.

Cross's activities for the rest of the winter and the spring of 1883 were mostly routine. He was reading instruments, measuring ice depth, working on boats, etc. During the summer and fall Cross was accused of being intoxicated more than once. The last entry concerning Cross's use of alcohol was on September 29, 1883, when Brainard wrote in his journal, "On returning they found him [Cross] intoxicated."

During the latter part of September, both of Cross's feet were frostbitten. He was barely able to walk.

By the first week in October, Cross was involved with hunting and did shoot some game. However, by late November, he was again troubled by frostbite on his foot. He continued to help with the woodcutting needed for cooking until December 29, when the doctor excused him from any work. Cross's health continued to decline from that time on. On January 16, 1884, Brainard wrote in his journal, "Cross is growing weak. He has failed greatly since yesterday morning. I think he is near the end." The next day Brainard wrote, "Cross is failing rapidly. He talks incoherently of his mother, of his birthday (next Sunday) when he will be forty years of age, and of the returning sun." Cross died the next day, January 18, 1884. He was the first of the members of the Lady Franklin Bay expedition to die. Biederbick's diary entry of January 18, 1884, describes the details pertaining to Cross's death:

> Cross, who has been sick and weak lately, died about 1:45 p. m. today. Cross had scurvy. His mouth looked dark brown and red under the gums and pulled up and swollen all over. His breath smelled very strong and bad. For the last few days he was very weak, and laying very much down in his sleeping bag. Dr. Pavy and the Commander tried their best to make him take exercise and sit up more. Last night (or rather afternoon) a matress and single sleeping bag was given him and he had to lay close to me that I might take care of him. He was then already very sick and asked a good many questions over again without seeming to recollect what was said. During the night Cross moved very much about and spoke to himself. I was unable to understand what except

that he sometimes referred to the next Sunday, the 20th, his birthday. I fell asleep again when he seemed to be quiet and was awakened by Jewell, about half past two this morning, to look at Cross, who was groaning much and had worked himself part way out his sleeping bag. He was unconscious and his hands and face cold. I called the Doctor, who ordered Aromatic Spirits of Ammonia and Brandy to be given, and hands and face rubbed slightly to warm Cross up again. I also heated water and put it in rubber bags on the sides of Cross, in his sleeping bag, but (although after several doses of medicine and our work on him, he seemed to breathe easier and was warmer), he never regained consciousness. His eyes were very much swollen and looked watery and dead.

In his journal, Sergeant Brainard describes the services that were held for Cross the following day:

> The remains were dressed for burial by Biederbick and myself, and wrapped in a large gunny sack. Lieut. Greely read the beautiful Episcopal burial service while we were yet in our sleeping bags, and about noon the solemn procession moved slowly across the lake and up the gentle incline to the grave. The body was covered with the Stars and Stripes and was borne on the small sledge which already has a history in connection with the Ellison disaster last fall. We carefully arranged a circle of stones about the grave, this being the only attention we could bestow on our comrade.
>
> One cannot conceive of anything more unearthly—more weird and solemn—than this ghostly procession of emaciated men moving slowly and silently away from their wretched ice-prison in the uncertain light of the Arctic night, having in their midst a dead comrade about to be laid away forever in the frozen ground. It was a scene that I can never forget.

Cross's body remained in the frozen ice until June 18, when the rescue ships arrived. His body was retrieved and placed in a barrel aboard the ship *Thetis*. The barrel contained a preservative. His body was taken to St. John's, where it was placed in a casket. From there he was returned to Washington, DC. He was buried in the Congressional Cemetery where his father was buried.

William H. Cross was truly a brave man for volunteering for the Lady Franklin Bay expedition. While he had some shortcomings, he used every opportunity to support the other members of the expedition. He was the first to die on the expedition, and he worked as long as his body would allow him. The following obituary was published in the New York Times:

> Washington, D.C. Aug. 10.—The remains of Sergt. William H. Cross, of the Greely arctic exploration party, which arrived in this city yesterday and were laid in state in the hall of Franklin Lodge, K. of P., of which the deceased was a member, were removed at 9 o'clock this morning to the residence of his widow, where the funeral services were held this afternoon at 8 o'clock. During the day the casket in which the remains are enclosed rested on trestles in the parlor of Mrs. Cross's residence, and fully 5,000 persons passed through the house to view it. The heavy metal casket was covered with the United States flag, on which lay the sword and regalia of a Knight of Pythias, and numerous floral decorations. Conspicuous among these was a small pillow of white roses, with the word "papa" in violets, which lay at the head of the casket, placed there by the 13 year old son of the dead explorer, and a large floral pillow, handsomely designed, the tribute of members of the Signal Corps. Crosses, wreaths, and other floral tributes were heaped in profusion about the casket.
>
> At 8 o'clock the Rev. Charles S. Andrews, of Christ Church, (Episcopal,) delivered and address in eulogy of the deceased, and was followed by the Rev. Joseph E. Nourse, United States Navy, who spoke briefly of the heroism displayed by the members of the expedition with which Sergt. Cross lost his life. The remains were then taken to the hearse and conveyed to the Congressional Cemetery. Two lodges

> and a Commandery of the Knights of Pythias, headed by the Marine Band, formed the escort, and a guard of honor of 16 men and two Sergeants of the Signal Corps walked beside the hearse. The pallbearers were two Sergeants of the Signal Corps and six Knights of Pythias. The streets along the route of the funeral procession were lined with spectators.
>
> On arriving at the cemetery the escort formed in double lines and allow the hearse to pass through, presenting arms as it passed. At the vault the Episcopal burial service and the burial service of the Knights of Pythias were read, after which the casket was place in the vault.

William's mother, Ann Maria Cross, died in 1900 and was buried alongside her husband in the Congressional Cemetery.

William's widow, Mary Ann Cross, received a pension from the government as a result of William's death. She also obtained employment as a clerk for the US Treasury Department, from which she retired. She died on March 15, 1924, from liver cancer at the age of seventy-seven years and was buried in the Congressional Cemetery next to her husband.

William and Mary's son, Charles Franklin Cross, enlisted in the Signal Corps on April 2, 1888, at Washington, DC. He served for three years and was discharged on June 3, 1891, at Nantucket, Massachusetts. He married Anna Marie Morell on November 2, 1891. They made their home in Arlington County, Virginia. After being discharged from the Signal Corps, Charles went to work as a clerk for the Treasury Department. For the remainder of his life he was employed by the government. Charles and Anna had five children: William Lawrence, Dorthea, Mary Louise, Morell, and Anne. Morell died shortly after his birth in 1902. Charles died on April 12, 1942, and is buried in Arlington National Cemetery.

William's oldest brother, James, married Laura Virginia Norton in Washington, DC, on August 15, 1861. They had four children: Ada, Henry, Anna, and Clarence. James ran a shoe business in Washington, DC. He died a year after his fourth child was born, on September 9, 1874. He was buried, like his father, in the Congressional Cemetery.

William's oldest sister, Catharine (Kate), never married. She died on May 3, 1910, in Washington, DC. She was living with her sister Roseana at the time of her death. She is buried in the Congressional Cemetery.

His next oldest sister, Roseana, married Phillip Otterback. After she had three children by him, Phillip died in 1869. Roseana died on September 14, 1923, in Washington, DC. Rosanna and her husband are buried in the Rock Creek Cemetery in Washington, DC.

William's next oldest brother, Thomas B. Cross, married Virginia Francis Hodges in Portsmouth, Virginia, in 1864. They had three children: Lilla, James, and Rosa. Virginia died in 1893. Thomas died sometime after 1900.

William's younger brother George Alexander Cross married Sarah Virginia Andrews. They had at least five children, including Irene, William, Ruth, and Mamie. They lived their entire lives in Washington, DC Sarah died in 1922, and George died in 1929. They are buried in the Congressional Cemetery.

Mary Virginia Cross, William's youngest sister, was born about 1851. A person with that name was buried in the Congressional Cemetery on December 12, 1922. This may be the sister of William.

Franklin P. Cross, William's youngest brother, was born about 1852. He was a store clerk. He died on March 30, 1895, and is buried in the Congressional Cemetery.

12

David L. Brainard

(1856–1946)

David Legg Brainard was born in Norway, New York, on December 21, 1856. He was the sixth of eight children born to Alanson and Maria (Legg) Brainard. His siblings, all born in Norway, New York, were Josephine, George, Henry, Joshua, Alena, Arthur, and Charles.

David's father, Alanson Brainard, a farmer, was born in Norway, New York, on September 9, 1820. His parents were Joshua and Freelove (Ellis) Brainard. David's mother, Maria Legg, was born in Norway, New York, on February 13, 1824. Her parents were Bailey and Mary (Benson) Legg. Alanson and Maria were married on January 1, 1844. The Brainard family moved to Freetown Corners in Cortland County, New York, in 1867, where Alanson continued farming and running a dairy.

David's sister Alena apparently died as an infant, and his only living sister, Josephine, married Asa H. Legg on September 29, 1867, the same year that the family moved to Freetown Corners. They had three children: Annie, Charles David, and Edna Marie.

David's oldest brother, George, was injured when he was two years old and remained crippled until his death in 1873. He is buried in the Marathon Cemetery in Cortland County, New York.

David's second oldest brother, Henry, enlisted in one of the New York Volunteer Regiments on August 17, 1864, and was sent south, where he served until the close of the war, being discharged on June 2, 1865. He married Carnelia (Nellie) Pullman on September 25, 1866. Nellie was born on July 11, 1844, in Norway, New York, to Isaac B. and Caroline (Bly) Pullman. They moved to

Ceder Bluffs, Nebraska, in 1870, where he owned a large ranch. Henry and Nellie had four children: Alanson, Charles, Edward, and Arthur.

David's younger brother Arthur married Florence A. (Carley) Colvin on March 22, 1879. Florence was born on July 17, 1851, in Marathon, New York. She was the widow of Otis P. Colvin. She had a child by her prior marriage, Katherine Ray Colvin. Arthur and Florence had no children together. Arthur died in 1918 and is buried in the Marathon Cemetery in Cortland County, New York.

David's youngest brother, Charles, married Isabel Eckeron on December 25, 1879. Isabel was the daughter of William Henry and Mary Annah (Hooner) Ecker. Charles died in 1937 and is buried in the Marathon Cemetery. David's brother Joshua never married.

In September 1876, nineteen-year-old David Brainard took the train to Philadelphia to visit the Centennial Exposition, a celebration of the one-hundredth anniversary of the founding of the United States. On the way back he had to change trains in New York City, but reaching into his pocket for the train fare home, he could not find his money. He took the free ferry to the US Army Post at Governors Island. However it happened, Brainard enlisted in the army on September 18, 1876, for a period of five years. He was listed as having black eyes, black hair, and a dark complexion; it also said he was five feet, six and a half inches tall and twenty-two years of age. He was only nineteen years old.

Soon Private Brainard was sent to Troop L, Second Cavalry, at Fort Ellis, Montana Territory, serving against the uprising of the Cheyenne and Sioux Indians. While serving under General Miles in May 1877, Brainard was injured. He suffered wounds to his right hand and a gunshot wound to his right cheek, which affected his eye.

Brainard was active in many battles of the Nez Percé War, which included areas in Oregon, Idaho, Montana, and Wyoming. In the fall of 1877, Brainard was selected to be one of four soldiers as escorts of General Sherman. This included escorting Sherman from Fort Ellis to Yellowstone and back to Fort Ellis, a trip of some three hundred miles. They returned on August 18, 1877. Two weeks later Brainard was assigned the duty of carrying an important dispatch to Lt. G.

C. Doane, who was reportedly camped at Henderson's Ranch near Cinnabar, Montana, about sixty-four miles from Fort Ellis. Brainard managed to make the trip in eight hours, a world record. Brainard was involved in many other Indian wars during the late 1870s. In 1878 he was promoted to sergeant.

On May 13, 1880, an order was sent to Fort Assiniboine, Montana Territory; part of it follows:

> In compliance with telegraphic instructions received from Headquarters Department of Dakota, 1st Lieut G. C. Doane, 2nd Cavalry, will take charge of Sergeant Francis Stewart, Privates William P. Johnston, James Ryan and Nicholas Saylor, Company "H"; Sergeant Daniel L. Brainard, Privates George B. Richardson, Julius Fredericks, and Blacksmith Frans Stotzel, Company "L". 2nd Cavalry, and will proceed, without necessary delay, to Washington, D.C., reporting on his arrival, to the Adjuntant General of the Army for instruction in connection with "Arctic Expedition".

His name is incorrect in the order; it should read "David L. Brainard."

Lt. Doane made arrangements with the Northern Pacific and Penn railroad companies to transport them to Washington. The party, led by Lt. Doane and including Brainard, departed Fort Assiniboine on May 17, 1880, and reached Washington on May 30.

But soon the plan for the military to sponsor the expedition was canceled because of lack of government support. The only ship available for this expedition was an English ship, the *Gulnare*. This ship was ill equipped to break through the ice, as would be required to reach Lady Franklin Bay. The navy declared it unworthy of the expedition. However, Captain Howgate would not hear of the expedition being canceled. He decided to privately foot the bill and use nonmilitary personnel for the expedition. Lt. Doane took a leave of absence from the army and led the expedition to Greenland. The military troops, including Brainard, who had been brought in from the frontier to be part of the expedition, were sent back to the frontier. As predicted by the navy, the *Gulnare* was unable to penetrate the ice fields and had to return after being damaged. Dr. Pavy and the material for the living quarters were left in Greenland.

A year later, in June 1881, Brainard was back in Baltimore to be part of the now government-financed Greely expedition to Lady Franklin Bay. This time they had contracted to use a more reliable ship, the *Proteus*. Brainard and thirteen other members of the expedition, commanded by Lt. Lockwood, left Baltimore on June 14, 1881, sailing on the steamer *Nova Scotia* bound for St. John's, Newfoundland.

At St. John's, after meeting up with the remainder of the expedition (except for Dr. Pavy and the Eskimo dog drivers), they loaded all the necessary supplies aboard the *Proteus* and set sail for Greenland on July 7, 1881. They reached the island of Disko on July 16 and stayed there until June 20, when Dr. Pavy returned from Ritenbenk to meet them. Here they loaded twelve sledge dogs.

The party arrived at Lady Franklin Bay on August 12, 1881. Brainard acted as first sergeant for the expedition. As the first sergeant he acted as a go-between for the commander and the enlisted personnel. Brainard was outstanding in this capacity. Not only was he aware of what was happening with the enlisted personnel, but he also set an example for them to follow. He only asked them to perform tasks in which he participated. At the onset, it appeared that the commander did not realize the asset he had in Brainard, but as time went on he seemed to fully realize Brainard's importance to the expedition.

The journals recorded on the expedition speak only positively of Brainard, except in one case, where he is accused of unfairly portioning the food. In this case, it was only the opinion of one person and had very little basis.

Brainard's participation while in the polar region covered several fields. His work included hunting, taking provisions to storage areas for later explorations, exploring, reading instruments, monitoring provisional supplies, preparing provisions for expeditions, hauling coal, constructing tents, working on buildings, and caring for the lost and injured.

Probably Brainard's greatest success was the trip during the summer of 1882 to reach the farthest point north that had ever been recorded, with Lockwood and one of the Eskimos, Frederick.

Another event that should be mentioned occurred during the move from Fort Conger to Camp Clay. The expedition's plans were quite clear. If no relief ship should arrive at Fort Conger in either the summer of 1882 or the summer of 1883, every attempt should be made to move the expedition party southward toward Littleton Island, where a rescue party would be there to meet them. Since the ships did not get through to Lady Franklin Bay in either of those years, Greely decided to follow his plan and depart the fort for Littleton Island. Some of the party members were skeptical of this plan. Pavy had wanted to take a trip along the shore, possibly five hundred miles, to check on the provisions that should have been left at the site where Camp Clay would later be erected. Greely did not agree to this plan, even though Pavy was willing to make the trip himself. During the trip southward it appeared to many of the party that they should reverse course and try to get back to Fort Conger. Pavy concluded that it was ill advised to continue southward and that Greely should be removed from his position as commander of the expedition. He declared that Greely must be insane in his desire to continue on such a disastrous plan and should be relieved based on his mental disability. Pavy conferred with Kislingbury, Rice, and Lockwood. They all agreed to the plan, but they realized they needed Brainard to accept the plan too. Brainard felt that it was treason, and he would not agree to the plan; therefore, it was abandoned.

While at Camp Clay, Brainard continued in his efforts to look after the party. Day after day he fished for the small shrimp. On June 6 he wrote in his journal:

> I fished over seven hours for the tantalizing little shrimps and caught only two and a half pounds. My baits are almost worthless. What are we to do? I have tried everything at hand, but with no favorable results. I would again drag for sea vegetation, but my failing strength is not equal to the task. I can do nothing more than to stagger down to the shrimping grounds and return.

The relief ship arrived sixteen days later and rescued Brainard and the six other survivors. Ellison, died on the way back. The party, along with the remains of the dead, reached St. John's on July 17, 1884. After placing the dead in caskets at St. John's, they continued on their journey back home. They stopped at Portsmouth, New Hampshire, where a welcome party was there to greet them. After the parade, Brainard was taken to the navy hospital in Portsmouth for recovery.

When Brainard was sufficiently recovered, he was transferred to Washington, DC. On September 17, 1886, Brainard's term of service expired. He reenlisted the following day. One month later, on October 21, he was discharged as a sergeant in order to accept a commission as a second lieutenant. He was commissioned in recognition of gallant and meritorious service rendered by him in the Greely Arctic expedition. He later received the Purple Heart in recognition of his injuries received in the Plains wars.

Brainard was transferred to Fort Walla Walla, Washington Territory. There he met Anna Chase. Anna was the daughter of Henry and Margaret (Raboin) Chase. Henry Chase, born in Pennsylvania about 1830, was an early pioneer of the Walla Walla area, arriving in 1851. Interesting stories are recorded about his dealings with both the friendly and unfriendly Indians in the Walla Walla area. One of the pioneers that remained in the hostile country near Walla Walla with Henry was Louis Raboin. Henry's wife, Margaret, was Louis Raboin's sister. Margaret was born in Oregon Territory about 1837. Henry and Margaret were married about 1855. They had four children, Anna being the youngest child. Anna's mother died when Anna was a young child. The 1885 census shows Anna as a student in Tacoma, Washington. The Washington census taken in 1887 shows that she had returned to Walla Walla.

David Brainard and Anna Chase were married on February 7, 1888, at the Saint Paul's Church in Walla Walla. During the next five years, Brainard served at several posts, ending up in New York by 1893. His marriage to Anna had not been a smooth one. They endured separations. Brainard received a letter from Anna's father, Henry, in August 1893. Henry, his sister Mary, and Anna were now living in Barnstable, Massachusetts. Henry wrote the following:

The Evergreens
Barnstable, Mass.
Aug 21, 1893

My dear Brainard,

Your letter of Aug 1st reached me in due course, and I have delayed a reply, thinking that you would soon write at greater length as indicated, and then I was so completely stunned with the purpose of your letter, that I have been simply unable to respond. I can hardly take in the fact of your permanent separation from Anna, your wife. I had for some time feared the consequences of her appetite for stimulants, but did not dream of anything of such far reaching character as to involve a separation. I knew that Anna is very willful, but hoped that your influence over her would in time correct that defect, as well as that of her unending love of wine. But again I must believe that your love for her, as exhibited in the better days, must have been always, exhibited for the best. It is hard for me to think, that her heart is radically wrong. How unfortunate for her was the loss of her mother, while yet a child of tender years, and her consequent [illegible] up in boarding school, deprived of that home influence which is so necessary for some characters in early life. While I do not yet know what act of Anna's may have impelled the act of separation, I must [illegible], from your determination of the matter, that it was of an unpardonable nature. This conclusion, as you must know both shocks and humiliates me, beyond the power of words to express, and has had a weakening effect upon me which I cannot describe. I shall try to do my duty, and what may seem to me to be for the best, and leave the rest in the hands of God. Mary will aid me and do all in her power to lead Anna in the right way, although her efforts may not be always appreciated. I fully realize that it may be difficult for us at all times to control Anna's movements as we would wish to do, as she is her own mistress, and her ideas may not always coincide with ours. God only knows what may be the [illegible] result of this great sorrow. I am glad to know that I have your affection and love, and I assure you that I entertain the same warm feeling toward you, as I have always in the happier days. When you come east I shall expect to see you and will leave you to designate the place. Mary [illegible] me in my grief and in my love to you.

Affectingly yours
H M Chase

During this period, Brainard was promoted to first lieutenant and was deeply involved in commissary stores. Henry sent him a second letter, a month after the previous letter:

Barnstable, Mass Sept 21/93

My dear Brainard,

I have your letter of 11th inst, and was pleased to know that you were at that [illegible], in good health and pleasantly located in camp; and as your letter brought to me the first direct information in regard to your [illegible], I take this opportunity to congratulate you, and to say, that I feel greatly pleased to know, that you have advanced another step, toward the high position which I trust you may finally reach in your chosen profession.

I am distressed to learn that you contemplate another journey to the north and most earnestly hope that you will change your mind, and conclude to remain with your troop. What can you hope to gain by again exposing health and life in the frozen [illegible]? You say that you must go to some place where your troubles are not known. Ah who has not trouble of some kind, and is it not better to face and live down our misfortunes? God knows that I pity and sympathize with you, and I must also feel great pity for Anna, no matter what she may have done. And then I feel that I too need the sympathy of all friends, for this [illegible] is hard for me to bear, and I do not know if I shall have strength to bear it. I do not yet know what has caused the separation, and only pray that it may be possible for the breach to be cured.

Anna, today, seemed to be frustrated, and tonight begs me to write you, and to say that she bitterly repents her misconduct, whatever it may have been. She sent the enclosed note to me, [illegible] her [illegible], and I send it to you, consider it, and if it be possible to reconcile past differences, and begin life anew. I pray that the effort may be made. I cannot write more, my feelings tonight overcome me. Since this dreadful affair came to my knowledge, life has presented a different aspect; and I look forward to care and grief instead of peace. I take no pleasure in life, and am even troubled in my dreams. Mary is in the same condition of mind, and her trouble adds to my [illegible]. I trust that you will write me very soon, and hope to see you before long.

Affectionately Yours
H M Chase

Brainard divorced Anna the following year. He continued to work in the quartermaster field throughout his career. He served across the world in this capacity. He was promoted to captain in 1896, to major in 1899, lieutenant colonel in 1905, and colonel in 1917. In December 1897 he was detailed for duty with the Alaska Relief Expedition for the destitute miners at Dawson City. In May 1898 he was ordered to the Philippine Islands as chief commissary of the military forces. He remained in the Philippines through 1911. In 1914, he went to Buenos Aires, where he served until 1917. He had been promoted to brigadier general. He retired from the army in October 1919, after serving forty-three years in the military.

After Brainard retired from the army he married Sara Hall Guthrie Neff. Sara was born in Arkansas on May 15, 1880. Sara had a child, Elinor, by a previous marriage. David, Sara, and her daughter resided in New York City for several years before moving to Washington, DC. David L. Brainard died on March 22, 1946, and is buried in Arlington National Cemetery. His wife, Sara, died on November 12, 1953, and is buried beside David in Arlington National Cemetery.

David's first wife, Anna, never married again. She died in a nursing home in Barnstable, Massachusetts, on November 2, 1952. She was cremated at the Forest Hills Creatorium in Boston, Massachusetts.

David's father died on March 12, 1887. His mother died on January 31, 1891. They are buried in the Marathon Cemetery in Cortland County, New York.

13

David Linn

(1854–1884)

DAVID LINN WAS born on May 7, 1854 at Philadelphia, Pennsylvania. He was the fourth of five sons born to Audley Linn and Margaret Ryan Linn.

David's father, Audley, was born about 1816 in Ireland. He immigrated to the United States in 1843, living first in Washington County, Pennsylvania, and later moving to Philadelphia. David's mother, Margaret, the daughter of Charles and Letitia Ryan (Rien), was also born in Ireland. She was born about 1818. Margaret immigrated to the United States and settled in Philadelphia, as did her parents and some of her siblings.

David's father and mother were married at the Union Presbyterian Church in Philadelphia on March 29, 1848. David's oldest sibling, Charles, was born in 1849; his brother James was born in 1851; and Alexander was born in 1852 or 1853. Then came David in 1854, and in 1856 another sibling was born; however, the child did not survive. David had a younger brother, Samuel, who was born in 1859.

The 1860 census shows that David was living with his grandparents, Charles and Letitia Ryan. His brothers, Charles and Alexander, were living with an aunt, Catherine Lynn, likely a relative of David's father. No trace of David's parents is found in the 1860 census record.

The mid-year census record of 1870 shows David's family living in Philadelphia in the Seventh Ward. The family consists of his father, Audley, working as a gas fitter; his mother, Margaret; his brother Charles, working in a dry goods store; his brother James, working as a brick mason; Alexander, working in a brickyard, and Samuel, his youngest brother. David is not listed with the family. In November 1870, a second census was taken in Philadelphia. This census record lists all of the family members, including David, living together.

Four years later, on January 1, 1874, David's father died. He was buried in the Mount Moriah Cemetery in Philadelphia.

On November 27, 1876, David enlisted at Philadelphia as a soldier in the "Army of the United States of America" for a period of five years. His enlistment record shows that he was twenty-five years old, had gray eyes, brown hair, and a ruddy complexion, and was five feet, eight and a half inches tall. His occupation was listed as that of a "paper stainer": someone making wallpaper.

Strangely, David is listed in the 1880 Philadelphia census as living with his mother and his brothers. He is listed as a "laborer." No mention is made that he is in the military.

David must have had contact with Lieutenant Greely or someone in the party in order to be requested to join the Lady Franklin Bay expedition. Linn, now a sergeant, met with a party headed up by Lieutenant Lockwood in Baltimore, in June 1881. The party departed Baltimore on the steamer *Nova Scotia* on June 14, 1881, heading to St. John's, Newfoundland, where they met up with Lieutenant Greely and the remaining party members.

They departed St. John's on July 7, heading toward Greenland. It was not long before Linn became involved with the activities of the expedition. When the ship reached Upernivik, Greenland, and most of the stores had been loaded, it was necessary to obtain the services of two Eskimo kayakers. The Eskimos recommended by the governor of Greenland, Governor Elberg, were at Proven, some fifty miles from Upernivik. A team consisting of Lieutenant Lockwood, Sergeant Rice, Sergeant Cross, and Sergeant Linn was assigned the duty of getting the Eskimos from Proven and bringing them back to Upernivik. The party, accompanied by Governor Elberg, departed from Upernivik on July 25 aboard the *Lady Greely*, their steam launch, and returned on July 28. They brought back Thorlip Frederick Christiansen and Jens Edward, the two Eskimos who would become part of the expedition. The Eskimos brought with them their kayaks and hunting implements.

This was only the first of many activities that David would be involved with during the expedition. His activities included exploration and exploration support, carpentry, rescue, bringing in musk oxen for food, hauling coal, reading and repairing scientific instruments, and cooking. From the time of the arrival at Lady Franklin Bay until his death, journals record him as having supported or having been on expeditions at least a half dozen times, many times acting as the cook. He made several sled trips to get musk-ox meat or coal, two of the bare necessities of life. In the spring of 1883 he was scheduled to go on a journey, but he had to cancel because of rheumatism.

One of the low points for Sergeant Linn was a demotion in rank. On October 1, 1882, expedition member Private Maurice Connell, returning from Bellot Island, had seen bear tracks on the island. On his way back to the station Private Connell met Sergeant Linn, Corporal Nicolas Salor, and Private Francis Long, who were on their way to Dutch Island, and he told them about the bear tracks. The trio rushed back to the station to get a rifle.

As soon as Connell reached the station and reported the sighting to the commanding officer, a hunting party was formed to pursue the bear. The commander, Lt. Greely, instructed Lt. Lockwood, who would lead the party, to catch up with Linn and his companions and take the guns away from them, as they were only going to Dutch Island and would not need them. The hunting party did not catch up to Linn and his companions until they had passed Dutch Island and Linn's party was already on Bellot Island, following the tracks of the bear. When the guns were taken from them, Linn was highly incensed, as they were very eager to follow up the bear, whose tracks were getting very fresh. Upon returning to the station, Linn, in naturally a very angry mood, went to Greely and asked if it was by his order that he had been disarmed. Lt. Greely resented the manner Sergeant Linn had assumed and answered in the affirmative. Greely told Linn that he would at once be reduced in rank and would be tried by court-martial when the expedition returned to the United

States. Upon reading the order for Linn's demotion from sergeant to private, Greely referred to Linn's act of insolence as mutiny.

Sergeant Rice, in his journal, states that he was rather surprised that Greely spoke of Linn's insolence as mutiny. He further writes that he feels that there was not a more subordinate and orderly member of the expedition than Linn, as was proven by his record during the more than a year that had elapsed. Sergeant Rice felt that Linn should have been disciplined in some manner, such as being placed under house arrest for a short period of time for his insolence, but Rice indicates that he feels demotion was inappropriate. A year later, Lt. Greely reinstated Linn's rank of sergeant.

While many events could be written about, the following event illustrates David Linn's compassion for his fellow comrades. It was a month or so after the party had reached Cape Sabine. Rations were so short that it appeared as though the entire party would die of starvation in a very few weeks. Fall weather had really set in, and the winter weather was not far away. The cold winds and low temperatures were something to be reckoned with. David Linn, now a sergeant, accompanied by Sergeant Rice, Corporal Ellison, and Private Frederick, volunteered to retrieve 144 pounds of meat that had been cached by the English at Cape Isabella on a previous expedition. The retrieval of this meat may have been the best chance for the members of the expedition to survive. They departed on the forty-mile trip on November 2, 1883. This account taken from the journal of Private Henry best describes the events of the journey:

> On November 2nd four men departed with the little altered sledge for Cape Isabella to bring on the 144 pounds of Australian beef. The trip proved for us a most disastrous one. The daylight was of only short duration now and they had to travel so as to take advantage of both sunlight and the feeble moon, which just there for the first time asserted its supremacy as the coming illuminator.
>
> The temperature was crawling down the bulb steadily during their absence and several bad storms caused us at home no little anxiety regarding them. Cape Isabella was reached in safety, but it was impossible to bring the sledge

nearer than two miles to it on account of the heavy conglomeration of crushed up ice blocks. Taking a few bags they ascended the rocky prominence wondering all the way up, how the Britons managed to come so close to such a place with a boat and carry the provender up such a terrible height among such fearful irregularity of boulders of granite and feldspar.

Picking up their load they scrambled down the acclivity against a cold piercing north wind. Before they reached their abandoned sledge, it was noticed that Ellison was not so spry and talkative as he used to be. His face and hands were partially frozen. Pausing long enough to restore circulation they proceeded on their way and succeeded in bringing everything to the sledge, not however without seeing that Ellison had again been visited by Jack Frost.

Resting a few hours they trudged on towards Esq. Point, but the reduced ration and the increase of cold and wind told already on them. Ellison staggered in his tracks like a drunken man, that portion of his face, which was not white from being frozen was of a livid blue color. His eyes stared vacantly and finally closed altogether. His hands remained in a permanent state of numbness; a pair of sleeping stockings pulled over his fur mittens failed to keep them warm, and finally they also turned white at the tips of the fingers and began to crawl gradually up his wrists. Presently he complained about his feet and commenced to walk as if on stilts. The poor fellows feet were froze already up to his ankles and still was gradually stealing up to his knees. They now placed him in the large sleeping bag, which itself was one solid sheet of ice and the old trick of thawing into it had to be resorted to. They [*Rice, Frederick and Linn*] crawled in alongside of him and placed his hands on their bare breasts and wrapped everything in the shape of clothing around his feet. His speech became incoherent and matter commenced to ooze out from his nose and eyes and to make it still worth he began to suffer from incontinence of urine and completely wetted the bag and his companions who were trying to save him.

They were now about eight miles south of Esq. Point in Baird Inlet and they concluded as it became now a question of saving a man's life, to drop the meat, gun and everything not actually needed. To haul Ellison on the sledge was out of the question as the other three became too exhausted, but they tagged along with their by no means light load and poor Joseph staggered blindly after them. Occasionally they would pause when they saw the poor fellow had lost the tracks and was leaning bewildered against an iceberg or wandering astray among the hummocks which with every step bruised his frozen limbs. They had finally adopt the seemingly cruel measure of tying him with a rope to the end of the sledge and to partially lead and drag him to Esq. Point. At the point they demolished the English boat and build a good fire and managed to thaw him out gradually and partially. Then loading their bag which was becoming heavier and heavier to them, on the sledge, they traveled slowly towards home, but had scarcely gone a mile, when Ellison was as badly frozen as ever and was indeed growing rapidly worse. To those versed with the English expedition the case reminded them of Peterson who died with symptoms similar to those.

Soon they had to drag him behind the sledge again and it was a pitiful sight to see the poor fellow hobble along on his frozen and helpless feet. He begged to be allowed to be let alone and lie down to die.

In such manner they traveled about seven miles and having to go over a sort of a divide there, they found themselves unequal to the task, and unrolling their icebag, they again thawed themselves with poor Joe in the middle, as the fourth man could not get into even if he wanted to.

Partaking of a small lunch Rice without waiting started for home to obtain help. [*Frederick and Linn stayed in the sleeping bag with Ellison.*] Not expecting that he would live until morning he left direction for his burial in the ice in a decent manner as duty to the living would permit.

Darkness had already set in when he (started on his dangerous mission. In Rice Strait the young ice had partially been broken again and in many other places it was so thin that it bend beneath his footsteps, but becoming reckless with hunger and exertion he cared little whether he perished or not. To make matters worse a fresh north wind howled through the strait and many a time he had to turn his back to it to allow his nose to thaw out a trifle. In Buchanan Strait condition of affairs on account of the moon being now completely hidden, assumed a different aspect. The danger of drowning or breaking through the young ice was over but in the total darkness, he stumbled among the terrible hummocks, falling many times and bruising himself badly on legs and body.

With such trouble and worry of mind he dragged himself wearily on; reaching home at midnight on the 10th. The building was in total darkness; and as we heard the slight noise Rice made in entering. Hearing but one some one inquired after the others, not wishing to alarm us at once he thoughtfully answered "oh they are behind" but his tremulous voice foretold that something was the matter. He finally told his story and the camp was in an excitement. It being the first serious accident, everyone desired to go out at once. At 4:30 a.m. the two fleetest walkers started in advance with spirits and food, and at 6:20 a.m. the English sledge with eight more men went to his relief.

From Rice's story we hardly expected to find him alive and to tell the truth, we hoped and prayed that the poor fellow would be dead and out of his misery, but in case that he yet was in the land of the living Lt. G. sent out a message to him to the effect, that he died doing his whole duty. The little Bay where they expected to find him interred in the ice foot was named after him Ellison Bay.

During their absence speculation was rife, everyone was in suspense and expectation but none more so then Rice, who as being in charge of that ill fated detail, felt a certain responsibility on his shoulders. After coming in the night before tired and hungry and thirsty, he never informed us of his real condition, on account of our being already on short rations and his failing to bring in the meat he refused to accept food or drink, except his weekly allowance of the moldy dog biscuits, and those only because they could be deducted from the regular issue. Before 9 a.m. on the 11th he was as if on a gridiron and could hardly be persuaded to remain and not go to their assistance.

It must be remembered that the party, who started out, had been on extreme reduced rations and the breakfast they took before starting was only a slight increase if any, and for the two days they were expected to be gone their rations was increased to about double, but it even then is hardly sufficient to support life, let alone to perform an exceedingly hard days work on.

At 5 p.m. on the 11th we were again startled by a noise outdoors in the darkness and presently the two men who had been left with Ellison in the bay entered our gloomy quarters. Both were nearly dead with fatigue and hunger and had it not been for the energy of one, the other would have lain down and died before reaching the shelter of the friendly hills. They reported Joe alive yet but in a critical condition. The party had reached them in one march and to release the two men out of their icebound sleeping bag they had to cut them out through the sides. While a draught of tea was prepared for them a hungry fox, probably aware of the helplessness of the inmates of the bag endeavored to crawl in with them.

On the 12th at 2 a.m. the party came in with the unfortunate sufferer and he was carried in tenderly and placed on a mattress. Stearine lamps were lit and between the Dr. and his faithful steward, they began to thaw the frozen limbs and commencing with cold water at first and gradually increasing the temperature of the same.

The condition of the sledging party was indeed pitiful to see. They had made the entire march with but one stoppage, and that only for only a few moments to eat. Wishing to make it in one march they ate up an extra allowance and were considerately reprimanded for it.

> Take this relief expedition as a whole, it stands without parallel in the annals of arctic history. The men sank exhausted upon their damp bags and laid like logs for a considerable length of time; nor were any of them fit or able to stir about for the next week.

The episode was so traumatic for Linn that he never really recovered his strength to do much more for the expedition. On April 6, 1884, nearly five months after this ill-fated attempt at retrieving the meat, David Linn asked the commander to take charge of his personal effects and send them to his brother, Charles C. Linn, at 1904 Lombard Street in Philadelphia. Shortly after noon Linn became unconscious. In the evening, after asking in vain for a drink of water that no one could furnish, he closed his eyes and quietly slept into a painless death. He died at 7:00 PM.

That night, since there was no other place to sleep, Sergeant Rice and Ralston crawled into the sleeping bag that contained Linn's body, one on each side of their dead comrade, and slept soundly for a few hours. The next day, April 7, Kislingbury scratched a grave six inches deep on Cemetery Ridge, the spot where the dead of the party had been buried. That was as deep as he could penetrate the frozen gravel of the ridge.

His body remained there until the relief party arrived two and a half months later, on June 22. David Linn's body was removed from Cemetery Ridge and placed in a barrel containing a preservative fluid aboard the *Thetis*, one of the three ships that would carry both the dead and the living to St. John's, Newfoundland. The ship departed Cape Sabine on the afternoon of the following day. After stopping at Godhaven, the ship journeyed on, reaching St. John's on July 17, about four weeks after leaving Cape Sabine. Linn's body was placed in a casket, and on July 26 the ship carrying Linn's casket departed from St. John's. The ship went to Portsmouth, New Hampshire, where a large celebration was staged. The remains of David Linn reached Philadelphia on August 8, 1884. The funeral for David Linn took place at the home of his mother on August 10. After the funeral services, many posts of the Grand Army of the Republic (GAR) accompanied the body to Mount Moriah

Cemetery, the cemetery where his father was buried and where he would be buried.

The news media had been suggesting that cannibalism might have taken place during the party's starving days.

In an newspaper interview with David's mother a few days after David's burial, the following was reported in the *New York Times*:

> Philadelphia, Aug. 16— "It is my wish" said Mrs. Linn, the mother of Sergt. David Linn, to-day, "that the body of my dear son be taken up and examined. I would like it to be done by our own doctor, and very quietly and privately. I only regret that it was not done before he was buried; but at any rate I shall not feel satisfied until I have seen the body. It is not so much that I expect to see his body mutilated; there is another cause. I would like to know if he was shot."
>
> "What makes you think he was shot?"
>
> "I have a sort of presentiment. It came in this way: About the time of his death I had a dream. I heard him cry out for warm water and hot clothes for his back. Oh, and I saw poor boy with a great lump as big as an egg, with blood oozing from it, on the left side of his back. I have always since then thought he was shot, and I would like to know. I cannot believe the story of the men eating each other's flesh, but it is horrible, if true. Why couldn't they all die alike or live together?"
>
> "Do your sons wish the coffin opened?"
>
> "Yes and no. My youngest son is very anxious about it, but the other three are against it. They think we should let well alone."

The coffin of David Linn was not opened for examination. There is nothing listed in the journals of his comrades that even suggests that David died of anything other than starvation. The four sons she spoke of were Charles (her oldest, about thirty-six years old), James, Alexander, and Samuel (her youngest, about ten years younger than Charles).

Margaret Linn, David's mother, died on May 19, 1904. She had remained in the house on North Lambert Street until the time of her death. Her sister, Rebecca Ryan, and her son Charles were living with her. She was buried in the Mount Moriah Cemetery. Charles and his brother James were still living in the North Lambert Street house with their Aunt Rebecca in 1910. Little is known after that about her sons except for Alexander. Alexander married Mary Ann Slotter in July 1883. They had several children, including Charles Audley, James Daniel, Ida Margreate, and Elwood Cornelius. They continued to make their home in Philadelphia.

David Linn's life was cut short by his volunteering for Arctic service. Even though he was demoted for what the commanding officer considered insubordination, in time his rank was restored. In each case, we find Sergeant Linn ready to assist his fellow comrades. His final action, which led to his death, was to risk his life in order to help his comrades survive. David Linn was truly a caring and brave man.

14

Nicholas Salor

(1849–1884)

Nicholas Salor was born in Steinfort, Luxembourg on December 24, 1849. He was the tenth of fifteen children born to Jean Pierre Salor and Catherine Grunen. His father, Jean Pierre, was born about 1804. His mother, Catherine, was born about 1815. Jean Pierre and Catherine were married in Steinfort on July 20, 1831. Jean Pierre was a farmer.

One of Nicholas's older siblings was also named Nicholas. He died as an infant. Also, one of his younger brothers was named Nicholas. He also died when he was young. More than one of his siblings bore the name Anne, and more than one bore their father's name, Pierre.

Sometime between 1861 and 1864, Nicolas left his family in Steinfort and moved to the French town of Kuntzig. This town is located only a few miles from Steinfort, Luxembourg. The reason for his leaving is unknown by the author, but he may have had relatives living there or found work in those rough times, or both. In 1870 Nicholas was working on a farm in Michigan, so his stay in Kuntzig was less than ten years. He is listed in the 1870 census record as having been born in Michigan, with foreign-born parents. He may have just said he was born in Michigan if he entered the country illegally. This may have been the case, as no record of his arrival has been found.

Eight years later, on February 23, 1878, Nicholas joined the United States Army at Cincinnati, Ohio. He enlisted for a period of five years. The enlistment record lists his birthplace as Luxembourg and his occupation as laborer, the same occupation that was listed on the 1870 census record.

Nicolas is listed in the 1880 census in Arlington, Virginia. He, along with ten other soldiers at Post Fort Wipple (now known as Fort Myers), was planning to depart on an Arctic expedition. The other soldiers were Frederick E. Server, Frances Steward, David S. Brainard, Daniel L. Starr, William H. Johnson, James Ryan, George B. Richardson, Julius Fredericks, Frantz Stotzen, and Frances Long. When the government failed to provide funding for the expedition, the army backed off, and the expedition was funded by private funds; consequently these soldiers did not go on the failed 1880 expedition. It would be the next year, 1881, before the government would provide the army with funding for the expedition. Some of these soldiers did accompany Salor on the 1881 expedition, including Brainard, Starr, Ryan, Fredericks, and Long. Starr and Ryan returned on the *Proteus* and did not remain in the Arctic with the expedition.

In June 1881, Salor joined a group of other solders under the command of Lieutenant Lockwood. On June 14, they sailed on the Allan Line steamer *Nova Scotia* for St. John's, where they would meet up with the rest of the party and the commander of the expedition, Lieutenant Greely. They departed from St. John's on July 7. The group reached Lady Franklin Bay on August 10, 1881, after stopping in Greenland to pick up supplies as well as the doctor and the dog team drivers.

As mentioned previously, Salor was a laborer. He had no particular trade, and as such, he was used to assist in a wide variety of activities. Salor's earliest activities were mentioned in Ellison's journal: "Wednesday, August 31. Sgt. Brainard, Jewell, Cross, Corp. Salor and Connell left this morning in the whale boat northward. Sgt. Ralson by order of the commanding officer watched the party from Cairn's hill but could not see them."

In September that first autumn at Fort Conger, Salor is recorded as going with Gardiner to St. Patrick Bay to check on the ice and going with a crew to assist Rice back to camp when he was suffering from rheumatism. In October he went with Lockwood, Linn, and Henry toward St. Patrick Bay to explore the valley, and later with Lockwood to Dutch Island to provide sledge support. In November, while Salor was filling an oil lamp in the lean-to, the oil caught fire, burning Salor, but not seriously.

Little is noted of his activities between November 1881 and March 1882 except for the celebration of his birthday on Christmas Eve, December 24. On March 5, he and Whistler circled Bellot Island, checking ice conditions. On March 23, Salor and Ellis left the station for Cape Beechey with the Hudson Bay sledge to stow 120 pounds of supplies in support of the upcoming "farthest north" trip. On April 3, 1882, the party that would reach a point farther north than ever recorded in history as of that time, along with the support teams, departed from Fort Conger. Salor was part of a support team. He was on that mission for over a month, from April 3 until after May 9, when he returned to the fort. The party sometimes traveled over twenty-four hours in one stretch. Besides moving supplies, Salor also acted as cook.

From June 24 until July 3, Salor was on a support trek with Greely as the team went westward, hoping to reach the western sea. During the remainder of 1882 and throughout the spring and summer of 1883, Salor helped with many tasks, including reading instruments, firing shots to determine the speed of sound at this latitude and at these cold temperatures, cutting holes in the ice to measure depth, and hauling coal. He also assisted in preparing specimens of plants and animals that would be saved for the Smithsonian Institute.

After the expedition departed Fort Conger in the fall of 1883 and reached safe haven at Cape Sabine, Salor continued to always give a helpful hand. He went on scouting trips in the area and worked at keeping the water hole open where small shrimp were being captured for food to supplement their meager supply. Rice, who was doing much of the shrimping, taught his methods to Salor, and Salor was soon involved in this activity. On April 4, Salor brought in twenty pounds of shrimp, and on the following day, over twelve pounds.

On January 19, 1884, when Cross died, Salor was part of a party of six that carried his body to Cemetery Hill for burial. He performed the same duties on April 7 when Lynn died.

Doctor Pavy reported on April 18, 1884, that Salor was very feeble, with a fluttering heart and pulse. But on May 9 it was reported that Salor and Schneider worked seven or eight hours daily cooking. By May 16 Salor was so weak that he had to give up cooking; however, by the nineteenth, he was back to cooking. Salor continued to grow weaker, until at three in the morning of June 3 he died. Lt. Greely wrote the following in his journal pertaining to Salor: "Corporal Salor died this morning about three o'clock. Salor was an honest, reliable, hard-working soldier, and was an energetic and important member of the supporting party toward attaining the Farthest North."

About six weeks later the rescue team arrived. Salor's body was not recovered. After the survivors and remnants of the expedition had returned to the United States and the newspapers carried news about the dead and living, on August 15 the secretary of the navy received the following letter from John Salor:

Hancock, Mich. August 11, 1884

Hon W.E Chandler
Secretary of the Navy
Washington, D.C.

Sir:

I most respectfully beg leave to inform you that I am a brother of the late Nicholas Salor, one of the Lady Franklin Bay expedition.

He wrote me from St. John July 5, 1881 saying that each member of the expedition had made a will and that his will bequeathed everything due or to become due to him to me. Will you kindly inform me of the proper steps to take in the matter. I hold his letters and other correspondence which I will forward. An early reply will much oblige.

Yours very respectfully
(signed) John Salor
Hancock, Mich
Please address in care of M. Fiem
Hancock, Mich Late of Leadville Colo.

John Salor, purporting to be a brother of Nicholas Salor, probably was indeed his brother. While no John Salor was born to Jean Pierre Salor and his wife Catherine Grunen, one of the children was named Jean Pierre, after his father, and was born in a year that matched John's year of birth closely. It is likely that John is in fact Jean Pierre, Nicholas's brother. Be that as it may, an official will was written by Nicholas Salor on May 9, 1884, just four weeks prior to his death:

> I, Nicolas Salor, Corporal U.S. Army, born at Steinfort, Grand-duchy of Luxembourg, being of sound mind, do declare this to be my last will and testament. I give and bequeath to my brothers and sisters who may be living all my property, real and personal, to be equally divided among them.
>
> I hereby appoint my father Pierre Salor, of Luxembourg, executor of this will. Given at Camp Clay, near Cape Sabine, Ellesmere Land, May ninth, 1884.
>
> Nicholas Salor (seal)

This will was witnessed by Greely, Ralston, and Israel. Nicholas's brother John was not mentioned specifically in this will, but it is likely that he received a portion of the estate.

It is difficult to discover much about Nicholas's family. His mother, Catherine (Grunen) Salor, died in 1885, the year following Nicholas's death. One of his sisters, Marie, married Joseph Servais in 1872 in Steinfort. Nicholas's sister Catherine married Pierre Clemen in 1861, and another sister with the same name married Juan Pierre Mauritus in 1867, both in Steinfort. Nicholas's brother Dominique died that same year. Another of his sisters, Marie, married Jean Pierre Wilmes in France in 1878.

Perhaps the most that is known about any of Nicholas's siblings is John. John married Elizabeth (Aurich) Schwartz on December 15, 1877. Elizabeth was the widow of Jacob Schwartz. Jacob and Elizabeth had five children prior to Jacob's death in 1875. John and Elizabeth had three children together. The oldest of the children was Nettie. Nettie was born in early 1878, and she died on July 7, 1880. Nicholas, the second child, was born about February 1880 and died on September 24, 1880. In 1884 they had a son they named

John E., sometimes using the surname Salor and at other times the surname Schwartz. Sometime prior to 1900 John and Elizabeth were divorced. John's whereabouts after his divorce are unknown.

Nicholas Salor was a hard worker. He worked on his father's farm in Luxembourg, possibly worked on a farm in France, and worked on a farm in Michigan prior to entering the army. He volunteered for service in the Arctic area and was prepared to go in 1880. He had an entire year to contemplate his decision before proceeding in 1881. He certainly realized the dangers of such a mission, yet he volunteered and was accepted. Nicholas Salor was indeed a brave man.

15

Joseph Ellison

(1849–1884)

THE MEMBERS OF the Franklin Bay expedition would reside in quarters made from pieces of lumber that had been precut prior to shipment. This preparation of the lumber was done to assist in the building of such a structure. To perform the task of assembling a building that would provide quarters for twenty-five people in the Arctic cold and snow required someone with carpentry abilities. It also required someone with the skills that would enable him to build and repair other structures such as furniture and outbuildings. Joseph Ellison volunteered for this duty and was selected.

Josepf (Joseph) Ellison was born in Orschweier, Ettenheim, Baden, Germany, on January 12, 1849. He was the fifth of eight children born to Joseph Ellison and Magdalena Obergeffel. His siblings, all born in Germany, were Aloysius (Alois), born in 1842; Joseph, 1843, living only eight days; Karl (Charles), 1844; Karolina (Carolina), 1847; Katharina (Cathrine), 1851; Anton, 1860; and Augustus (August), 1863.

Joseph Ellison's father, the senior Joseph Ellison, was born on January 10, 1810. He married Magdalena Obergeffel on January 18, 1841. Magdalena was born on May 25, 1818. The senior Joseph Ellison was a wheelwright, making and repairing wheels. He eventually turned his attention to farming, which he continued throughout the remainder of his life. Magdalena died on May 19, 1876, having lived her entire life in Germany. The senior Joseph died in Germany two years later, on January 11, 1878.

Some of Joseph and Magdalena's children came to America, and some decided to stay in Germany. Alois (Aloysius), the oldest of the children, was the first to come to the United States. He immigrated about 1862, settling in Pottsville, Schuylkill County, Pennsylvania. He worked for the Pottsville Rolling Mill, rolling wrought iron, which was used for the construction of the rails on the Central Pacific Railroad. These rails were also laid on the first continental railroad in 1869 near Wells, Nevada.

Joseph immigrated to the United States in 1867, going to Pottsville, where his brother Alois lived. His brothers Carl and Anton followed closely, Carl in 1868 and Anton in 1870. Upon his arrival in Pottsville, Joseph went to work with his brother Alois in the Pottsville Rolling Mill. He worked there for about a year and a half.

About 1868 or 1869 Joseph moved to Newark, New Jersey, where he worked as a carpenter. He also improved his natural talents of architecture and drafting. He went to Chicago after the Great Fire of 1871 and helped with the architecture and carpentry needed to restore the city.

On February 7, 1875, he enlisted in the United States Army in New York City. During the next five years he was involved with the building of many government buildings, ending up in Fort Wayne, Indiana, where in 1880 he reenlisted for another five-year term.

Joseph departed Fort Wayne in May 1881 on his way to Washington, DC, to meet up with other members of the expedition. En route from Fort Wayne to Washington he visited family members in Pottsville, Pennsylvania, for about ten days. While visiting his brothers in Pottsville, he told them of his plans for after he returned home from the expedition. He planned to visit the Holy Land and then visit his two sisters, Carolina and Cathrine, in Germany. On his return from the Holy Land and Germany, he hoped to marry and make his home in Pottsville.

In Washington he met Lieutenant Lockwood, one of the officers Lieutenant Greely had assigned to oversee the enlisted men. Lockwood was gathering together the members of the party assigned to him. Lockwood would be in charge of them while traveling to their final destination, Lady Franklin Bay. On June 13 they traveled the short distance to Baltimore, and the next day they boarded the steamer *Nova Scotia* for the trip to Saint John's, Newfoundland. They stopped at Halifax en route. There the steam launch, which they would carry on their journey north, was christened. Miss Lillian Gary, a prominent lady from Baltimore, did the honors, christening the launch *Lady Greely* in honor of the commander's wife.

The party arrived in St. John's on June 22 and assisted in the loading of supplies aboard the *Proteus*, the ship that was to transport them to the site on Lady Franklin Bay where they would construct their quarters. From this site they would perform a number of tasks related to exploration and meteorological, temperature, and other research.

They completed the loading of the ship on July 4 and departed on their journey on July 7, 1881.

The next stop on the journey was Disko, Greenland, an Eskimo village of about two hundred inhabitants. They arrived at Disko on July 16, some nine days after departing St. John's. Of big concern to Ellison was the "rafting" of lumber to be used for building their living quarters at Lady Franklin Bay. The precut lumber for the construction of their quarters had been aboard the ship *Gulnare* that headed for Lady Franklin Bay in 1880 but was damaged by the ice and had to return. The lumber had been unloaded at Disco and stored in a government warehouse. Ellison assumed a lot of responsibility for the handling of this lumber. Once it was rafted out to the ship, it had to be loaded aboard.

They left Disco at about ten o'clock on the night of July 20 and eleven hours later arrived at Rittenbenk, some seventy miles northwest of Disco. Rittenbenk was an Eskimo village of about one hundred and fifty people. There they picked up Dr. Pavy, Henry Clay, and another seven dogs. Ellison helped Dr. Pavy, packing and transferring Pavy's goods to the ship. They departed Rittenbenk on July 22, heading for Upernavick.

The ship arrived at Upernavick on July 24. Upernavick, another Eskimo village, had about two hundred inhabitants. The steam launch *Lady Greely* was unloaded from the *Proteus* for the purpose of going to Proven, about sixty miles from Upernavick, where the two Eskimo dog-sledge drivers, Jens Edwards and Thorlip Frederick Christensen, would be picked up to accompany the expedition.

Many of the expedition members were involved with duck

hunting while at Upernavick. They brought in literally hundreds of ducks, which Ellison helped skin and stuff for shipment to the Smithsonian Institute. On July 29, after taking aboard another eleven dogs and loading the steam launch back on the *Proteus*, they departed Upernavick.

The ship reached Littleton Island on August 2. They were now only about two hundred and fifty miles from Lady Franklin Bay, their destination. The prospects of reaching Lady Franklin Bay were not very good. They encountered great ice fields and bergs. By August 7 they were trapped in the ice, and it looked as though they would be crushed. For four days, they drifted with the ice. Finally, on August 11, they were released from the ice and were in open water. They reached their chosen landing point the next day, August 12, at Lady Franklin Bay. Ellison was now involved in unloading the ship. The first to come off was the lumber to be used for the quarters' construction. It had to be rafted again, this time from the ship to the coast, a distance of about one hundred and fifty yards. This rafting process meant that the lumber got wet, leaving it in a bad condition to work with. A team would work for four hours, then a second team would work four hours, after which the first team would return for four more hours of work. This unloading of the lumber lasted for two days.

On August 14 work began on construction of the quarters. Ellison wrote this in his journal:

> I have a great deal of trouble in finding the different parts as there is a great deal missing. I would rather not have any of it framed. It takes almost as long to hunt it up as it would be to make it.

With the temperature between thirty and forty-five degrees, Ellison worked fourteen hours each day on the quarters. The quarters were finally enclosed on August 27. All the supplies had been unloaded, and the *Proteus* was heading back to St. John's.

Besides constructing the quarters, Ellison was also involved in other carpentry tasks. He built a table for the cookhouse, put in the kitchen range, put a stove in the officers' room, and erected a small observatory.

Throughout his entire time with the expedition, very few days passed without Ellison being involved with some type of carpentry activity. He was continually repairing or making sledge runners and sometimes even sledges. He repaired doors, windows, observation buildings, etc. This did not keep him from being involved with other activities. He helped take instrument readings, he helped cut fresh ice for water, and frequently he served as room orderly and occasionally as second cook.

On November 10, 1881, he was involved in a disaster. While he was in a tent filling a gas lamp, the gas lamp caught fire and exploded. His hands and face were badly burned. He ran out of the tent and put out the fire by rolling in the snow. For the next week he suffered terrible pain from the burns. Nearly all the skin rubbed off his face. From then on he had difficulty facing the cold. He was able to go back to work on the twenty-first.

It is likely that the events of November 10 had a lasting impact on the ability of his body to withstand the cold weather. On February 2, 1882, while helping Jewell place thermometers in the ice and in the officers' lean-to, he froze the tips of three of his fingers. Three days later, while taking an hourlong walk to Dutch Island with the temperature at fifty-four degrees below zero, his eyes got watery, and the lids froze together. Ellison stated that this was the first time he felt the cold in his eyes. And a few days later, while on a trip to Cape Murchinson, he stated that he had a hard time keeping his nose and face from freezing.

On March 12, 1882, when he was asked by the commanding officer if he had any objection about going out into the field, Ellison replied that he had come up for that purpose and had no desire to be lying around the station. On a forty-mile, weeklong trip to Newman's Bay a few days later with seven other members of the expedition, Ellison froze all of his fingers when the temperature dipped to sixty degrees below zero. But this would not stop him from volunteering to go on future journeys.

In April and May 1882 he traveled over a hundred miles, pulling sledges with supplies in support of a team that would break the record, at the time, of the farthest point north ever reached.

Throughout the summer of 1882, he did relatively routine tasks. He did garden work, pressed flowers and other plants to bring back as specimens, walked to hilltops to see if any sign of a relief ship could be seen, made frames and fastened Eskimo relics to them, and helped recover meat from hunted animals. In August he actually killed two musk oxen.

When the winter weather returned, more of his work was indoors, making tables, wallpapering, working on doors, etc. He did travel to take temperature and other types of readings. He was also involved with making sound measurements. A party, usually two people, would go to a hill a half mile or so away from camp and fire several shots. A record would be made of how long it took from the time the person at camp saw the flash from the shot to the time that the shot was heard at the camp. This information was analyzed with respect to different temperature and barometric readings. Ellison froze two fingers while firing shots on one of these occasions.

In March 1883 it was time for another trek to the north. Again Ellison volunteered to be a part of the support team. On the second day of the trek, he "stiffened up," the first time anything of this nature had happened to him. He could not eat. The next day he still had no appetite. After three days he was still sick, and the trek leader, Lieutenant Lockwood, decided to send him back to the station. It was hard for him to get back to the station, and it was several days before he was well again.

In April he was on another short trip, and his face was badly frostbitten. The remainder of his time before the party departed the station was spent preparing flowers as specimens to bring back with them on their return from the expedition.

The party departed from the station, Fort Conger, on August 8, 1883, aboard the steam launch *Lady Greely*. They abandoned the launch a month later after it had been jammed by the ice floes and traveled by foot over the floes until they reached land at Cape Sabine.

By November their meager food supplies were getting low. The English had cached about 144 pounds of meat at Cape Isabella, some twenty-five miles away from their makeshift camp. Among the four people who volunteered to make the trip to Cape Isabella to recover the meat was Ellison. The party, consisting of Ellison, Rice, Lynn, and "Shorty" Frederick, took a sledge with them on which to carry the meat back to Cape Sabine. The following are Ellison's journal entries, made by Schneider as Ellison dictated them:

Camp Clay, November 2, 1883

> Sergeant Rice in charge and Sergeant Lynn, Private Frederick and myself left camp about 8 a.m., it being quite dark yet, with a lightly laden sledge for Cape Isabella, for the purpose of getting the 144 pounds of English canned meat left by Capt. Allen Young in 1876.
>
> Travelling is quite bad, snow being soft and deep. Met Long and the two natives in Rice's Straits.
>
> Went into camp about 4 p.m., one mile from the southern tip of the strait; having no tent, it took a very short time to spread our sleeping bag, which was frozen quite hard, and caused us some difficulty to get into.
>
> We sat up in the bag cooking our frugal meal consisting of ½ pound of pemmican, 4 ounces of hard bread, a cup of tea, and a half gill of rum, after which we retired. It was very cold during the night.

November 3

> Arose at 7 a.m., it being quite dark yet. Had the same meal as the previous day. Broke camp at 8 a.m. Travelling quite fair and went into camp at 4 p.m. at Eskimo Point, in the broken [illegible], which is partly covered with the ice boat. Used part of the boat for fuel to cook the meal. Spent the night moderately comfortable.

November 4

> Broke camp at 8 a.m. Found traveling from here very bad, owing to days soft snow and hummock ice. Went into camp

about 5 miles north of Cape Isabella, myself quite worn out and the others very tired. Had much difficulty in preparing our meal owing to the strong wind and having no shelter, this about 3 p.m.

November 5

Spent a miserable night. Broke camp about 8:30 a.m. Only took 1 cup of tea, 1 biscuit, started for Cape Isabella.

Left our sleeping gear about 3 miles north of the Cape and went on with the empty sledge.

From here the traveling was very bad, the ice being forced up 40 feet against the cliffs, we climbed along the best we could. Reached the cache and obtained the 4 boxes meat and with great difficulty started back to the sledge, which it took us 5 hours to do.

Took our meat on the sledge and then proceeded to where we had left the sleeping bag, having worked 13 hours in all this day. I was completely exhausted. Sergeant Rice, with great difficulty, after about two hours work with the wood from the meat boxes succeeded in cooking a cup of tea; the pemmican we ate cold.

Here I froze my hands so that I was unable to use them. Tried our best to thaw them out in the sleeping bag, but owing to the high wind which was blowing at the time we did not succeed, the bag being frozen so stiff that we were hardly able to move. From this time out I had to be fed.

November 6

Spent a most miserable night. I froze both my feet. Broke camp about 9 a.m., myself still able to walk with great difficulty, but not able to assist any on the sledge, and thus making it very hard on the others.

Went into camp at 4 p.m., it being quite dark, and after preparing our frugal meal we retired.

November 7

Spent a most miserable night, it being very windy and the temperature about –30. Broke camp at 9 a.m., weather cloudy and snow drifting badly. I still am struggling along, my legs being like stilts and entirely unable to bend my ankles, and it was only by the greatest efforts and exertions that I got along at all. This day I froze my nose badly on account of not being able to use my hands. Went into camp at Eskimo Point about 4 p.m., having abandoned the meat about 5 miles from here, the party being unable to drag the load any farther.

We now started a good wood fire with some of the boat Beaumont. After supper, party partly thawed my feet by warming stockings, which occupied about 2 hours, and then we retired for the night.

November 9

Broke camp about 9 a.m., myself yet able to struggle along, but becoming weaker and weaker until I finally had to give in after traveling a distance of 7 miles, it being now utterly impossible for me to get along any farther. Compelled to go into camp at the head of Ellison's Bay. Party concluded that it would be impossible to get me to Camp Clay without assistance. They tried to cook supper but were unsuccessful, owing to high wind.

Sergeant Rice started for Camp Clay 3 p.m., having taken with him a frozen piece of meat to eat on the way, with a 15 mile march ahead of him.

November 10

Spent a most miserable night, unable to move in our bag. My hands and feet frozen now so bad that I had no use of them whatever. A high wind blowing. We were unable to cook breakfast. Feet frozen solid into the bag. We cooked us a meal consisting of English meat, myself only able to drink the broth. We also had a can of oxtail soup, some hospital brandy for my use, which revised me somewhat. My sufferings about this time more horrible, shortness of breath, begging for water and ice which could not be obtained.

Sergeant Brainard stayed with us a few hours. The next morning a party headed by Lieutenant Lockwood arrived and putting me on their sledge, hauled me to Camp Clay. My sufferings on the way there were horrible.

Sergeant Ellison was brought back into Camp Clay at about 1:00 am on November 12, 1883, with his feet and legs badly frozen up to the knees. His hands and wrists and his nose were also badly frozen, so that they appeared like pieces of ice. He was taken into the hut and put on a mattress over which a sheepskin sleeping bag, cut open, was spread, and then covered with three woolen blankets. For the next four days Schneider and Doctor Pavy took turns thawing out Ellison's frozen limbs with cloths soaked in cold water and gradually raising the temperature of the water. Ellison's frozen body parts were then oiled with carbolic oil and glycerin and wrapped in flannel to ensure warmth. After about ten days a line of demarcation showed itself just above the ankles, and two days later on the hands. His nose was very sore, and part of the flesh sloughed off later.

The wounds were washed and dressed daily using the oil on hand until it was exhausted. Eventually two of the fingers on his left hand fell off. The remaining fingers on his left hand died but did not fall off. The fingers on his right hand died but did not fall off. The instruments necessary for their removal had been lost under the snow. Eventually one of his feet was removed, through the ankle joints, with only a small pair of scissors being available for the procedure.

On May 7, realizing that he might not survive his ordeal, Ellison dictated to Lieutenant Greely the following letter:

Alois Ellison, Pottsville, Pa.

There being a chance of my surviving the spring I write by Lt. Greely's hand a few lines to say that all deaths have been so far easy and quiet, I shall die quiet and contented never repining at my fate. I lost my feet and hands doing my duty in a manner of which you need never feel ashamed. I have always tried to do right by you all but if I have failed I hope and feel confident of your forgiveness. You will I know write my brothers and sisters of my death. I have to regret not seeing you again but feel certain my last wishes and hopes will be for the welfare of you all together with your families.

Joseph Ellison by Lt. Greely"

Greely added the following:

I can say of Sgt. Ellison (promoted for extraordinary services for the expedition) that he is one of the most faithful, manly, courageous and patient men I have ever known. His family may well be proud of him.

A comment made by Schneider of June 9, 1884, only a few days prior to the rescue, is as follows:

The wounds are to this day running and the bones protruding about one to one inch and a half, needing amputation. What makes the case so very remarkable is the short rations on which the patient has to subside and the cold, damp and dark at most here in which he had to live.

On June 12, 1884, Lieutenant Greely recorded in his journal that Ellison had bedsores and was getting weaker. This condition seems likely, as he had been lying in the cold makeshift bed for nearly seven months.

The rescue ship arrived ten days later. An attempt was made to amputate the rest of Ellison's dead limbs while aboard the rescue ship, but he was too weak to withstand the procedures. He died near Godhaven, Greenland, on July 8, 1884. His body was brought back to St. John's, where it was placed in a casket and returned to the United States with the other bodies.

At the request of his brother Alois, his body was returned to

Pottsville, Pennsylvania. On August 10, 1884, the Ellison's funeral and burial took place. The funeral procession was made up of a large, diversified group of about four thousand people. It consisted of the Marshall and his aides, various societies, bands, military regiments, relatives, and friends, escorted by the Pottsville Police Force. He was buried in the German Catholic Cemetery in Pottsville.

On the day of Ellison's death, Greely wrote the following:

> Sergeant Ellison died at Godhavn, July 8th, consequent on secondary amputation, which was absolutely necessary and equally hopeless. Though both hands and both feet had been lost by natural amputation, his indomitable will power and naturally fine physique kept him alive for seven and a half months. Utterly helpless, fed with double our ration, cared for and nursed by his starving comrades, no open word or secret insinuation ever came to me that this drain on our strength and supplies was useless—this man a burden. I hardly know now whether most to admire the courage and will which kept Ellison alive, or the devotion and charity of his comrades who gave so freely of their strength, food, and tender offices, knowing all the while that their sacrifices were in vain, except as a concession to their spirit of humanity and Christian charity.
>
> Sergeant Ellison was an honest, faithful man, who never spared himself when the interests of his comrades or of the expedition could be advanced. He was equally valuable in the workshop or field, as botanist, carpenter, or sledgeman.

Joseph Ellison truly was a man who gave his all in order to do whatever he felt was necessary. He ended up giving his life in order to obtain food so that others could live. Although the venture failed, no one can question that Joseph Ellison was truly a brave man.

16

Charles Henry Buck, alias Charles B. Henry

(1856–1884)

CHARLES HENRY BUCK, baptized as Carl Heinrich Friedrich Buck, was born in Hannover, Germany, on February 27, 1856. He was the first of six children born to Johann Heinrich Buck and Wilhelmina Christina Dorthea Grosstruck. His brother Johann Heinrich Buck was born on April 16, 1858, and died a week later, on April 23; his sister Wilhelmina Dorthea Elizabeth Buck (Dora) was born on May 11, 1859; his brother Wilhelm Buck (William) was born about 1861; his sister Mimmi (Mini) was born in 1862; and his youngest sister, Frida, was born in 1866.

Carl Henry Buck immigrated to the United States when he was just fifteen years old. He arrived in New York on July 17, 1871. After his arrival, Carl wandered around the United States and resided for a brief period in almost every state of the Union. He found work as a newspaper reporter as well as working in the newspaper print shop. In 1875 and 1876 he worked for the Daily Monitor in Moberly, Missouri, but by September of the latter year we find him living in Philadelphia. On September 11, 1876, five years after his arrival in the United States, Carl enlisted in the army at Philadelphia, Pennsylvania. He was assigned to the United States Seventh Cavalry, Troop G, as a clerk under the command of Lieutenant Wallace. He was assigned duty at Fort Buford, Montana Territory, as a post purchasing agent. On August 13, 1878, while at Fort Buford, Carl was found guilty of forging the commander's signature in order to purchase liquor for his own use. He was sentenced to four years' imprisonment at Fort Leavenworth, Kansas. He was released after serving one year and discharged from the army.

Some newspaper accounts, although not documented, claim that shortly after his discharge from the army, Carl was involved in a barroom brawl in Deadwood, Dakota Territory, where a "Chinaman" was killed. Carl reportedly fled from the area.

Carl most likely went to Chicago where one of his sisters, Dora, who had emigrated from Germany to the United States, lived. She was residing with another relative, William Helms, whom Carl would later designate as executor of his will.

On December 23, 1879, Carl enlisted as a clerk in the army at Cincinnati, Ohio, under the alias Charles B. Henry. The army was unaware that this was the same man who had served under his real name and had been discharged because of the forgery conviction. Carl Henry Buck, now known as Charles B. Henry, was sent to Sidney, Nebraska, where he was assigned duty as a letter carrier under the command of Captain George Frederick Price. Price and Greely had been friends since 1877 when they were competing for the hand of Henrietta Nesmith in marriage. Greely won her hand, but a relationship developed between Greely and Price. Price thought quite highly of Henry and was willing to support him in his endeavor to join the upcoming polar expedition. In April 1881 Henry wrote a letter to Captain Price, asking him to intercede for him:

> My object, in addressing this letter to you, is to request you to intercede in my behalf and use your influence to procure the detail for me. I have always been accustomed to cold climate, and am desirous of distinguishing myself by extraordinary service.
>
> Hoping for a favorable consideration of the much coveted detail,
>
> I am, very respectfully, your obt. Servant,
> Charles B. Henry
> Private, Co. E. 5th Cavalry
> Fort Sidney, Neb.

Greely finally accepted Henry as one of members of the expedition, based on Price's recommendation. Henry obtained permission to stop in Chicago again, en route from Sidney to Washington, to visit his sister Dora and William Helms. While in Chicago he made arrangements with the Chicago Times for him to act as a special correspondent with the Lady Franklin Bay expedition. Henry continued on to Washington, DC, where he met up with Lieutenant Lockwood and others of the expedition party. They left Washington on June 13, 1881, traveling to Baltimore, where they boarded the steamship *Nova Scotia*; they then headed for St. John's by way of Halifax. Henry was seasick during much of the four-day trip to Halifax. The party spent three days at Halifax before departing for Saint John's, arriving there two days later, on June 22, 1881.

After loading the supplies at St. John's, the steamship *Proteus* departed St. John's on July 7, 1881, for Lady Franklin Bay, with planned stops in Greenland to pick up additional supplies, dogs, and some more of the party, including Doctor Pavy, and Henry Clay. Pavy and Clay had gone to Greenland the year before and stayed when their ship had to return to St. John's because of damage. The expedition would also pick up two Eskimos to manage the dog teams. Henry's seasickness returned immediately, and he was sick for at least the first three days of the trip on the way to Lady Franklin Bay.

Once they arrived in Lady Franklin Bay and set up their house, Henry helped with any project for which he was needed. Projects included hauling coal, moving supplies, reading meters, and most of all hunting. Henry was probably the best shooter in the expedition party. He won first place in a shooting contest held in November the first year they were at Lady Franklin Bay.

Also in November, Lockwood, Rice, and Henry began publication of a newspaper, the Arctic Moon, which they planned on publishing semimonthly. Henry, with his past experience in writing for a newspaper in Missouri as well as being a correspondent for the Chicago Times, was a natural for this type of activity. The first issue was published, and it was a hit, except for the personal column that Henry wrote, which offended many of the readers. Henry was also part of the Christmas program held on December 26, during which he sang many comical songs.

Henry continued to be a loyal worker; however, on March 19, 1882, Henry complained for the first time about his rheumatism. This would be a problem that would plague him for the rest of the expedition. He complained of rheumatism a couple of times in April and then again in June, but he continued to provide support for the expedition. Henry continued to be an outstanding hunter, rivaled only by Long.

On February 2, 1883, both of Henry's feet froze while in bed. But the next day he went with Ellison to Proteus Point, where they fired forty-two pistol shots as part of a sound experiment. The temperature that day was fifty-one degrees below zero!

Throughout the summer of 1883, things were pretty routine for Henry. He continued to assist in many details, from reading meters and measuring water depths to hunting.

The very first time there were suspicions that Henry could not be trusted was after the expedition had left Fort Conger, where food was ample, and had settled down in Cape Sabine, where the food ration was sparse. On November 9, 1883, Lt. Lockwood discovered an opened but full can of milk hidden away. It appeared, from the marks on the can, that the knife used to open the container belonged to Henry. Henry was confronted, but he denied having opened the container. The theft question seems to have abated for some time.

While Henry had a gift of poetic writing, he would at times resort to obscene language. In January 1884 the commander reprimanded both Henry and Bender for their use of insubordinate language.

The next mention of theft came in mid-February. A small piece of butter had been taken from a can on the overhead shelf. Brainard noted in his journal, "Henry keeps his candle molds on the same shelf."

On March 21, Greely accused Henry of making blasphemous remarks. Four days later, Henry was accused of stealing bacon from their meager supplies. Everyone of the expedition was asked their opinion; on hearing testimonies, they all declared Henry's guilt. Henry was not allowed to leave the hut without a guard. This order apparently did not hold up very long, as a few days later he was out helping retrieve the bear that had been shot. But in between chores such as chopping wood or cooking, Henry often seems to have been accused of taking food or drink not allocated to him. It was as though he thought, "I see it; I want it; I'll take it."

On May 9, 1884, Henry wrote his will:

> Camp Clay, Ellsmere Land,
> May 9, 1884.
>
> I, Charles B. Henry, being of sound mind and health, do hereby declare this to be my last will and testament. All the property, pay due and that may become due, I bequeath to my parents, brother, and sisters now alive, to be equally divided among them. William Helms, No. 20 South Water street, Chicago, I appoint as my Executor.
>
> Charles B. Henry,
> Private Fifth Cavalry, United States Army.
>
> Witness: Frederick Kislingbury, First Lieutenant Fourth Infantry,
> United States Army'
> Jacob Bender, private, general service.

The letter that Lt. Greely wrote to the adjutant general of the army concerning Henry, after Greely's return to the United States, best relates the details of what occurred next:

> Sir: I have the honor to report that on June 5th 1884, at Camp Clay, near Cape Sabine, Grinnell Land, it became necessary for me to order the military execution of Pvt. Charles B. Henry, Fifth Cavalry, for continued thieving. The order was given in writing on my undivided responsibility, being deemed absolutely essential for the safety of the surviving members of the expedition. Ten had already died of starvation, and two more lay at the point of death.
>
> The facts inducing my action were as follows: Provisions had been stolen in November, 1883, and Henry's complicity therein was more than suspected. March 24, 1884, the party nearly perished from asphyxia. While several men were unconscious and efforts were being made for their res-

toration, Private Henry stole about two pounds of bacon from the mess stores. He was not only seen by Eskimo Jens Edward, but his stomach being overloaded, he threw up the undigested bacon. An open investigation was held and every member of the party declared him guilty of this and other thefts. A clamor for his life was raised, but was repressed by me. I put him under surveillance until our waning strength rendered his physical services indispensable. Later he was found one day intoxicated, having stolen the liquor on hand for general issue. A second time his life was demanded, but I again spared him.

On June 5th thefts of provisions on his part having been reported to me, I had a conversation with him, in which I appealed to his practical sense, pointing out that union was necessary to our preservation. He promised reformation, but distrusting, I issued a written order that he should be shot if detected stealing. On June 6th, he not only stole part of the shrimps for our breakfast, but visiting, unauthorized, our winter camp, stole certain sealskin reserved for food. I then ordered him shot. On his person was found a silver chronograph abandoned by me at Fort Conger and stolen by him. In his bag was found a large quantity of sealskin and a pair of sealskin boots stolen a few days before from the hunter. Suspecting complicity on the part of several, I ordered his execution by three of the most reliable men. After his death the order was read to the entire party, and was concurred in by every member as being not only just, but as essential to our safety. To avoid public scandal, I ordered that no man should speak of this matter until an official report was made of the facts. I have the honor to request that a court of inquiry be ordered, or a court martial convened, should the Honorable Secretary of War deem either advisable in this case. I have thought it best not to ask the written statements of the surviving members of the party for appendices to this report, least I might seem to be tampering with them. I have not asked since our rescue—June 22—whether their opinions concurring in my action have changed or not, leaving such questions to your action, if deemed requisite. I necessarily regret that circumstances imposed such a terrible responsibility upon me, but I am conscious that I would have failed in my duty to the rest of my party had I not acted promptly and summarily.

After the recovery of the survivors, the remains of those who died that could be recovered were placed in barrels containing preservative fluid and placed on the rescue ships. These bodies were removed from the barrels at St. John's and placed in caskets. The ship containing these caskets arrived at Governor's Island, New York, on August 8, 1884. The body of Private Henry was among those recovered. His body was taken to Cypress Hills for interment in the national part of the cemetery devoted to the burial of soldiers. The ceremony was conducted by Reverend Goodwin, chaplain of Fort Columbus, and was attended by General Hancock as well as Captain Price, who was Henry's commander prior to his Arctic journey. Also in attendance was Robert Oberfelder, an intimate friend of Henry's while he was stationed at Sidney, Nebraska. After the ceremony, which was quite extensive, Mr. Oberfelder was asked to comment on Henry.

> "Ah!" said Mr. Oberfelder, "how earnestly we all entreated this young man not to join the arctic expedition. You know all his ideas on the subject were gained from books. He was a splendidly educated young man and read deeply. He was employed as letter carrier in the company at Sidney, Nebraska. I remember Captain Price's words to him when he stated his intention of joining Greely's expedition. Said the Captain: 'If I had a yellow cat, and was mad with her, I wouldn't send her out to the arctic seas.' Couldn't stop him. He had set his mind on it. And now we're following him to the grave. I think he must have left some letters with Lieutenant Greely, and I am anxiously waiting for them. I know he must have written to me. We were always such old chums—poor old boy!"

Was Private Henry brave? Anyone who would put their life at risk to explore the Arctic would certainly be brave. Any person who would continue to steal food after being warned about the consequences would certainly be brave, although not in a smart way. Yes, Henry was a brave man. He might have survived the first act of bravery, that of going to the Arctic, had he not lost it by the second act of bravery, taking that which was not his, even though warned of the consequences.

Henry's will was probated in Cook County, Illinois. His estate was divided equally between his father, John Henry Buck; his mother, Mina Buck; his brother, William Buck; and his sisters Mina, Frida, and Dora.

Dora returned to her home in Hannover and married Louis Ferdinand John on April 29, 1890. Her sister Mina married Georg Heinrich Otte on the same day in Hannover. Frida married August Hermann Karl Saloman Sievers on October 11, 1892.

17

Maurice Connell

(1852–1921)

MAURICE CONNELL WAS born Maurice O'Connell on February 2, 1852, on the shores of Lake Killarney, possibly in the town of Killarney, County Kerry, Ireland. His father's name is thought to have been Daniel O'Connell. His mother's name is unknown; however, according to some census records, she may have been born in the United Sates, and possibly in Rhode Island or Pennsylvania. Maurice's father was born in Ireland. Maurice is known to have had a sister, Bridget, nicknamed Bridgie. Little else is known of Maurice's parents or of his childhood. He was orphaned when he was young. At age twelve or thirteen he hired on as a cabin boy on a ship headed for New York City. Upon reaching New York, Maurice left the ship. According to information passed down to his descendants, he then joined the Union Army. The roster of Union Army members does include a Maurice Connell who served with the 168th Regiment, New York Infantry. According to information passed down in the family, Maurice enlisted in the New York 169th Infantry in 1864, when he was just twelve years old.

By 1871 he had somehow reached the western coast of the United States. He enlisted in the US Army at San Francisco, California, on July 25, 1871, for a period of five years. During the next ten years, while serving in the army, Connell was involved in numerous battles against the Indians. He fought against the Apaches in Texas and Arizona and the Sioux in Nebraska; he served under General Cook, a famous Indian fighter, and fought with General Custer. He was serving under Cook when he reenlisted at a camp on Goose Creek in Northern Wyoming Territory on July 26, 1876, only a month after General Custer was killed at the Battle of Little Bighorn. The camp was located about seventy miles south of the Little Bighorn battle site.

Many of the members of the Lady Franklin Bay expedition were at or near Little Bighorn during that famous battle. It is likely that Connell had already made a name for himself during these Indian battles, as he was asked to join the expedition. He was highly recommended for this expedition by his company commander.

His second five-year enlistment was completed when the party reached Upernivik, Greenland, on the way to Lady Franklin Bay. He was reenlisted there by Lieutenant Greely on July 25, 1881, for another term of five years.

Most of Connell's activities while at Lady Franklin Bay were in a support function, such as hauling coal or reading instruments. He was involved in exploration support, providing support on three different journeys during the first two years at Fort Conger.

On the last day of August during their first autumn in the Arctic, a team was designated to move provisions to Cape Beechy, some distance to the north of Fort Conger. The provisions were to be used at a later date. Since the steam launch was cut off by heavy ice, it was necessary to use the whale boat for this operation. The crew designated for this operation consisted of the leader, Sergeant Brainard, with Connell, Cross, Jewell, and Salor. Nearly two thousand pounds of provisions were transported to the whale boat over the harbor flow and loaded on the boat. The crew then paddled the boat northward with great difficulty, owing to the violent currents in the vicinity of Distant Cape. They succeeded in reaching Cape Beechy the next day, but the conditions made it impossible to land at the cape. They moved back south about two miles and managed to land the stores at that point. The heavy ice, which had come down from the north and settled in Robeson Channel, precluded their return by boat. They cached the boat and returned to the fort overland, which they reached on September 3.

The early part of April in 1882 brought them to the most famous journey during their stay at Fort Conger. On this journey, three of the members reached a point farther north than anyone from the civilized world prior to that time. Lieutenant Lockwood was in charge of this expedition, and he selected some of the most energetic people to act as the supporting parties for those who would continue northward. To haul the goods needed for the journey, the supporting parties used four sledges. Three men were assigned to each sledge team. Connell was one of the twelve men selected for this assignment. Unfortunately, on about the third day out, Connell froze one of his toes and was forced to return to the fort.

In order to determine how far west of the fort a party could go overland, a crew was established to make an exploratory journey. A party was sent sixteen miles to the west to cache some of the supplies for the use of the party making the trip. The exploratory party consisted of Lieutenant Greely, Connell, Bender, and Whisler. They left the fort just after midnight on April 26, 1882. The supplies they took with them included rations sufficient to last for twenty days. Loaded on two sledges, the supplies weighed four hundred and fifty pounds.

This party was gone for twelve days and traveled over two hundred and fifty miles. They were able to chart elements of the land where no person was ever known to have gone. On the last day of this journey they traveled thirteen hours, making a distance of thirty miles. Connell had severe cramps in his legs and knees and had a very difficult time making it back to the fort. Soon after, he recovered from his cramps.

One of Connell's side duties was hauling coal. Sometimes the party would bring in nearly half a ton of coal. Other duties were reading the instruments and measuring the depth of the ice over the sound. Neither of these tasks was easy, as at times they required him to brave the wind and low temperatures, which made him susceptible to frostbite, from which Connell frequently suffered. Connell was also involved a lot in hunting.

The commanding officer thought highly of Connell—highly enough to give him a promotion.

After the party had left Fort Conger and established their home in the tent at Cape Sabine, Connell continued to hunt and scavenge for food whenever he could. In this respect he was at least partially credited with prolonging the life of some, and possibly he contributed to the survival of those who made it back home.

When the rescue ship finally arrived, it was none too soon, as

Connell was in such a state that in a few more hours, he probably would have died. Connell appeared to have a complete recovery after the rescue.

After appearing in a few presentations in some of the eastern states concerning the Arctic life, Connell moved back to San Francisco. Upon completion of his five-year enlistment, he was discharged from the army with the grade of corporal on July 24, 1886.

In an interview with a news reporter, Connell made some statements that caused some alarm. He asserted that Doctor Pavy was falsely accused of stealing food while at Cape Sabine, when suspicion pointed to Greely, and also claimed that Greely ordered Henry to be shot for an offense that he condoned in others. He also stated that the records claiming that the Greely expedition reached a point "farthest north" raised the question of whether the observations to determine the latitude, on which the claim was based, were not wholly erroneous.

These statements did not fit well with the other survivors. Julius Fredericks, a member of the expedition, said to a reporter, "These statements are almost entirely false." In response, Connell replied, "The department at Washington has done all in its power to humiliate me since my return from the Arctic, simply because I attempted to speak the truth. This has all been owing to the machinations of Greely, whose statements and mine differ on many points in the story of the expedition. At last I could stand it no longer, and although I have no other occupation, I determined to leave the service. Lieutenant Greely, hearing of my intention of retiring from the army and signal service, wrote me a letter several days ago. The communication was of a very conciliatory nature, insinuating the greatest friendship and offering me very advantageous positions if I changed my intention of leaving. These offers I refused. He has heard that I was about to write a book on the expedition and has become alarmed. Thank God I am able to tell my story now." Connell did not write a book about the expedition.

In 1888 Maurice went to work for the weather bureau at Eureka, California. It was there, on January 16, 1890, that he was married to Hettie Louisa Bast. Hettie was born in Schuylkill Haven, Pennsylvania, on February 12, 1864. She was the daughter of Ulysses Augustus Bast and Jane Davies.

Maurice and Hettie had three children, born in Eureka. Their first, Maurice Best Connell, was born on October 6, 1890. He died of convulsions a year and a half later, on April 19, 1892. Their second child, George Albert Connell, was born on April 16, 1892, just three days prior to his brother's death. The third child was born premature and died as an infant on February 3, 1894.

In 1894, Maurice and his wife and only living child, George, moved to Red Bluff, California, where Maurice was put in charge of the weather bureau operations there. Maurice and Hettie's only daughter, Leonore Connell, was born eight years later, on May 24, 1902. She died soon after her first birthday, on June 13, 1903. George would be the only child to reach adulthood.

In 1905, Maurice was transferred to the weather bureau at San Jose. There he would continue to work until the month before he died. Maurice died on June 3, 1921, as a result of colon cancer. His body was cremated and his ashes stored in the Mt. Olivet Cemetery in San Mateo County, California. His wife, Hettie, died on November 28, 1946, in or near Los Angeles. Their son, George Albert Connell, married Ruth Alice Smith on June 4, 1917, in Chico, California. George died in Los Angeles, California, on November 19, 1972. His wife, Ruth, also died in Los Angeles, on June 17, 1985. George and Ruth had two children: George Albert Connell and Elizabeth Ruth Connell. Maurice's sister, Bridget Griffin, was living in Brooklyn, New York at the time of Maurice's death.

Maurice Connell had an interesting life. He was born in Ireland during extremely difficult economic times. Protestants were at odds with Catholics. Either because of the economic times or because he had no one to care for him, he left home at twelve years of age to gain employment by being a cabin boy on a ship. The ship took him to the United States, where he got off and was left to fend for himself. He spent many a year putting his life in peril by battling in the wars with the Indians. Then he risked his life further by volunteering to serve in the Arctic, where many lives had been lost in the years ahead of his journey. He was one of the six that survived that ordeal. The knowledge that he gained from that journey allowed him to work with the weather bureau for the remainder of his life, until it was taken by cancer. Maurice Connell was truly a brave man.

18

George Leyerzapf, alias Jacob Bender

(1854–1884)

Jacob Bender was born George Leyerzapf on July 5, 1852, in Friedberg, Germany. He was the youngest of five sons born to Johann Conrad Leyerzapf and Cristiane Kessler Leyerzapf. His siblings, Johann Conrad Wilhelm, Ernst, Karl, and Phillip all remained in Germany, except for his brother Karl. Johann (junior) was born on June 25, 1837; Ernst on May 5, 1839; Karl on February 27, 1842; and Phillip in 1849.

Hardly anything is known of George Leyerzapf's childhood. Entries in the journals of lieutenants Lockwood and Greely shed a little light on the matter. On December 1, 1883, Lockwood wrote, "Tonight Bender is giving a general description of Germany." Two days later, on December 3, he wrote, "Last night Bender finished his travels in Germany as a journeyman tinsmith." And on January 5, 1884, Greely wrote, "Bender talked to us for an hour or more this evening regarding his tramps through Germany while an apprentice, and gave an interesting account of gambling life at Baden-Baden." These entries at least suggest that he spent his childhood in Germany and learned his trade as a tinsmith while still in Germany.

George's brother Karl immigrated to the United States, departing from Germany on May 22, 1869. He arrived in New York City eighteen days, later on June 9. Two days after his arrival, he married Julie Lemp, the daughter of Jacob and Elsie (Jung) Lemp, in Manhattan. Julie was from Butzbach, Germany, a village about eight miles from Friedberg, the place where Karl grew up. No record has been found of Julie's arrival in New York City; however, the evidence is compelling that Karl and Julie had known each other in Germany.

Karl and Julie continued to make their home in New York City until 1878, when they moved to Idaho. Julie had a brother living in Boise City, Idaho, who had immigrated many years before.

No record has been found of George Leyerzapf's emigration, or that of his alias, Jacob Bender, to the United States. On March 15, 1872, nearly three years after his brother arrived in New York City, George enlisted in the army in New York City under the alias Jacob Bender. It seems obvious that he was in New York as a result of his brother being there, or vice versa. The question comes up why he used an alias when he enlisted in the army. The first answer comes very easily to our minds: he was running away from something! While this may be true, another explanation seems to be more likely. Since no evidence was found of his entering the country, he may have entered illegally. If he did enter the country illegally, it would make sense that he would use someone else's name in order to join the army.

Although George Leyerzapf enlisted in the army in New York, by the time his term of two years had expired, he was stationed with Company G of the Third Cavalry Regiment at Omaha Barracks in Nebraska. He was discharged on March 5, 1874, and reenlisted ten days later, on March 15, for a term of three more years. He was present with his company at the Battle of Little Bighorn in 1876. Also present at that battle was another person who would be part of the Lady Franklin Bay expedition: William Ellis. Leyerzapf held the rank of corporal at this time. He was discharged from the army on March 26, 1877, and reenlisted for a five-year term, this time with Company F of the Ninth Infantry Regiment. He was still at Omaha Barracks at the time. It was listed on his enlistment papers that he had gray eyes, light hair, and a fair complexion and was five feet, six inches tall. The papers indicated that he was twenty-six years and three months old. He was in fact a year and six months younger. This age may have been calculated from his earlier enlistment, which he may have used to conform to the alias Jacob Bender. He was listed in each of these commitments as Jacob Bender.

Leyerzapf's last duty station before joining the Lady Franklin Bay expedition was either Snake River in Wyoming or Omaha Barracks in Nebraska. On June 10, 1880, Leyerzapf was listed on the federal census as being stationed at Snake River. His commanding officer was Major Leonard Hay. Major Hay was relocated to Omaha Barracks the next month, July 1880. Whether Leyerzapf's unit moved with Major Hay is not known. If the unit did move with Hay, then it is likely that Leyerzapf's last station, before meeting up with the expedition team, was in Nebraska.

While it is not known what trade Leyerzapf had up to this time during his military service, he was accepted for duty with the Lady Franklin Bay expedition because of his training as a tinsmith. He met up with Lieutenant Kislingbury and some other members of the party and sailed to Saint John's, Newfoundland, where the entire party gathered. On July 7, 1881, the party departed for Lady Franklin Bay via Greenland, with George Leyerzapf aboard.

During the trip to Lady Franklin Bay, Leyerzaph had very little involvement in activities. He indicated that he was sick part of the time, something that would be repeated many times. When they reached their destination, Leyerzapf immediately became involved in construction of their quarters. Within a week after their arrival, Leyerzapf wrote in his journal, "Starr is relieved and will go home. I wish I could go too." This seems to indicate that he felt he had made a mistake by volunteering for this mission. He certainly had been briefed on the hardships that they might encounter, yet only because he felt brave enough to endure did he join the expedition. He would express his longing to be back home many times in the future. Leyerzapf shared an area with Salor, Long, and Ellis on the east side of the quarters. They slept in two-tiered bunks.

Leyerzaph was a good worker and willing to help others. He had a problem when he disagreed with the decisions of those appointed over him. At one point, a couple of years after he arrived at Lady Franklin Bay, he objected to the decision of the commander and was threatened with death for mutiny if he didn't get in line.

As a tinsmith, Leyerzapf's primary duty was the construction of things made out of tin and other products. These included chimneys for the buildings, stoves, lanterns, candles, and holders, as well as some carpentry work. He was also called upon a lot to do the cooking. As an example, Leyerazapf states in his journal on August 20, 1881, "I finished the chimneys and started to make some stove pipe out of old cans left by the English." Even with this type of work around the quarters, Leyerzapf found himself involved in many support functions.

On September 16, 1881, Lieutenant Greely, Sergeant Brainard, and Leyerzapf started on a three-day journey toward the northwest in the hope of learning something of the physical conditions of the interior of Grinnell Land. Private Connell accompanied the group the first day. Greely's knee was giving him problems, and as a result he had to return to Fort Conger after going about six miles. The rest of the party, including Connell, continued on. They traveled nearly twenty miles that first day. Then they encamped for the night. Connell, who had not anticipated the amount of traveling or the length of time he would be away from Fort Conger, was not clothed for the trek. Adding to this problem, they had only one two-man sleeping bag to accommodate the three of them. They resolved this problem as best they could by one of the men sleeping with his feet to the other mens' heads. Leyerzapf was the person who slept with the other two's feet at his head. Leyerzapf cooked breakfast for the men the next morning. They traveled about nine miles before they were stopped because of a snowstorm and set up camp for the night. Brainard concluded that they should return to Fort Conger the next morning. Leyerzapf made breakfast, and at seven o'clock they started for home. Even though they had a hard time seeing because of the storm, they reached home after traveling about twenty-eight or twenty-nine miles that day.

In October, Leyerzapf, along with sergeants Brainard and Rice, went to the Bellows, some distance away, to bring in musk-ox meat that had recently been killed by a party led by Lieutenant Greely. It took three days for them to recover the meat, with temperatures dipping to twenty-five degrees below zero. Leyerzapf was the cook on that trip. A few days later he went on a trip with Lieutenant Lockwood and Ellis to store about three hundred and fifty pounds of rations at Cape Liever, which would be used for a later exploration. They were gone two days on this trip, with Leyerzapf doing the cooking, and they returned with their noses frozen.

The remainder of 1881 was quite routine for Leyerzapf. He

spent his time working in the shop, making stove pipes and lanterns. Part of the time he acted as cook, and part of the time he was sick.

On Christmas Day the party had a feast and a big celebration. Each person received a present, personally addressed to him, that had been donated to the expedition by well-wishers. Leyerzapf was elated to receive a gift from a lady by the name of Lizzie A. Garther.

The year 1882 started out the same way for Leyerzapf. Part of the time he worked in the shop, making things such as cooking lamps, spirit lamps, and cooking utensils. He also served as cook at times, and his illnesses continued. On March 1 he was so sick that he was moved to the officers' quarters and Doctor Pavy stayed up all night with him. In a few days he was better, and he went back to his normal routine.

On March 25, George Leyerzapf wrote in his journal, "My term of service expired today, and I reverted to my rightful name, George Leyerzapf, Bender being an assumed name." Nonetheless, he reenlisted under the name Bender, and everyone on the expedition continued to refer to him as Jacob Bender.

In April, Leyerzapf went on a four-day trip to cache stores in preparation for a northward trip later in the season. The party departed on the nineteenth and returned on the twenty-second.

Three days after their return, Leyerzapf accompanied Lieutenant Greely, Connell, and Whisler on a trek toward a place referred to as the US Mountains; the trip lasted two weeks. They had with them two sledges loaded with supplies. The first day they traveled sixteen miles, pulling the sledges over the ice. This distance traveled would be the norm for each day's effort. While on this trek, Leyerzapf was ordered by Greely to cross a lake and see what was on the opposite side of it. Leyerzapf reported that he had discovered an island there, and having the right to name it, he called it L. A. Gather Island, apparently after the lady that he had received a gift from the previous Christmas. In Greely's writings the island is referred to as John's Island, so it appears that Leyerzapf did not get his request to name the island after all.

For most of the remainder of 1882, Leyerzapf performed routine duties at the station, mostly working in the shop. On Christmas

Day, Leyerzapf states in his journal that it is "the most miserable Christmas" he ever passed in his life.

During the first half of 1883, Leyerzapf continued with routine duties. He made lamp chimneys out of medicine bottles; soldered lamps, putting new burners on them; soldering up some specimens for the National Museum, etc. His illnesses continued. He was reported sick in February, March, and July. During the July illness he had pains in his chest. He was sick for at least three days that month.

In August, as no support ship had arrived, the party departed Lady Franklin Bay in the steam launch *Lady Greely*. All the journals and other important documents, such as reenlistment papers, were packed into a metal container, and the tinsmith, Leyerzapf, soldered it secure so as to protect them from all damage from rain or snow. Most of the members of the expedition began keeping new journals at the time of departure from Fort Conger. Leyerzapf recorded his notes in what was called the Memorandum Book. Most of these later recordings were recovered by the rescue crew and were a valuable source of information.

Leyerzapf continued to do his share of the work at Cape Sabine; however, very little tin-work could be done in their new quarters without the proper equipment and materials. He did, however, help with cooking, reading gauges, digging water holes, etc. He continued to have periods of illness. During the last couple of months, some of the members of the expedition were suspected of taking some of the scanty food supply without permission. Leyerzapf was among both the accused and the accusers.

Leyerzapf died, primarily from lack of food, but probably hastened by his seemingly poor health, on June 6, 1884, less than two weeks before a rescue party reached the site. His body was not recovered, and as such there was no funeral, parade, or other activity honoring him.

When word of his death was announced, a lady from Lebanon, Pennsylvania, claimed that Leyerzapf (Jacob Bender) was her husband who had abandoned her some years back. She stated in a letter that she desired that all his back pay be sent to her. This was rather troublesome for the officers who were involved with settling the accounts with relatives of the deceased, as they needed to respond to her and point out how this man could not possibly be the person that she believed to be her husband. Layerzapf had made a will the day before his death and had dictated it to Lieutenant Greely. The will read as follows:

> Camp Clay, Ellsmere Land,
> June 5th 1884.
>
> I, George Leyerzapf, now serving in the U. S. Army under the Name of Jacob Bender being of sound mind and health do hereby Declare this to be my last will and testament.
>
> All my property, both real and personal I bequeath to my Four brothers, Conrad Leyerzapf, Friedberg near Frankfort on Maine Germany, Ernst Leyerzapf of same place, Carl Leyerzapf Boise City Idaho Terr, Philip Leyerzapf Friedberg Germany.
>
> George Leyerzapf
> Pvt. Gen. Service, U.S.A.
> Witnesses:
> C. B. Henry
> H. S. Gardiner
> Henry Biederbick

George Leyerzapf's journals and other personal effects were sent to his brother Karl in Boise City, Idaho. Karl suggest to the chief signal officer that George's back pay should be sent to his mother, who was still living in Germany. Apparently the father of the four brothers had already passed away.

George Leyerzapf's brother Ernest married Regine Fueller in Friedberg on February 25, 1872. His brother Johann Konrad Wilhelm married Margaretha Knocke, also in Friedberg, on July 27, 1873. His brother Karl and Karl's wife, Julie, had four daughters: Helena (Lena), Anne Margaretha (Annie), Jennie, and Lizzie. The three oldest girls were born in New York, and Lizzie was born in Boise City. Helena and Lizzie died prior to reaching adulthood. Karl and his daughter Annie made a trip to Germany in 1896, presumably to see his brothers; however, it may have been for the funeral of his mother. Karl and his wife made another trip to Germany in 1904, likely to visit family. Jennie married Martin Klinge in Boise on May 28, 1902. Annie married Carl Hipp, also in Boise, on May 18, 1920. Karl Leyerzapf died in Boise on March 19, 1917. His wife, Julie, died five years later, on July 24, 1922.

While George Leyerzapf seemed sorry at times that he had volunteered for Arctic service, he was a brave man for doing it. He contributed much to the expedition, and in the end he gave his life for it. Many of the documents that have been referenced, not only in this writing, but also in others pertaining to the Lady Franklin Bay expedition, might not have survived the conditions of the last year without the expertise of George Leyerzapf, the tinsmith.

19

Francis Long

(1852–1916)

FRANCIS LONG WAS born in Bohmenkirch, Germany, on June 9, 1852, under the name of Franz Joseph Lang. His parents, Jacob Lang and Creszenz Ruehle Lang, were also born in Bohmenkirch. He had two brothers: Jacob, who was about three years older than Francis, and Johann.

Francis immigrated to the United States in July 1869, settling in New York City. He found employment and living quarters with a saloon and boarding house owner, Henry Fisher. Henry was of German descent, as were most of his employees. Francis, still going by the name of Franz Lang, worked as a "malt man."

After living in New York for about four years, Francis enlisted in the army. He enlisted under the name Francis Long, by which he would be known for the rest of his life. He was assigned to Company G of the Second Cavalry Regiment with a term of service of five years. He would be later transferred to Company F of the Ninth Infantry Regiment.

In July 1876 he was stationed in Montana Territory under the command of General Custer. His immediate superior was Lieutenant Doane. Lieutenant Doane gained notoriety for his discovery of the grounds where Yellowstone National Park is now located. Doane was also the officer who was selected to command the failed attempt to reach Lady Franklin Bay in 1880.

According to a sworn document written some years later by Francis's widow, once General Custer realized the seriousness of the situation he was in at Little Bighorn, he instructed Francis to ride to the encampment of Major Reno and appeal for immediate reinforcements. The document further states, "Major Reno started but went into camp at sunset. In the meantime General Custer's force was surrounded and annihilated. Mr. Long was the first to arrive on the battlefield and was able to find and identify the bodies of General Custer and his principal officers."

Two years after the massacre at Little Bighorn, Francis reenlisted at Omaha, Nebraska for an additional five years of military service, committing him to serve until July 1883. He remained with Company F of the Ninth Infantry Regiment.

In 1881, Francis was offered the opportunity to be part of the Lady Franklin Bay expedition. He accepted the invitation and was transported to Baltimore and from there to St. John's, Newfoundland, where all of the expedition members met, excepting those that would board in Greenland.

Once the expedition reached Lady Franklin Bay and the quarters were erected at Fort Conger, Long was assigned to an area in the quarters, which he shared with Salor, Bender, and Ellis.

While Long did not have a particular trade for which he was recruited, he did have a couple of talents that would become real assets to the expedition. His cooking skills were demonstrated at Christmas their first winter at Fort Conger. Greely wrote in his journal, "The preparation of the Christmas dinner was commenced several days in advance, as from its extensive character much extra labor was entailed upon Frederick, who was the regular cook. Unfortunately he burned his arm quite badly on the 22d, but, despite his condition requested that he be permitted to complete his tour of duty. Long, who was considered the especial cook of the party, with his customary cheerfulness, assisted Frederick in the preparation of this important meal."

On February 22, 1882 the party had a shooting contest. Long won the contest hands down, making a score of thirteen out of a possible fifteen. He would later exhibit his skills in this area for the good of the entire expedition. A review of the journals of expedition members reveals entry after entry pertaining to Long's hunting:

> June 17,1882—Long shot one and Cross got a male ring duck near the station.

July 1, 1882—Long shot the first eider duck this season.

July 3, 1882—Long went to Lake Alexander for the purpose of hunting.

His expertise in this craft is exemplified in this journal entry of August 13, 1882:

> Long, on going out last evening, saw fresh musk ox track. He followed them [...] and killed nine of them and skinned all [...] He traveled ten miles each day.

Lt. Greely wrote in his journal on August 13, referring to the same event:

> Long returned at 6 P.M., having been gone twenty-two hours hunting. His prolonged absence caused much alarm, as he was alone. Several parties had been sent out to search for him, when he was met returning. He had fallen in with a herd of musk-oxen in the valley, about two miles above the head of St. Patrick Bay. He had sixteen rounds of ammunition at starting, and, shortly after, fired two at an owl. With the remaining ammunition he killed eight musk-oxen, and wounded two others; four escaped. He had delayed to skin the eight before returning to the station, in order that the meat should not taint.

Greely further stated that Long's record as a hunter had always been a fine one, but with this success Greely noted that Long's patience, coolness, and skill made him an outstanding hunter.

While the meat obtained by Long's hunting abilities was not necessarily required for their survival while at Lady Franklin Bay, it became an essential element of their survival after departure and setting up camp at Cape Sabine.

Upon arriving at Cape Sabine, the party's food supply, even rationed, would last less than two months. The food supply that they anticipated finding at Cape Sabine was not cached there. Every means possible was considered in order to increase the length of time that the food supply would last. Hopes of finding cached food supplies were explored. They were aware that 144 pounds of meat was cached some thirty miles from where they were, and two attempts were made to retrieve it. Each attempt resulted in the eventual loss of a person's life without the retrieval of the meat. They waited and waited to see if the possibility existed of crossing over Smith Sound to Littleton Island, some twenty-seven miles away, where a supply of food might be found. The sound never froze over sufficiently to make the crossing, and even if it had, they would have been disappointed at the lack of food that was there. Lowering the allocation of food consumed each day sapped the party of their strength. Something more had to be done.

The food supply was supplemented somewhat by what was called shrimping. A hole was dug in the ice, and a net was placed in the water beneath the hole, and as a result, miniature shrimp were captured. These shrimp were added to the food supply and resulted in prolonging the period that the food supply would last.

Game was not nearly as bountiful as it was at Lady Franklin Bay. It consisted mostly of a fox now and then and some fowl; nonetheless, Long continued to hunt. The hope was to capture a bear, a seal, or a walrus. The sightings of these creatures were few and far between. Usually one of the Eskimos, Jens Edward, assisted Long. They would look for a seal that had left the water and was lying on an ice floe. They would try to get close enough to the seal that, after shooting it, they could capture it before it rolled back into the water and disappeared. Doing this was a tricky proposition. The hunters had two choices; either trying to get close to the seal and shooting it without scaring the seal and causing it to go back into the water, or shooting it from a distance and rushing to reach it before it got back into the water. In either case they generally lost the seal.

In the first part of November 1883, Long was able to shoot a seventy-pound seal and recover it. This added about three pounds of meat for each member of the party. In the latter part of November he shot a fox that weighed a little over three pounds. During the winter months of December through March, little game was spotted. Long managed to shoot some dovekies periodically. Long and Jens went out almost daily to check for game on the ice floes. They usually spotted nothing, but they kept looking. On March 28 Long and Jens went out hunting and brought back thirty-three dovekies; they brought back fourteen the next day.

On April 11, 1884, a bear was spotted. Long and Jens went after the bear and managed to shoot it. This bear weighed about four hundred pounds when it was dressed. This game seemed to ensure the party's future, as only four of the party had perished so far. The added food supply came too late for Jewell, as he died the next day. Greely promoted Long to sergeant for his "coolness and skill" in shooting this bear.

Two days later, Long and Jens again went hunting. They went to the open water, and while Long waited on the ice, Jens went ahead with the kayak to stalk a large seal resting on a pan across several open leads. In launching the sealskin craft, Jens must have scraped the hull on a sharp projection and ripped it. Suddenly Long saw his comrade paddling furiously as the bow of the kayak tilted downward and its stern rose in the air. Without uttering a single cry for assistance, Jens stood upright for a few moments before falling forward in the icy water. From the edge of the ice, Long desperately tried to rescue him, at risk of his own life. The body of Jens sank from his view.

With the loss of Jens, the expedition now was down to eighteen men. Long, realizing the possibility that none of them would survive, wrote a letter to his family in Germany. He hoped, as was the case of many on the expedition, that letters and wills that they left would be preserved and recovered upon the discovery of their camp. The letter, written in German, was translated by Doctor Thomas Seibel, a man well versed in both German and English:

Camp Clay, near Cape Sabine
Lat. 78 degrees 46 ' N. long 73 degrees W.
Thursday, May 13, 1884

Dear parents and siblings!

Albeit I am at present in good health and in good heart, I think it is about time to get back to you now, probably for the last time. Three years ago, in the summer of 1881 I joined the Lady Franklin Bay north-arctic expedition, under command of Lt. Greely. You will learn best about the complete story of our work and fortune through newspapers. Our existence now depends so much on hunting so that I hardly can take time to write elaborately. If it should be God's will that we depart this life here, I am able to present to you in all boldness that I discharged my complete bounden duty. As proof of how much I am held in great esteem by Lt. Greely, I can instance my promotion to a Sergeant's rank, as well the naming of a cape that I had discovered in the spring of this year. Furthermore I am able to claim that there are only thankful friends around me. Death is man's fate, do not grieve over me being overtaken by death some years earlier than expected, and forgive me for any pain that I ever may have caused you.

My testament will be reposited in the keeping of the Chief Signal Officer, U.S. Army, Washington, DC, U.S.A., from whom you can obtain more thorough information about me. It is my will that my watch and my fob chain will be allotted to one of my nephews. Some pictures and arctic plants will also be conveyed to you.

Now if I am destined to die here, I hereby send you and all my relatives my compliments for the last time. With all my love.

Francis Joseph Lang
Sgt. General Service, U.S.A.

Please do not take my death to heart too much. F.J. L.

To be mailed to Jacob Lang
Boehmenkirch, Wurtemberg, Germany

The bear meat and the shrimping sustained them until the latter part of May, when four more of the expedition members died. Four days after Long wrote the letter to his family, he wrote his will:

I, Franz Joseph Lang of Boegmonkirch, Germany, (now serving as a Sergeant in the United States Army under the name of Francis Long), being of sound mind do declare this to be my last will and Testament. I leave all of my property, real and personal, to be equally divided between my father, Jakob Lang, my mother Kresenz Lang, and to my brothers Jakob Lang and Johann Lang, all originally of Boehmenkirch, Wurtemburg, Germany. In case my mother should be dead the property reverting to her is to be divided between my two brothers Jakob Lang and Johann Lang. In case either brother should be dead the property reverting by this will to each brother will be given to the surviving brother.

Given near Cape Sabine, Ellsmere Land, this seventeenth day of May 1884.

Franz Joseph Lang (Seal)

A.W. Greely, U.S. Army (Seal)
Edward Israel, Kalamazoo, Mich. (Seal)
David C. Ralston, Sig. Ser. Howard, Ohio. (Seal)"

Two of the witnesses, Israel and Ralston, died the following week.

When June arrived, the deaths seemed to accelerate. Kislingbury died on June 1, Salor on June 3, and on June 6, Bender, Pavy, and Henry died. Schneider died on June 18, four days prior to the rescue. The remainder survived, except for Ellison, who died just after the rescue.

On June 22 the rescue crew had discovered a cache that the Greely expedition had left in October the previous year. In the cache was a note describing their condition. Upon finding the note, the captain of the rescue crew, Schley, ordered that all rescue ships should be recalled so that they could continue on to Cape Sabine. The recall signal was given—three long blasts of the steam whistle. This recall signal was not only heard by the captains of the other two rescue ships, but also by Greely in the tent at Cape Sabine. He asked Brainard and Long if either of them had the strength to check if any vessel was in the area. They crawled up to the crest on their hands and knees in the fierce storm that was raging. They saw nothing. Brainard crawled back to the tent and noticed that the top was off of one of their water cans, and the wind blowing over it made a whistling sound. He crawled back into the tent and reported that there was nothing to be seen and that the sound that Greely heard most likely came from the wind blowing over the water can.

Meanwhile, Long noticed that their distress flag had blown down. He crawled back up the crest to set it up again. He erected the distress flag with some difficulty in the driving wind. As he was erecting the flag, he stared in disbelief as one of the ships came around the point of land. The captain of the ship caught sight of Long standing on the ridge. The ship docked, and the crew approached Long. He directed the crew to where the six other survivors were. They then took Long aboard the ship.

The survivors of the expedition were welcomed home with parades and other festivities. After these were over, Long was assigned work in Washington, DC. This must have been a far cry from being out in the Montana Territory wilderness as well as the Arctic wilderness. On the day before Christmas, the anniversary of the day he helped prepare a Christmas feast for his comrades in the wilderness of the Arctic three years before, he married Anna Dora Weiler in Brooklyn. Anna, known by her middle name, Dora, was born in Kitzingen, Bavaria, on January 9, 1859 to Christoph and Margaret Fuehrlein Weiler. She lived in Brooklyn at the time of her marriage.

Francis continued his military service in Washington, DC, until his discharge on July 23, 1888, but this time was not without suffering. Long's health problems became evident in March 1885, less than a year after returning from the expedition. Exposure to the elements at Lady Franklin Bay and at Camp Clay had left him with acute rheumatism. He was laid up for nearly three months from this attack. In July and September of the same year he had more subacute attacks of rheumatism that disabled him for an additional two months in 1885. These attacks continued during the remainder of his military service. During this period while he was still in the army, two of his three children were born. The older was named after the place where he suffered the greatest hardship, Cape Sabine. Cape Sabina Dorathea Long was born on October 6, 1885. The second child, Lena Anna Long, was born May 25, 1887.

Upon his discharge from the army, he was given duty as a meteorologist with the US weather bureau in New York City. On October 4, 1891, his youngest child, Adolph Francis Long, was born, his name honoring the Lady Franklin Bay expedition leader, Adolphus Greely.

Long's medical problems did not go away after he left the army. His rheumatism attacks continued. In 1891 he applied for a pension because of his medical problems. A battle over his pension went on for several years, as the affidavits from various physicians would support his claims and the pension bureau would deny them. He finally received a pension of two dollars a month starting in 1891, which was later increased to six dollars a month.

Long continued to work for the weather bureau in New York City. In May 1903 Long participated in another expedition to the Arctic. This expedition, which was called the Fiala-Zeigler polar expedition, left New York on the steamship *Heligolaf* on May 27, 1903. Fiala, the leader of the expedition, was already in Trondheim, Norway, with the Zeigler Arctic steamship, *America*, awaiting the arrival of the men who sailed. The party consisted of William Peters, the representative of the National Geographical Society, who had charge of the scientific work and was the second-in-command; Doctor George Shockley, chief surgeon, and his wife; Doctor Charles L. Zitz, assistant surgeon; Doctor H. N. Newcomp, veterinarian; Francis Long, meteorologist; Charles E. Rilliet, quartermaster; and R. R. Tafel, John Vedoe, J. E. Moulton, and Spencer W. Stewart of the quartermaster's department.

They sailed to Christianna (Oslo), Norway, and rode by rail to Trondheim. From Trondheim, they set sail aboard the *America* to Tromsø, where they took on additional supplies and then went to Archangel, where they took on about thirty Russian ponies and two hundred dogs.

Others members were added along the way until the total number of expedition members reached thirty-nine. It did seem kind of strange that Long, after his near miss on the Lady Franklin Bay expedition, would risk his life again to go on another polar journey. The object of this expedition was similar to the Lady Franklin Bay expedition in that meteorological readings were made and recorded. But the main purpose of the expedition was to attempt to reach the North Pole. Unlike the Greely expedition which went toward the pole following the western side of Greenland, the Fiala-Zeigler polar expedition followed the eastern side of Greenland to Franz Josef Land, located at the far north of Russia. It was a series of uninhabited islands (191) between latitutde 80° and 82° north. The islands are located about six hundred miles from the North Pole. The only other land closer to the pole is Ellsmere Island, where the Greely expedition was stationed, and Greenland.

The expedition spent the first winter in Teplitz Bay, where it deposited fifty tons of provisions and a hundred tons of coal on the ice. In the severe weather of November 1903, the ship *America*, which carried the Zeigler explorers, broke up, and the provisions and coal were lost. Part of the wreckage remained until January 22, 1904, when it disappeared in a storm. The loss of the provisions was seriously felt, and but for the stores left by the expedition in Teplitz Bay, the men would have been in bad straits.

The following spring, they made repeated attempts to force a passage to the pole, but the conditions were insurmountable. The expedition found much open water and, day after day, encountered fresh dangers and difficulties. Ultimately the supply of provisions ran short, and a painful journey southward began, the members of the expedition finally reaching the supplies that had been cached at Cape Flora. With these limited supplies, when supplemented by catches of walrus and bear, they were able to eke out a living.

All of the expedition members, as in the Greely expedition, were buoyed up by the knowledge that relief ships would be sent to their rescue. All were most hopeful until the fall of 1904, when the solid ice fields stretching in every direction seemed to preclude the possibility of help reaching them. Then they became despondent. The leaders of the expedition had considerable difficulty throughout the hard winter months, but hope returned in the spring, when the ice conditions became more favorable.

On June 14, 1905, the *Terra Nova* sailed from Tromsø, Norway, and headed northward toward the ice fields in order to rescue the stranded expedition members. Everything went fine for about two weeks. Then they reached the ice fields, and the ship had to force its way through the floe of ice. By July 25 it struck open water. The next day, the ship encountered thick ice again, and the captain of the crew began to doubt that they could reach the expedition in 1905. A few days later, however, the *Terra Nova* reached Cape Dillon and found six members of the Ziegler expedition safe and well. From this outpost sleds were dispatched to notify Mr. Fiala, at the headquarters camp, of the arrival of the rescue ship. The *Terra Nova* reached Cape Flora on July 30 and found more members of the expedition. These had become weakened by the hardships they had endured, and some of them were so ill that they could not have held out for another winter. The ship sailed for home the next day and arrived back in Tromsø on August 11, 1905, all members of the party surviving.

The expedition leader, Anthony Fiala, wrote in his book, Fighting the Polar Ice, the following pertaining to Long:

> Our weather observer, Sergt. Francis Long of the U. S. Weather Bureau, was the Arctic veteran of the party. He had been a member of the famous Greely Expedition and it was his fortunate shooting of a bear, which saved the remnant of that company from starvation. Sergt. Long mounted his instrument shelter, the "chicken coop" as it was jocularly termed by the members of the party, on the deck over the *America*'s upper cabin, and his anemometer on the bridge, and began his weather observations. He was generally known among the explorers as "Obs", from the signature he attached to his memorandum slips. All sorts of jokes were cracked at his expense, but he kept serenely and good-naturedly at his work, setting many a younger man an example of diligence and faithfulness in the performance of duty.

Like the Greely expedition, numerous weather-related problems were encountered. Fiala wrote the following pertaining to Long's working in the storms:

> Storms were many and the members of the Scientific Staff, in their walks to and from the observatories, often had to face winds of high velocity with driving snow and low temperature. Observer Long was often obliged to crawl on his hands and knees through the drifted passage from the hut, and in the whirling blast of frigid, wind-driven snow particles find his way to the "Chicken coop" where he kept his thermometers. No matter how bad the storm, every evening he brought me the little slip of paper signed "Obs.", containing the weather instrument reading for the day.

Long returned to his work at the weather bureau in New York City. He continued to work there until his death. He died while at work on June 8, 1916. His combined service in the army and the weather bureau was forty-four years. He was a very loyal and caring man. When in starving or hazardous positions, Long was busy trying to solve the problem. He was not only brave enough to risk his life in the Montana Territory wilderness, as well as the wilderness of the Lady Franklin Bay expedition, he again risked his life on another Arctic journey. Francis Long was truly a brave man.

After Francis's death, his wife, Dora, needed financial support. After two and a half years and numerous letters and affidavits, including those of Greely and Brainard from the Lady Franklin Bay expedition, Dora Long was given a widow's pension of twelve dollars per month. She continued to reside in Brooklyn and receive the widow's pension until her death on July 10, 1922.

Cape Sabina, Francis and Dora Long's oldest child, married Caryl Hutzelman about 1910. Caryl and Cape Sabina had a daughter, Aline. Cape Sabina Hutzelman died in January of 1936 in Queens, New York City. Aline Long, Francis and Dora's second child, married James Christopher Howerton. Aline died on February 5, 1971. Francis and Dora's son, Adolphus, died in New York City on October 28, 1954. Adolphus had a son, Arthur F. Long.

20

William Henry Whisler

(1857–1884)

WILLIAM HENRY WHISLER was born in Carroll County, Indiana, on September 10, 1857. Although all of the family members, except William, spelled the last name Whistler, William was known by his comrades as William Whisler. He was the second of eight children born to Christian C. Whistler and Leah Catherine (Snyder) Whistler. His parents, as well as his grandparents, William and Hannah Whistler, were born and raised in Franklin County, Pennsylvania. His parents were married in Franklin County, Pennsylvania, on February 22, 1854. The following year, 1855, both of his parents and his grandparents relocated to Carroll County, Indiana. William's older brother, Clarence, was born in Indiana on February 24, 1856.

William's parents moved back to Pennsylvania prior to the birth of their third and fourth children. Eunitia Virginia (Jennie) was born on February 28, 1859, and Elmer Ellsworth was born on May 11, 1861.

The next two children were born in Virginia. Emeline (Emma) Kate was born on January 18, 1866, and Charles S. Whistler was born on May 28, 1868. The family returned to Carroll County, Indiana, before August 16, 1870, when their seventh child, George Oliver Whistler, was born. Their eighth child, Elsie, was born on September 8, 1872.

Five years later, on March 27, 1877, William's mother, Leah, died in Shelby County. It seems that the family had been in disarray for some time. Some accounts say that the two older boys, Clarence and

William, were raised by their grandparents, William and Hannah Whistler. Still other accounts have them being raised by their aunt, Lydia Funkhauser, a sister to their father. Both of these families lived in Carroll County, Indiana, and both families probably had a hand in raising them.

After their mother's death, the family seems to have dispersed. Both William and his brother became carpenters. This would change, as Clarence took up wrestling as a career. He was to challenge some of the most famous wrestlers of the time, and he was gaining popularity all the time. It is reported that he took on the famous boxer John L. Sullivan in a wrestling match and won.

William's uncle, Jacob H. Whistler, lost his wife sometime during the late 1870s. Jennie, William's sister, moved in with Jacob and his children, and she married Jacob on July 27, 1880, at Belle Plaine, Kansas.

Meanwhile William, now twenty-two, began his military career on September 4, 1878, by enlisting in the army for five years at Omaha Barracks, Nebraska. His occupation on his enlistment papers is listed as carpenter. By the middle of 1880, he was stationed at Snake River, Carbon County, Wyoming. He was assigned to Company F of the Ninth Infantry. When the Signal Service began looking for volunteers for the Lady Franklin Bay expedition, William volunteered and was accepted. The claim was that he was picked out of five hundred applicants. Another member of the expedition, Jacob Bender, was from the same company.

Meanwhile, his brother Clarence, who had been wrestling in Kansas City, Missouri, married a lady there named Minnie Gallagher. Little is known about this wife, but William must have had a place in his heart for her, as when he made out his will in Washington, DC, on June 6, 1881, he wrote the following:

> "I, William Whisler, being of sound mind and body,
> Hereby declare this to be my last will and testament.
> Should I not return from the Expedition to Lady Franklin Bay,

All Pay & Allowances due me, as a soldier, from the Government I bequeath to Mrs. Minnie Whisler of Kansas City Missouri.
All Personal property belonging to me I bequeath to Mrs. Minnie Whisler Kansas City Mo.

William Whisler
Pvt. Co F. 9th Infantry

Witnesses
Charles B. Henry, Pvt. Co. E. 5th Cavalry.
Nicholas Salor, Pvt. Co H. 2nd Cavalry."

It appears that at this time, his sister-in-law Minnie took preference over his father and his seven siblings as far as his estate was concerned. The will also points out, by the words "should I not return," that William realized that such an expedition was extremely dangerous and that he might not return.

After meeting up with all the expedition members at St. John's and stopping at Greenland for supplies. William, along with the rest of the expedition members, reached Lady Franklin Bay on August 10, 1881. William, a carpenter, was very active in construction of the quarters. Once the quarters were completed, he was assigned a living area on the south end of the quarters, which he shared with Biederbick, Connell, and Henry.

Private Whisler played a support role during most of his time at Fort Conger. Early in September the first year, Doctor Pavy and Sergeant Rice went on an exploratory trek, and Rice needed extra help to get Pavy back to the fort. Whisler was one of the men that went to his rescue, and in the process one of his feet froze. The next week, Whisler was out again with Doctor Pavy, searching for English caches.

In between his treks around the area, Whisler was involved with his carpentry skills. On September 19, he and Linn put up a shed at the south end of the building.

On October 2, with the winter weather beginning to set in, Whisler, along with Doctor Pavy with one dog team and another driven by the Eskimo Jens, departed for Cape Joseph Henry. Their plan was to search for any sign of the *Jeannette*, a ship that had vanished the year before, as well as to cache provisions for spring travel in that direction. While on this trek, Whisler had a nightmare that caused him to believe that the ice foot, with tent, was being carried into the straits. He got up and rushed with fright to his comrades, awakening and alarming them. They returned to Fort Conger on October 9, after being gone for a week. They cached some provisions; however, they saw no sign of the *Jeannette*.

On January 13, 1882, one of the Eskimos, Jens Edward, walked away from the camp. It was dark and dreary, with the temperature around thirty degrees below zero. After locating Jens' tracks, several people, including Whisler, went in pursuit of him. During the pursuit, Sergeant Rice fell and seriously injured his shoulder. Whisler was detailed to assist Rice back to the station. In his zeal to find Jens, Whisler had left the station without properly dressing for the weather. When near Distant Cape, about five miles from camp, Whisler began to complain of the cold. A few moments later he began to talk incoherently, and soon he was delirious. He became unresponsive, and it took all the will and ingenuity of Rice to induce him to walk. Rice and Whisler got within about half a mile of the station when a team met them, and they were put on a dog sledge and returned to camp. They had been out about eight hours and had traveled at least twenty miles on one of the darkest days of the winter. Whisler was delirious for several hours, his nose and cheeks frozen, but otherwise he suffered no bad consequences.

Whisler was involved with many other treks while at Fort Conger, including acting in support of the team that broke the record for reaching the farthest north point ever documented by man. On that trip, like many of the others, Whisler seemed to be prone to having his hands and face frozen.

But he was not only performing support duties for travels. Any time any carpentry work was required, he was involved in it. He was frequently involved with hunting, reading instruments, and hauling coal. On April 17, 1883, Whisler, along with Biederbick, Schneider, and the Eskimo Jens, left the station at eight in the morning for the coal mine, with two dog teams. They returned from the mine, which was about half a mile away, just after noon with sixteen hundred pounds of coal.

After the party had departed from Fort Conger in the fall of 1883 and set up camp at Camp Clay, Whisler was again called upon to help with numerous tasks: checking caches, carrying water, cutting holes in the ice for water, etc.

By October 21, 1883, Whisler began to show more signs of physical problems. He was on the invalid list, but he still managed to work. On January 9, 1884, he sawed wood for their cooking and heat. On January 19, at the death of expedition member Cross, Whisler and five others carried the body to its grave on Cemetery Hill.

On April 15, 1884, Brainard wrote in his journal, "Whisler appears to be failing rapidly and converses but little." But on April 22, Whisler set about ripping out the wooden lining of the boat for fuel, and on the next day he made a trapdoor in the roof of their boat-hut to let in some light.

On May 3, 1884, the weak side of Whisler came to light. Bender and Henry had caught Whisler outside the storehouse. The door was open, and Whisler had nearly a pound of bacon in his jacket. When he was reported to the commander, he hung his head and was crying. "I couldn't help it, I couldn't help it. The door was open and I couldn't help it." Whisler claimed that "the door was open. I saw the food and I just couldn't help myself." No action was taken against Whisler.

On May 9, 1884, Whisler made his final will, which was greatly changed from his will of 1881:

> I, William Whisler of Lafayette, Ind. Being of sound mind do declare this to be my last will and testament. To my married sister Mrs. Jennie Powell, I give one hundred dollars to be expended in some article for her own use; no more is given her as she is not in pecuniary need. I give and bequeath to my remaining brothers and sisters, viz Clarence Whisler, Elma E. Whisler, Charles Whisler, Oliver Whisler, Elsie Whisler and Catherine Whisler all my property real and personal. (except the one hundred dollars above mentioned)

to be equally divided. It is desired that the greater part of the amounts hereby bequeathed to Charles, Oliver and Catherine be expended on their suitable education, and it is requested that Lt. A. W. Greely, U. S. Army, who is hereby appointed executor of this will pay particular personal attention to this matter. God bless them all.

Given near Cape Sabine this ninth day of May 1884 in Ellesmere Land.

William Whisler (seal)

Witnesses:

D.L. Brainard	Sgt.Sig. Ser'ce Marathon, N.Y (Seal)
D.C. Ralston	Sgt.Sig. Ser'ce Howard, Ohio (Seal)
Edward Israel	Sgt.Sig. Ser'ce Ann Arbor, Mich. (Seal)
Fred F. Kislingbury	2d Lt. 11 Inf.U.S.A. Detroit, Mich. (Seal)

It should be noted that "Elma E." is in fact referring to Elmer Ellsworth, "Oliver" refers to George Oliver, and Catherine refers to Emeline Kate (Katherine). Also note that nothing is left to his father.

Whisler continued to weaken, and he died at noon on May 24, 1884. Greely comments, "Whisler was a man of fine physique, who had always labored his best to advance the interests of the expedition." He was truly a brave man, entering upon this expedition even though he understood the risk to his own life.

When the rescue party arrived on June 22, 1884, Whisler's body had lain on the ground, slush, and snow for nearly a month. It was recovered and placed in a tank in the *Bear*, one of the three rescue ships. From there it was transported to St. John's, Newfoundland. There the body of Whisler was placed in a metal coffin and transported to Governor's Island, New York. From there it was transported to Delphi, Indiana, for burial.

The body of Whisler arrived in Delphi, Indiana, on Sunday, August 10, 1884. It was placed in the corridor of the courthouse, where it was kept under guard until Tuesday when the funeral would be held. Numerous dignitaries attended the funeral, including the governor of Indiana. Numerous bands and military units honored the dead hero. It was reported that over three thousand people followed behind the casket of Whisler. The military stood at rest on arms during a prayer given by Rev. J. N. Martin, pastor of the family. Rev. J. W. Hett of Dayton, Ohio, preached the funeral sermon. After the sermon, the casket was lowered and covered. On the casket was the following inscription:

> W. H. Whisler, private 9th Infantry,
> U.S.A.
> Died May 24, 1884, age 27

It would have been wonderful if this were the end of it. It wasn't. The New York Times had been publishing articles throughout the year pertaining to cannibalism. The reporters attempted to find evidence of it from the survivors of the *Jeannette* but could get no proof. Likewise, when the surviving members of the Lady Franklin Bay expedition were questioned, most of the answers were that "there could have been; however, I have no knowledge of it." This translated to the reporters as "There likely was cannibalism; they were hungry, so they ate their fellow soldiers." Several of the bodies were exhumed as investigators looking for traces of cannibalism. Whisler's body was one of them. The following account of the exhumation was printed in the Hoosier Democrat, Flora, Indiana:

> A blanket was removed and the ghastly sight of a mere skeleton was seen. There was nothing of the body left, save the head and the trunk. All the flesh had been cut from the limbs. The arms, legs, and shoulders were bare bones.
>
> Strips of flesh had also been taken from the breast. The left foot, which had been frozen, was not touched, and the left hand was unharmed. The face was sunken, but not unlike the ordinary corpse, and the red hair and short beard made it easy for Whisler's friends to identify him. It was particularly noticeable that the bones were picked entirely clean; not a

> vestige of flesh is left on them. The back had nothing on it. In fact, the only thing left on the man are his head, breast, intestines, and the left hand and left foot.
>
> The appearance would show that an expert had done the cutting of the flesh. A thorough examination by the physician showed that the stomach was entirely empty. The head and neck were unharmed by blows. The head was incased in a knitted cap, over which was a sealskin. The skeleton hands wore mits—a mitten covering half of the hand. When the coffin was opened there was a strong odor of alcohol, but no further very bad stench.

One of the survivors, Connell, stated, "I do not believe that any of the bodies were used as food, but still the fact of the mutilation is undeniable, and as a matter of course some conclude that the survivors had subsisted on the bodies of their dead companions. I have talked with the men who survived and who are supposed to have eaten human flesh, and in the utmost confidence, yet they have all emphatically and strenuously denied ever having eaten of the bodies of the dead." Connell expressed his opinion that the bodies may have been cut for bait to catch shrimp, the hope of their survival. None of the journals kept by the survivors or those who died prior to the rescue give any hint to the likelihood of cannibalism. And if the journals had been doctored to remove all references to cannibalism, then why were they not doctored to remove references to the execution of Private Henry, which required more of an explanation of the commander? The question is in limbo.

After the funeral of William H. Whisler, the disposition of his personal property was of great importance. Two parties were mainly involved: his sister Jennie, and an attorney for his father, Christian. Greely having been designated the executor of the will made it even more complicated. Greely did not want to have that duty; however, he could not find a way out of it. The first letter was written by Frank Hench on behalf of Whisler's father on August 22, 1884, little more than a week after the funeral:

Delphi, Ind., Aug 22,1884
To the Hon. Secretary of the Navy, Washington, D.C.

Dear Sir:

I would on behalf of Mr. C. C. Whistler, father of Private Whisler of the Greeley Expedition beg an indulgence of your time, and would ask of you if you can inform him what contract if any was entered into by his son on the one hand, and the U. S. Government on the other—Was he to receive only the same wages per month, as he received while a soldier in the Army—or was he to receive extra compensation and remuneration for his services while along with the Expedition—Private Whislers father was a faithful soldier, and carries the effects of the conflict, and depended partially on his son for support in his declining years.

If the Government obligated itself to pay these men extra, Mr. Whistler would like to be so informed, and if so what steps he will have to take as his son was sole and unmarried—

Keenly appreciating the tender and commendable solicitude that you have manifested both personally and officially towards the friends of, as well as of that noble band of our Nations heros itself—I have as the personal friend of Mr. Whistler seen fit to address you personally.

Any information you can import I will communicate to him, he having entrusted the matter in my lap to investigate the same for him—Presume you have been informed officially of the exhuming of Whislers body—his identification, and the condition of the remains—please give this letter your personal attention and address.

Yours respectfully,
Frank P. Hench.
Delphi, Carroll County, Indiana

It is highly likely that William's father was not aware of the will at this time. In a second letter, undated, Hench asks what steps William's father needs to take to recover William's back pay. In September, William's aunt, Lydia Adams, wrote a letter requesting a copy of William's will. William's sister Jennie's correspondence commences on October 25, 1884:

El Dorado, Kansas
October 25, 1884

Chief Signal Officer
Washington, D.C.

I write you concerning the will of the late William Whisler of the Lady Franklin Bay Expedition who was my brother and whose will is on file in your office. What evidence will be required of us as the proper heirs and to who or where are we to apply. There are seven legal heirs to the estate, four of whom are of age brothers and sisters of the deceased. The following are the proper names. Clarence Whistler, Mrs. Jennie Whistler (myself, having married a distant relative of the same name) and Elmer and Katie Whistler. The minor heirs are Charley, Oliver and Elsie.

Hoping you will instruct me in full regarding our Dear Brothers last wishes.

I remain respectfully,
Mrs. Jennie Whistler
El dorado
Butler county
Kansas

P.S.

Please state as to the best course to pursue in making direct application as an heir to the above named estate.

Mrs. Whisler

In March and April 1885, both Hench, Whisler's father's attorney, and H. S. Hamilton, representing Jennie, wrote letters to the chief signal officer asking about the distribution of the estate, which had not yet taken place. You can see a certain amount of frustration in the letters. In September 1885, Jennie wrote another letter to the Signal Corps asking about the distribution of the estate of her brother and about a monument to be put up in his honor.

To add to the frustration Jennie was feeling, her brother Clarence died mysteriously. His wrestling career had taken him to Australia. He was challenged, by William Miller, to a match between them that would decide the championship. He beat Miller. In celebration of his victory, he engaged in a reckless, monthlong celebration and contracted pneumonia. He died on November 6, 1885. The cause of death was never identified. He was buried in the Melbourne General Cemetery. He was memorialized by the sports world as the most courageous athlete of his time.

The effort to settle the estate went on. As late as 1889, Jennie was still trying to get the estate settled. About 1890, Jacob, her husband, decided to leave her and their three children, Odessa, Adella, and Lea. Jacob remarried and lived for another twenty years. He died on November 4, 1910, and is buried beside his wife Anna in the Fredonia City Cemetery in Wilson County, Kansas. Jennie spent the next forty-six years as a schoolteacher, teaching in Wellington and Wichita, Kansas. She died in Wichita, Kansas, on February 20, 1956, at the age of ninety-four. She is buried in El Dorado, Kansas.

Christian, William's father, continued to live in Carroll County, Indiana. He died in Rockfield, Indiana, on February 23, 1915, at the age of eighty-six.

William's brother Elmer married Anna Mahahan in 1887. He relocated to St. Paul, Minnesota, where he worked as a teamster and raised his eight children. His wife died on June 26, 1935; however, Elmer lived until April 11, 1959, near his ninety-eighth birthday. They are buried in Ramsey County, Minnesota.

William's sister Emeline Katharine married Daniel Walters on January 31, 1888, in Shelby County, Iowa. The family moved to Pender, Nebraska, where they raised their four children—Daniel, Lowell, Leola, and Russell—and spent the rest of their lives. Daniel died in 1924, and Emeline died twelve years later, in 1936. They are buried in the Pender Rose Hill Cemetery.

William's brother Charles was living in Shelby County, Iowa, in

1885. He later moved to Utah and worked in the mines at Park City. He married Ellen Hancock in Midway, Utah, in 1914. Ellen was born in Midway, Utah, on December 22, 1864. Ellen was a granddaughter of Levi Ward Hancock. Levi was not only a relative of the famous John Hancock, but he was also a cohort of Joseph Smith, the founder of the Mormon religion. Charles died at Pleasant Grove, Utah, in December 1931, following an illness of several years of miner's consumption. His wife passed away at Orem, Utah, on March 29, 1940.

William's youngest brother, George Oliver Whistler, was living with the Myers family in Shelby County, Iowa, in 1885. From 1887 through 1892 he served with the US Army. During 1893 and 1894 George farmed in Shelby County, Iowa; however, in 1894 he moved to Pender, Nebraska. He farmed there until 1898. From 1899 through 1905 he was a hardware and implement dealer. During this time he met, and on June 2, 1902, married, Elizabeth Bayer at Pender. In 1906 he became an undertaker. Elizabeth died in 1953, and George died six years later, on June 18, 1959. They are buried in the Croften City Cemetery in Knox County, Nebraska. They had a daughter, Ouido, who was born on October 6, 1915, and died in May 1987.

William's youngest sister, Elsie, lived with her sister Jennie in Kansas after her mother's death. Sometime before 1900 she moved back to Pennsylvania, where she lived with relatives. She later moved to Bristol, Virginia, and lived with a cousin. Elsie never married. She died in Bristol on October 18, 1945. She was buried in Beautiful View Cemetery in Middleburg, Maryland.

This little red-haired boy grew up seemingly being shuffled around between relatives. He lost his mother when a teenager and did not appear to have a relationship with his father. He joined the army and volunteered for the Arctic journey even though he knew the dangers it presented. While on the journey, he was one of the lesser of the group, performing menial but needed tasks. He gave his all. William Henry Whisler was truly a brave man.

21

Henry Biederbick

(1859–1916)

HENRY BIEDERBICK WAS born in Waldeck, Germany, in the village of Sudeck, on January 25, 1859. His father was Christian Friedrich Biederbick, and his mother was Louise Friedrika Christiane (Pohlmann) Biederbick. Henry's birth name was Georg Heinrich Christian Biederbick; however, he would use the name Henry throughout his life upon leaving Germany.

Henry's father, Christian, was also born in Sudeck, on September 23, 1819. His mother, Louise, was born in Sudeck on June 29, 1813. They were married on February 18, 1844. Christian had the responsibility for maintenance and providing for the poor people in the small village of Sudeck. It was situated in a very poor region of Germany, and many of the people left in the 1800s, hoping to find a better future in the New World. This would be the case for Henry Biederbick.

Henry was the seventh of eight children born to Christian and Louise Biederbick. His oldest brother was Christian, born on March 14, 1845. Next was his oldest sister, Caroline, born on April 4, 1848. The third child was Carl, born on September 21, 1850. The fourth child died in infancy on June 7, 1853. The next child was Louise, born August 4, 1854. The sixth child was Wilhelm, born on March 16, 1857. Wilhelm died when he was a year old, on April 4, 1858. Henry's younger brother, Albert, was born on August 8, 1861.

Henry studied in the field of medicine while still in Germany. His primary fields were chemistry and pharmacy. In February 1879, twenty-year-old Henry sailed from Liverpool to the United States, arriving in New York on the February 25. It would be less than five months before he enlisted in the army at Cincinnati, Ohio, on June 14, 1879. He listed his age as twenty-one years and five months; in actuality he was twenty years and five months old. His occupation was listed as druggist. What brought him to Cincinnati to enlist in the army? Why not enlist in New York, his point of entry into the United States? There is only one reasonable answer: he must have had relatives living in or near Cincinnati that he stayed with prior to enlisting in the army.

Henry volunteered for the Lady Franklin Bay expedition. Besides the surgeon, Octave Pavy, Biederbick was the only member of the expedition that had any medical training. He went to Baltimore, where he met up with many of the expedition members, and on June 14, 1881, they sailed for St. John's, Newfoundland. After loading all the supplies aboard the ship, the entire party departed St. John's on July 7, 1881. The first three days of the journey found Biederbick seasick, as were others of his party. After that, things seemed to run quite smoothly for him.

After stopping in Greenland to pick up more supplies, the lumber for the quarters, sledge dogs, the two Eskimos, and the doctor, they arrived in Lady Franklin Bay on August 10, 1881. They erected their quarters and moved from their tents into the building. Mountain peaks hemmed in the quarters on the north, south, and west. The coast to the west for many miles consisted of inaccessible cliffs, with a height in many places of nearly two thousand feet. To the east was Robeson Channel, which was broken by the steep and repellent mountains of the Greenland coast. Biederbick shared an area of the quarters near the south end of the building with Connell, Henry, and Whisler.

The activities during the fall and winter months were routine. Biederbick was always there to help. He helped move provisions to be stashed away for later use, he helped people with medical problems, he hauled coal, he fished, he went to different places to read scientific instruments, and he taught the German language to those desiring to learn it. In November the first year, 1881, he was part of a party, led by Lieutenant Lockwood, whose mission was to cross Robeson Channel and reach the Greenland coast. While on this trip, Biederbick froze one of his feet quite badly. He was still able to perform his duties.

One of the goals of the Lady Franklin Bay expedition was to attempt to travel nearer to the pole than anyone had before. In March 1882 preparations were made for a long journey to the north, along the Greenland coast. This entailed moving supplies from Fort Conger to various places along the planned route. Biederbick was very active in this venture. The time came for the departure: April 3, 1882. The party consisted of Lockwood, Brainard, Ralston, Whisler, Linn, Ellison, Connell, Biederbick, and Salor. After eight days out, Biederbick became ill and had to return to the fort. The party went on and reached a point farther north than any explorer had traveled before.

Over the next couple of months, Biederbick performed routine duties. He did a lot of hunting, as well as moving stores. On June 24, Biederbick, Linn, Salor, and Whisler accompanied Greely on an exploratory trip to the west. Again some of the party, including Biederbick, became ill and had to return to the fort.

For most of the rest of the summer, Biederbick hunted. During the second autumn of the expedition, he again was doing routine duties: hauling coal, reading instruments, helping Rice with the photographic equipment, etc. In the early part of January, Biederbick complained of having rheumatism. A week later he was still sick. But on January 17, 1883, he was assigned the duty of cook. So besides his other duties throughout the winter, he also helped with the cooking.

In April it seemed that his primary duty was hauling coal. The following are entries from Ellison's journal:

> April 2—Biederbick and Schneider went to the coal mine.
>
> April 17—Biederbick went with Whisler, Schneider and Jens to the coal mine.
>
> April 25—Biederbick and Schneider went to the coal mine.
>
> April 30: Biederbick and Schneider went to the coal mine.
>
> May 5—Biederbick and Jens went to the coal mine.

Much of the remainder of the time at Fort Conger, Biederbick hunted.

After they left the fort and traveled south, Biederbick continued to complain of rheumatism. On September 9, 1883, Lockwood wrote in his journal, "Biederbick is perhaps an invalid, as he complains of rheumatism." And in the next month, on October 17, Greely wrote in his journal, "Biederbick troubled with a bad attack of rheumatism."

But Biederbick did not forget his duties as a hospital steward. Concerning Ellison, who was badly frozen during an attempt to recover a cache of food a long distance from the camp, Biederbick wrote the following:

> Ellison was brought into Camp Clay on the 12th of Nov. 1883 with his hands and legs badly frozen up to nearly his knees, his hands wrist and nose also badly frozen so that they appeared like a piece of ice. He was put in our miserable camp on a mattress over which a sheepskin sleeping bag cut open was spread and then covered with three woolen blankets. I was set to work at once thawing out the frozen parts with cloth steeped in cold water, which was gradually raised to a higher temp. All attention possible in our miserable condition was paid to the patient. After about ten days a line of demarcation showed itself just above the ankles, and two days later on the hands. The nose was very sore and part of flesh sluffed off. One foot was removed through the ankle joints, nothing being used but a small scissors, the disjointing coming through the natural process. What makes this case so very remarkable is the short rations that which the patient had to subsist, and the cold dark and damp atmosphere in which we had to live.

Greely wrote in his journal on March 5, 1884, concerning Biederbick and Ellison, "Biederbick was quite sick this afternoon; he has been working too hard lately, being indefatigable in the care, not only of Ellison and Lockwood, but of others who are stronger than he is himself." Biederbick was sick throughout the last half of April and into May, yet by the latter part of May and into June, he seemed to be involved with anything that was being done. On June 20, he was dressing Ellison's wounds, and on the twenty-first he was "suffering terribly from rheumatism." The next day, June 22, the rescue team arrived.

Back home, after the welcomes were complete, Biederbick was assigned duty in Washington, DC. He managed to go to New York City and participate in the show Storm Beaten at the Grand Opera House in that city. Storm Beaten was a sensational melodrama with a shipboard fire, passengers shipwrecked in the Arctic, and the breakup of ice floes upon which passengers had taken refuge. Biederbick only made an appearance, representing the survivors in the "Great Arctic Rescue Scene."

But things were not going well for Biederbick. In a letter published in the Newark Daily News (Newark, Ohio) on August 27, 1884, Biederbick is quoted as saying, "I shan't live a great many years—probably not until I am fifty. I am completely broken down, and the rheumatism contracted in the North will probably never leave me. With every change of the weather, it is exceedingly painful. The Government ought to do something for me, as I will never be able to labor again. If I ever get money enough to keep me, I shall go back to old Germany."

Biederbick was discharged from the army on January 6, 1885, based on a surgeon's certificate of disability. By an act of Congress declaring Biederbick an invalid, he was put on the pension roll in February. In early May he began to confer with the US Pension Office in an effort to receive disability retirement payments. On November 18, 1885, Biederbick was placed on disability for rheumatism and disease of the heart and eyes. He was given twenty-four dollars per month, retroactive to March 1885.

Henry's mother, Louise, died on November 19, 1885. In April 1886, Henry became a naturalized American citizen. On May 20, 1886, Henry married Augusta Lehmann in Brooklyn, New York.

Henry and Augusta had twin daughters, Johanna Elsa and Marguerite Anna, born in Brooklyn on March 6, 1891. On April 3, 1895, Henry's father, Christian, died. Henry must have wanted very badly to go to Germany, as on May 21 he obtained passports for himself, his wife, and his two children. The family had moved to Jersey City, New Jersey, sometime prior to May 1895.

On May 24, 1900, his third daughter, Ruth, was born. By this time Henry was secretary of the Arctic Club in New York City. He was also associated with the National Geographic Society, the Polar Star Lodge, the Polar Research Club, and other clubs and societies.

Biederbick was eventually given a job working as an inspector at the US Custom House in New York City.

In 1910 Henry Biederbick's wife, Augusta, died. Six years later, on March 25, 1916, Henry died. He was laid to rest in the Lutheran Cemetery in Jersey City, New Jersey.

His daughters left the country on two or three occasions, presumably to visit relatives living abroad. At least two of his daughters, and possibly all three of them, became schoolteachers.

Marguerite was found dead in an apartment in Brooklyn, New York, on March 28, 1934. Along with her body was that of a male acquaintance. It was concluded that the case was a murder and a suicide.

Ruth moved in with her aunt (her mother's sister) after her father's death. She continued to live with her aunt and uncle for many years. After they died, she was involved with a lawsuit over the estate of her aunt, which lasted for several years. Ruth died in New Haven, Connecticut, on May 10, 1980.

Johanna was still living at the time of her father's death in 1916; however; nothing is known about her after that time.

Henry Biederbick was a caring man, devoted to duty. He was certainly brave to place himself in the Arctic after he was aware of the dangers it involved. He was certainly a brave man. Fortunately he did not have to suffer the pain of one of his daughters being found murdered.

22

Julius R. Frederick

(1852–1904)

Julius Robert Frederick was born in either Germany or Ohio on July 21, 1852. Many documents have him listed as being born in Ohio; however, a like number of documents list him as being born in Germany and coming to Ohio when he was about two years old. The place of his birth in Ohio has been designated as Dayton, and the place, if he did indeed migrate to this country from Germany was Lima, Ohio, some sixty miles distance from Dayton. In either case, his parents were of German origin. He grew up in the St. Mary's area of Ohio, located between Lima and Dayton, some twenty miles from Lima.

When he was a young man, possibly no more than thirteen years of age, he left Ohio to become a messenger in Chicago. He eventually got a job with the Pennsylvania Railroad, performing the duties of a brakeman, fireman, and engineer. He worked in this capacity until he volunteered for the army in 1876.

On September 11, 1876, Julius Frederick, at the age of twenty-four years, enlisted in the United States Army at Cleveland, Ohio. He agreed to serve for five years. He was described on his application as five feet, three inches tall, with brown hair, a ruddy complexion, and "a mole on his left groin." He was assigned duty with Company L of the Second Cavalry Regiment under the command of Captain Randolf Norwood. Company L, along with Companies F, G, and H, formed a battalion known as the "Montana Battalion." This battalion, under the command of Lt. Col. Brackett, was formed in 1869 and transferred to Montana Territory, remaining there for the next fifteen years, through 1884.

The number of battles against the uprisings of various Indian clans was staggering. These battles included those against Chief Joseph of the Nez Percé and the Sioux. In the spring of 1877, Frederick's outfit, the Montana Battalion, accompanied by troops from the Fifth and Twenty-Second Infantries, attacked Lame Deer's camp on Little Muddy Creek, a tributary of the Rosebud in Montana Territory. Among the wounded on that battle was another member of Company L, Private D. L. Brainard. Brainard would serve with Julius Frederick on the Lady Franklin Bay expedition. Lt. Kislingbury and Private Ellis also were involved with these battles, as well as being part of the Lady Franklin Bay expedition. Lt. Doane, the leader of the 1880 failed attempt to reach Lady Franklin Bay, also served at these battle sites.

Private Frederick's last duty station in Montana Territory was at Fort Assiniboine. After volunteering for the Lady Franklin Bay expedition party, he departed Fort Assiniboine on April 26, 1881, for Baltimore, where he met up with some of the members of the expedition. This part of the expedition left Baltimore on June 14, 1881, aboard the Allen Line steamer *Nova Scotia* for St. John's, Newfoundland, to team up with the remainder of the expedition members. Frederick's party reached St. John's, and after loading the equipment and supplies aboard the *Proteus*, the entire expedition departed for Greenland, en route to Lady Franklin Bay, on July 7, 1881.

Julius describes in his papers the welcome they received upon their arrival at Disko, Greenland. He describes this welcome better than any other known source:

> The Kayakan of Greenland
>
> We were escorted into the harbor of Disco by the strangest fleet of boats and the strangest looking boatsmen that ever conveyed a ship. They were the far famed kayakers of Greenland and they deserve a passing notice. The kayak of the green land is the frailest specimen of marine architecture that ever carried human freight. It is eighteen feet long and as many inches wide at its middle and tapers with an aftward

curving line to a point at either end. The skeleton of the boat is made of light wood. Covering is of tanned sealskin sewed together by the native women with sinew thread and with a strength and dexterity quite astonishing. Not a drop of water finds its way through their seams and the skin itself is perfectly waterproof. The boat is about nine inches deep and the top is covered like the bottom. There is no opening into it except a round hole in the center, which admits the hunter as far as his hips. Their hole is surrounded with a wooden rim over which the kayaker laces the lower edge of his watertight jacket and thus fastens himself in and keeps the water out. He propels himself with a single oar about six feet long which terminates in a blade or paddle at either end. This instrument of locomotion is grasped in the center and is dipped in the water alternately to right and left.

The boat is graceful as a duck and light as a feather. It has no ballast and no keel and it rides almost on the surface of the water. It is therefore necessarily top heavy and long practice is required to manage it and no tightrope dancer ever needed more steady nerve and skill of balance than this same savage kayaker. Yet in this frail craft he does not hesitate to ride seas which would swamp an ordinary boat or to break through surf which may sweep completely over him. But he is used to hand battles and in spite of every fortune he keeps himself upright.

After picking up Doctor Pavy, the two Eskimos, the dogs, the precut living quarters, and supplies in Greenland, the expedition departed for Lady Franklin Bay. They reached their destination on August 10. After unloading their equipment and supplies (and, of course, the expedition members), the *Proteus* departed Lady Franklin Bay. The expedition was now in a remote area of the world without communications or transportation to the civilized world.

Julius shared an area in the quarters with Brainard, Ralston, and Gardiner. It seems that with their prior service in the Montana and Dakota area, they would have a lot in common.

Private Frederick had many valuable skills to offer the expedition. These included cooking, mending clothing, hunting, and the experience he had from the Pennsylvania Railroad; i.e., as engineer, fireman, brakeman, etc.

Due to his five-year enlistment terminating on September 10, 1881, Julius Frederick reenlisted on September 11, 1881 for a term of five more years. He was pronounced physically fit by Doctor Pavy and given the oath by Lt. Greely.

Frederick was to be involved in several treks. The purpose of the trek he joined in November 1881, the first year they were at Lady Franklin Bay, was to determine if they could cross Robeson Channel over the ice to get to the Greenland shore. The party, led by Lt. Lockwood, departed the home base on November 2. The temperature was six degrees below zero. In addition to Lockwood and Frederick, the party consisted of Brainard, Lynn, Biederbick, Salor, Connell, and Ellis. They took an eight-man English sledge that carried camping gear and fifteen days of rations. They returned within a few days, unable to cross the channel due to ice breaking and drifting away and the area between the floes being filled with new ice and snow. This new ice was not strong enough to hold the men and their supplies. The average temperature during the trip was thirteen degrees below zero. The coldest was twenty-six degrees below zero. Four of the men suffered frostbite.

Frederick was the expedition cook. Lt. Greely wrote in his journal, "The preparation of the Christmas dinner was commenced several days in advance, as from its extensive character much extra labor was entailed upon Frederick, who was the regular cook."

Three days before Christmas, Frederick burned his arm quite badly; however, this did not deter him from preparing the Christmas meal. Maurice Long assisted him in this endeavor.

A journey in the spring of 1882 was one of the most memorable, and it was a trip that would give a high degree of credibility to the expedition. It would be made along the coast of Greenland, led by Lt. Lockwood. Five sledges in all were to be used for this journey. About a dozen men, including Frederick, were selected for the trip. The third sledge, the Hudson Bay sledge Hall, was drawn by Sergeant Jewell and Private Frederick. They carried about three to four hundred pounds of supplies on each sledge, except for Lockwood's sledge, which was drawn by a team of eight dogs and carried about eight hundred pounds. The purpose of the expedition was to cross Robeson Channel to Greenland, if possible, and follow the Greenland coast northward as far as possible. Most of these teams were to be support teams for the lead team. The party departed Fort Conger (Lady Franklin Bay) on April 3, 1882. This time the party was able to cross Robeson Channel, reaching the Greenland coast in about five days, with temperatures dipping nearly to fifty degrees below zero at times—very unusual for April. By April 16, after weathering many storms, the party reached Boat Camp on the Greenland coast. They continued on their journey.

Sergeant Brainard wrote in his journal on April 20, "The majority of the party complain of sleeping cold, and the rest assert that they obtain no sleep at all. This no doubt is owing to the condition of the sleeping-bags, which were frozen so badly on camping this morning that three men were required to unroll them, and we were obliged to thaw ourselves gradually into them."

By April 28 the party was nearly worn out, after eleven straight hours of dragging their supplies. Some of the men had already been sent back, and others were suffering from snow blindness. Private Frederick had an injured knee. They had reached Cape Bryant, about ninety to one hundred miles from Fort Conger. Here some of the support party waited while Lt. Lockwood, Sergeant Brainard, and the Eskimo Thorlip Frederick Christensen traveled north, reaching a point farther north that any person had been known to reach as of that time.

The supporting party, including Julius Frederick, reached Fort Conger on May 9, 1882. They had been away from camp for over a month. Frederick relates his view of Greenland in his papers:

> Greenland had been for some time regarded by my companions as a sort of myth, for although frequently only a few miles from its coast so thick and constant had been the clouds and fogs that except for a few brief minutes it had been wholly hidden from our view. Here, however, it was at last shaking off its cloud mantle and standing squarely out before us in austere magnificence its broad valleys, it deep

> ravines, its noble mountains, bleak butting cliffs, its frowning desolation. As the fog lifted and rolled over the sea to the westward, iceberg after iceberg bust into view like castles in a fairy tale. It seemed indeed as if we had been drawn by some unseen hand into a land of enchantment, rather then that we had come of our own free will into a region of stern realities in pursuit of stern purposes, as if the elves of the north had in sportive playfulness, thrown a veil about our eyes and enticed us to the very seat eternal of the gods.

Frederick was involved in many other activities besides taking part in excursions. We find several journal entries referring to his work on footwear. On February 3, 1882, Bender wrote in his journal, "Frederick making canvas shoes," and on February 8 the following year he wrote, "Shorty Frederick is getting ready to go into the shoe business." Some of the members of the expedition called him "Shorty" because of his height. On another day Bender wrote, "Shorty Frederick is working on old Eskimo boots and moccasins."

He was also involved with hunting. Lt. Greely makes note of a hunting trip Frederick was on from February 7 to 21 in 1882. On June 13, 1882, Rice relates an incident where four young musk oxen, their prime source of meat, were captured. He states that the captured animals were only two or three weeks old. The smallest of the four animals was caught by Shorty Frederick, and he named it "John Henry." Upon discovering that the animal was in fact female, Frederick received lots of kidding from his comrades. On June 15, 1882, he went hunting with Brainard, and they killed three musk oxen, two hares, and two geese.

Frederick's skill with locomotives was displayed on several occasions. On August 5, 1882, Cross, Frederick, and Rice brought the steam launch *Lady Greely* from Proteus Point to the station. Frederick took care of firing the engine, Cross was engineer, and Rice steered. On August 20 and again on the thirtieth and thirty-first of August 1882, Frederick is again mentioned in journals in connection with the steam launch—in the latter days as engineer on the launch.

When the relief ships failed to arrive in either 1882 or 1883, the expedition took as many supplies as practical and entered the waters of Smith Sound in the steam launch. They had hoped to go far enough south either to meet up with a relief ship or to find a point where provisions were stored and rescuers would find them.

Initially Cross was the engineer on the steam launch; however, because of a disagreement between him and Lt. Greely, he was replaced by Frederick. Frederick continued in this capacity until the launch was beset by ice floes and the party had to abandon her and find safety atop a floe. After a month aboard the floe, they finally managed to reach land at a point they called Camp Clay. There was no rescue team there, and they found only a few provisions cached, contrary to the plans constructed prior to the expedition's departure from the United States. A means of finding more food was essential, as the food they carried would only sustain them for a few weeks. They also needed a means to endure the winter weather, as it was already September, and the winter temperature could drop to as low as sixty degrees below zero.

An inventory of their stores was taken on October 2, 1883. Only thirty-five days of full rations of bread and meat remained. These rations could be extended to fifty days (until November 15) if the party subjected itself to a greatly reduced diet; however, the suffering would be extreme in the low temperatures where a person requires two or three times the normal diet. Also, the labor of building winter quarters would require more energy, thus more food.

Already Frederick had been designated the prime cook, as well as being assigned the duty of the distribution of rations. He was not content to wait out the fifty days of rations and then hope for the best. He had already been on several hunting trips. Brainard wrote in his journal on September 16, 1883, "Frederick shot a large seal this evening. It will net us about 125 pounds of meat." On October 8 Brainard wrote, "Frederick shot two seals, but both sank before he could squeeze himself into his kayak and secure them. It is heart-rending to see this food which is our very life disappear before our eyes."

A cache of food was found by a party sent to Cape Isabella in October; however, this party of two had no means of transporting the food to Camp Clay. As the rations at the camp became scarcer, a party led by Sergeant Rice was selected to go recover the meat at Cape Isabella. On November 1, 1883, Sergeant Brainard wrote in his journal, "Ellison has cut down the six-man sledge to a four-man sledge for Rice's comtemplated journey to Cape Isabella. Frederick, Lynn and Ellison have been detailed to accompany Rice. They are brave fellows and the entire party feels that if there is a chance of bringing the meat to Camp Clay they will do it. God grant that they all will come through safely. I have issued them provisions for eight days."

The party departed for Cape Isabella the next morning. They reached Cape Isabella after three days of travel, all in fair condition. On starting back with the load of meat, Ellison became exhausted. For several days his hands and feet had shown a tendency to freeze, but on each occasion his comrades were able to thaw them out. Now, though, his whole body seemed to lose all power to resist the cold, and his hands, arms, legs, and feet quickly froze up stiff. The men carried and dragged him nearly across Baird Inlet, making double trips, first for him and then for the meat, weakening their strength and exposing themselves to the merciless cold. Frederick even carried Ellison on his back until he could bear the burden no longer, and all the while the frozen man was crying out in pain.

Seeing that they could not continue to carry both Ellison and the meat, the load of meat was left in the snow, with one of their rifles standing upright in the snow to mark the spot. They managed to get to an old camp at Eskimo Point. It took fourteen hours, when they had hoped to reach it in six. On reaching their camp, Frederick says, "Ellison had frozen both his hands and feet, and our sleeping bag was no more nor less than a sheet of ice. I placed one of Ellison's hands between my thighs and Rice took the other, and in this way we drew the frost from his frozen limbs. The poor fellow cried all night from pain. This was one of the worst nights I ever spent in the Arctic."

Here Frederick and Lynn crawled into the sleeping bag with Ellison, one on each side, to thaw him out. Rice then left them and walked the seventeen miles to Camp Clay to get help.

After Rice's arrival at Camp Clay, sledge teams were sent out to rescue Ellison, Frederick, and Lynn. Brainard, part of a rescue team, writes in his journal, "About noon we reached the camp and found Ellison a little better than when Rice departed. Lynn and Frederick had done a good job in thawing him with the heat of their bodies, but had greatly weakened themselves and severly frozen their faces and extremities." It was a couple more days before they all got back to camp. Brainard writes. "Lynn and Frederick arrived at 4 p.m. last night, badly broken down physically. Lynn almost went out of his head again, eating handfuls of snow as he grew more exhausted. Frederick, though, bolstered him up and was able to get him into camp without any serious effect from the snow."

Greely writes, "Frederick makes no special mention of their sufferings from cold and hunger. Such was the stamp of this man."

Not only did Frederick serve as cook, but he also had the responsibility of measuring out the portions. When Frederick was accused of unfairly distributing the rations, not only were the complaints determined to be unfounded, but he also offered to let each man select from the rations he meted out, and he would take the ration remaining.

On February 14, 1884, Greely wrote in his journal, "Frederick had the misfortune to spill the rice belonging to the mess this morning, but gathered it up without considerable loss. It is remarkable that the cooks have been able to prepare their food with so few accidents, considering the darkness and other disadvantages under which they have necessarily labored."

By April food had became so scarce that several of the party had already died of starvation. On April 6, 1884, as a last-ditch effort to save the remaining members of the party, Sergeant Rice and Frederick departed the camp in an attempt to find and recover the meat left by the party when Ellison became frozen. Brainard had wanted to go on this search; however, Rice insisted that he was stronger than Brainard, and Frederick believed that he needed to go, as he was better qualified to find the place where the meat had been left. Both Rice and Frederick asked that no special ration be provided to them for this trip. Besides rations, they took along a sledge that they would use to haul back the meat, a two-man sleeping bag, a rifle, an ax, an alcohol lamp, and a small cooking pot.

For the first three days of the trip the weather was so bad that they spent twenty-two hours in the sleeping bag at one sitting. By the morning of the fourth day they were about six miles from where the meat had been left. They decided to leave most of their gear at this point and return to it after retrieving the meat. After traveling the six miles to where the meat should have been, they saw no sign of it. At this point Rice became too weak to move. Frederick tried to comfort Rice by taking off his jumper and wrapping it around Rice's feet. Frederick held Rice in his arms. Rice soon passed away. Although he was extremely weak, Frederick tried to scrape a hole in the snow and bury his friend. Frederick somehow made it back to Camp Clay. He brought back with him the portion of Rice's rations that Rice had not eaten. No meat was recovered.

On May 19, when he went outside their tent to get some ice to use in cooking, Frederick spotted a bear only a few feet away from him. He ran back into the tent to report the presence of the bear, their lifeline of food, as he did not have a rifle with him. Frederick and Long went in pursuit of the prize; however, they were unable to get close enough for a shot at the bear.

By June the rations had been nearly depleted. They had taken to eating their shoes and other items that might have some nutritional value. They had been finding some shrimp about the size of fleas, hardly enough to sustain them for very long. A dozen of the party had already perished, mostly from lack of food.

Private Henry had been accused of stealing food from their meager stores. On June 5 Lt. Greely gave the following written order:

Near Cape Sabine, June 5, 1884.
To Sergeants Brainard, Frederick, and Long:

> Private Henry having been repeatedly guilty of stealing the provisions of this party, which is now perishing slowly by starvation, has so far been condoned and pardoned. It is, however, imperatively ordered that if this man be detected either eating food of any kind not issued him regularly, or making caches or appropriating any article of provisions, you will at once shoot him and report the matter to me. Any

other course would be a fatal leniency, the man being able to overpower any two of our present.

(signed) A. W. Greely, Lieutenant Fifth Cavalry, U.S.A., and Assistant."

According to Greely, Henry continued to steal from the stores, and he ordered him shot, issuing the following order on June 6:

Near Cape Sabine, June 6, 1884.
To Sergeants Brainard, Frederick, and Long:

Notwithstanding promises given by Private C. B. Henry yesterday, he has since, as acknowledged to me, tampered with seal-thongs, if not other food at the old camp. This pertinacity and audacity is the destruction of this party, if not at once ended. Private Henry will be shot to-day, all care being taken to prevent his injuring any one, as his physical strength is greater than that of any two men. Decide the manner of death by two ball and one blank cartridge. This order is imperative, and absolutely necessary for any chance of life.

(signed) A. W. Greely, Lieutenant Fifth Cavalry, U.S.A.,
and Assistant.
Commanding L. F. B. Expedition."

Greely's orders were carried out that same day. The three men agreed among themselves that they would forever hold it a secret which one of them fired the fatal shot.

Two weeks later, Greely wrote, "The morning of the twenty-first broke with the gale still raging, and it was with the greatest difficulty that Frederick was able to cook our wretched stew of lichens and heat up some stewed seal-skin." The following day, he wrote, "By the morning of the twenty-second we were all exhausted, and it was only through the devotion of Frederick or Brainard, I do not remember which, that we obtained, about noon, some water."

Three ships, the *Thetis*, the *Bear*, and the *Alert*, were being prepared some time before this in order to attempt a rescue of the expedition party. Ample supplies would be aboard these ships to last the 115 men aboard for two years. The ships were especially rigged to break through the ice of Melville Bay and Smith Sound. The *Bear* sailed from New York Harbor on April 24, 1884. The *Thetis* departed New York Harbor on May first. By the later part of May the ships had reached Upernivik in Greenland. The next landmark to head for was Littleton Island. The *Thetis* arrived at Littleton Island on June 21. A party went ashore and realized that the Greely party had never reached Littleton Island. By the morning of the twenty-second. the *Bear* had also reached the island.

Twenty-seven miles away, at Cape Sabine, were the remainder of the Greely party, seven men in all. Schley, commander of the rescue ships, falsely concluded that since no sign of the Greely party was found at Littleton Island, the expedition had not reached Cape Sabine, as was planned in the event of a retreat from Lady Franklin Bay. But Schley concluded that a supply of goods should be deposited at that point for future use, as they passed by Cape Sabine on their way north. The ships reached Cape Sabine on June 22, 1884, and discovered the seven survivors of the Greely expedition. Frederick was among those survivors.

The men of the rescue recovered as many of the bodies as they could find and placed them aboard the ships. The survivors were brought aboard the ships and fed and cared for. They then retreated to St. John's, Newfoundland, arriving on July 17. Ellison had died on the way back. After building metal caskets for the dead comrades and attending a service to commemorate Sergeant Rice, whose family now resided in St. John's, they departed for Portsmouth, New Hampshire, arriving there on August 1.

It was here that Frederick transferred from the "line of the army" to the meteorological branch; he would stay at Portsmouth until February 9, 1885, when he was transferred to Indianapolis, Indiana, to work in the Weather Bureau of the Signal Service. Julius was in Indianapolis in September 1884, reportedly "visiting a brother," J. W. Fredericks, according to one newspaper account. Another newspaper refers to Julius as visiting the Honorable J. W. Fredericks and makes no mention of him being Julius's brother. Julius was discharged from the army on May 11, 1885.

On June 4, 1885, Julius married Laura Kettler in Augulaize County, Ohio. Laura was born November 9, 1866, to Augustus and Natalia (Orphal) Kettler. August and Natalia were married on October 14, 1862, in Augulaize County. It is interesting that Julius and Laura got together. Laura was possibly not even born, or at least just a young child, when Julius left the St. Mary's area where they grew up. He went back to Ohio to enlist in the army in 1876; Laura was only thirteen at that time. It seems that he did not return to Ohio until after he was reassigned to Indianapolis in February 1885, or after his discharge in May; however, he may also have visited St. Mary's during the trip to Indianapolis in September 1884. He had maintained correspondence with Frantz Orphal, one of Laura's relatives, during his military service. How long he was away from Indianapolis to court Laura is not known; however, it had to be less than four months, and probably only a month. It shows that he still had contact with his Ohio family and friends.

It was on May 1, 1885, that Julius's sister Caroline Koehler, her husband, Charles William Koehler, and her family arrived at New York City en route to Indianapolis from Germany. They most likely went to Indianapolis because Julius was there.

While at Lady Franklin Bay, Julius had stated that his desire was to open a bar in Minneapolis. He partially met his desire, as the 1886 Indianapolis city directory shows Julius working in a saloon located at 665 Virginia Avenue. He is listed in the directory as living at 16 Shelby Street.

The oldest child of Julius and Laura, Thetis, named after the ship used in the rescue of Julius and the other members of the party in the Arctic, was born on June 23, 1886. The 1887 city directory lists Julius as a confectioner living and working at 53 North Pennsylvania Street, still in Indianapolis. In 1888 they moved to 336 S. Alabama Street, where they lived until 1892 or 1893, when they moved to 104 Middle Drive, Woodruff Place, where Julius would live out the rest of his life. In the years preceding 1893 his occupation was listed as engineer and clerk; however, in 1993 he is listed as being an observer for the Weather Bureau.

Julius and Laura's second child, Sabine, was born on February 24, 1889, while they lived at 336 S. Alabama Street. They named their daughter after Cape Sabine, where Julius had spent the winter of 1883–84 before the rescue. It was obvious by the naming of their children that the Arctic experience, after nearly five years had passed, was still burning at Julius's heart.

Apparently Julius continued to work for the Weather Bureau. In a letter to the chief of the Weather Bureau, Frederick asked for an increase in salary, because the work of the messenger at the station over the past four years had increased considerably and the cost of living had increased. The letter is undated.

Every effort was made by the expedition leaders, Greely and Brainard, to obtain a pension for Frederick. Legislation was finally passed in 1902 that gave Frederick a pension of about one hundred dollars per month. In order to receive this retirement pay, he was reenlisted in the army on July 14, 1902, and retired from the army the same day.

Frederick was involved with P. E. McDonnell of the McDonnell Odometer Company in Chicago, Illinois. McDonnell's ambition was to construct an airship that could reach the North Pole. He conferred with Frederick about this subject on several occasions.

While Frederick may have suffered health problems stemming from the Arctic expedition, he became quite ill in 1903 with a stomach problem. He was injured by a runaway horse that fell on him that same year; however, it probably had nothing to do with his stomach problem. He died as a result of stomach cancer on January 7, 1904, before reaching his fifty-second birthday.

The relationship between the surviving members of the expedition and Frederick had continued throughout his lifetime. Most either came for his funeral or wrote messages of condolence to his family. He was buried in Crown Hill Cemetery in Indianapolis.

At one time a neighbor and friend offered to help him edit and publish his journal, but when he brought it out to give it to the friend, he sat for a long time before the fireplace, staring into the flames, the journal unopened in his lap. Then he leaned forward and deliberately laid the journal on the coals. When his well-meaning friend leaped forward to rescue it, Frederick shoved him roughly aside. "Let it burn," he said. "It is stupid, crude and illiterate."

When we look at the flowing descriptions that he recorded while in the Arctic—the ones that survived burning—we find them extremely poetic. I'm sure that his journal entries were not stupid, crude, or illiterate, but he apparently set such high standards for himself that he never felt he could meet them. When we look at the sacrifices he made for the good of the members of the expedition in the Arctic, we can surely see that Sergeant Julius Robert Frederick was indeed a brave and humble man.

Julius and Laura's daughter Thetis married James Armour Calderhead in Marion County, Indiana, on June 23, 1908. James, whose parents were born in Scotland, was born in Indiana on January 3, 1885. He was a car salesman. On a trip he made to Europe in 1919, he was listed as being single; however, he was living with Thetis in 1920 in Indianapolis. By 1923 Thetis and James had separated. James married Stella Williamson on October 4, 1923, in Marion County, Indiana. James died in Alameda County, California, on September 11, 1962.

On July 23, 1924 Thetis married John Morgan Dils in Marion County, Indiana. John was born in Indiana on August 20, 1881. He married Missouri P. Morgan in 1906. They had a son, John P., who was born in 1909, so he was about fifteen years old when Thetis and John married. John, like Thetis's first husband, was a salesman. He was also a druggist. He had separated from Missouri prior to 1917–18 when he registered for the draft. The family moved to Florida. Thetis died in Dade County, Florida, on May 12, 1970. John died seven years later in Miami, in November 1978, at the age of ninety-seven years. John's son, John P., died in Bradentin, Florida, on February 9, 1995.

Sabine, the second daughter of Julius and Laura, married Harry Jacob Epply in Marion County, Indiana, on October 20, 1910. Harry was born in Ohio on May 29, 1883, to Harry C. and Marry Epply. Harry and Sabine had three children: Evelyn, born about 1912; Harry F., born July 18, 1914; and Ruth, born October 17, 1916. They made their home in Indianapolis, where, at least some of the time, Harry was a bookbinder. He was described as tall and slender, with brown eyes and dark brown hair. Harry died on March 1, 1946. He is buried in Crown Hill Cemetery in Indianapolis. Sabine died in November 1977 and is buried beside her husband in Crown Hill Cemetery. Harry's sister, Ruth, is also buried in Crown Hill Cemetery.

Laura Kettler Frederick, Julius's widow, continued to live in Indianapolis, with periodic trips back to visit family in Ohio. In 1910 she was living with her daughter Sabine at 863 Middle Drive in Woodruff Place. By 1920, Sabine was married, and James Calderhead and her daughter Thetis were living with her at 863 Middle Drive. She began drawing a widow's pension in 1921. By 1930, she was still living at 863 Middle Drive, now with her daughter Sabine and Sabine's husband, Harry, and their two children. Laura continued to live out her life in Indianapolis. She died in January 1962 at about ninety-six years of age, never having remarried, having been a widow for fifty-eight years. She is buried beside her husband in Crown Hill Cemetery in Indianapolis.

23

William A. Ellis

(1850–1884)

WILLIAM A. ELLIS was born in Seneca Falls, Seneca County, New York, on October 22, 1850. He was the elder of two boys born to William Henry Ellis and Eliza A. (Fulkerson) Ellis. Little is known of his childhood; however, 1860 census records reveal that he and his eight-year-old brother, David, attended school in Fayette, a neighboring town in Seneca County. Neither of the two brothers lived with their parents. At the time of the census William was living in the county poorhouse, and David was living with a family in a house near the county poorhouse. The reason given in the census record for William residing in the poorhouse was that he had "intemperate parents." Intemperate is defined in the Collier's dictionary as "being characterized as unrestrained or given to or characterized by excessive use of alcoholic drinks." Most of the people living in the poorhouse with William were dysfunctional. While a couple of people were living there because of old age, most were there because they were orphans, crippled, idiots or lunatics. This was not a very good environment in which to grow up.

While little is known about William's father, his mother probably had a very tough life. She was born in New York, and according to the birth date listed on her grave marker, she was only twelve years old when William was born and fourteen years old when David was born. The birth year of William's mother, however, is in dispute, as it varies widely from record to record. A census taken a few months prior to William's birth lists her age as eighteen years old. Based on 1870 census records, his mother, Eliza, had married Peter Smith.

While a marriage record has not been located, the marriage ended upon the death of Peter on April 10, 1875. Peter was thirty-nine years old.

William married Mary Ione Brace sometime prior to 1875. Mary was born in Seneca Falls on October 11, 1853, to Charles Brace and Hannah (Fulkerson) Brace. While both the mother of William and the mother of his wife, Mary, had the maiden name Fulkerson, the relationship between William's mother, Eliza A. Fulkerson, and Mary's mother, Hannah Fulkerson, is unknown. It is conceivable that they were related.

By the early 1870s, William and Mary Ellis had moved to Galen, Wayne County, New York, a county adjoining Seneca County. William and Mary had two sons, Charles Henry Ellis and Edward Allen Ellis. Charles was born about 1871, and "Eddie" was born in March or April 1875. In the early part of 1875 Charles was baptized in the Ellis home. According to the baptismal certificate he was "baptized in sickness." This suggests that Charles was of poor health and possibly not expected to live. His brother, Eddie, was baptized two or three months later.

William entered the United States Army in Buffalo, New York, on July 8, 1875. It seems strange that William would leave his wife with an infant child and a sick four-year-old son; however, it may have been that he left for economic reasons or that he just wanted to get away from it all. While nothing is known about William's occupation, he must have been involved with making or repairing clothing. His occupation is listed as "seamster" on his application to enter military service.

He was sent to Dakota Territory, where he served with the Gatling Gun Battery, Twentieth Infantry Detachment, during the famous battle of Little Bighorn in 1876. In this battle, which was an attack upon a group of Indians, General George A. Custer and the members of his unit were all killed. William Ellis was assigned to Company C of the Twentieth Infantry Detachment, which was led by Major Reno. The initial planning would have placed Reno's unit right up front with Custer; however, Custer decided that the unit should attack from another direction. While ninety-five soldiers of Major Reno's party were killed or wounded, Private Ellis emerged uninjured. The news of this famous battle was soon to be reported in the newspapers. The headlines of the Port Jervis, New York, newspaper read, "The Indian Butchery. The news of the terrible massacre confirmed. Annihilation of Gen. Custer's command." The newspaper further reported, "Major Reno lost ninety-five killed and wounded. Gen. Custer's command was annihilated."

Meanwhile, back home in New York, many things were happening. William's son Charles, who was "baptized in sickness," died on January 12, 1876, six months after William went away. His wife, Mary, perhaps concluding that her husband was no longer alive, married John W. Pausley in Cayuga, Cayuga County, New York, on June 2, 1876.

The following year, in 1877, William A. Ellis's unit, the Twentieth Infantry Regiment, Company C, was transferred from Dakota Territory to Fort Clark, Texas. The railroad terminated in San Antonio, and as such, his unit had to march 126 miles to its destination. In 1878, on two separate occasions, his unit crossed the Rio Grande in pursuit of cattle thieves. In the autumn of 1879 and during the 1879–1880 winter, his unit occupied the Indian country south of Fort Davis and between the Rio Grande and Pecos rivers, and opened a military road from San Philipe northwest across Devil's River.

William's five-year enlistment was completed in July 1880; he was discharged from the army at Fort Clark, Texas. He returned to New York. In a New York Times article about Ellis, it was reported that in Seneca Falls, "Ellis surprised his aunt here, Mrs. Edwin Relyea, and other acquaintances by appearing in flesh and blood." It must have been quite a shock to see him come back home after the assumption was made that he was dead. Can you imagine the shock to his wife and the embarrassment it must have been to her to tell him she had married someone else? There was also the pain in telling him that his oldest son, Charles, had died. It must have been devastating for William to learn that his son had died and that his wife, assuming him dead, had remarried. He also learned that his mother, who was widowed from his stepfather, Peter Smith, had again married, this time to George Vanderpool, on March 4, 1880—her third marriage. His mother must have been joyful about his return. William's brother, David, had joined the army and left the area. This did not look like the home William had left five years before.

After being home for about a month, perhaps living in the home of his Uncle Edward and Aunt Mary Relyea, William decided to rejoin the army. He enlisted in New York City on August 13, 1880, and was assigned to the Second Cavalry. Some months later he was selected to join Lieutenant Adolphus W. Greely and twenty-three other men on an expedition to the Arctic. The standards and requirements for being selected for this mission were high. Greely writes, "Long and hazardous duty on the Western frontier had inured the greater part of the men to dangers, hardships, and exposure, and developed in them the quality of helpfulness so essential in Arctic service." Most had a special talent to offer. William's tailoring ability may have been one of the things that qualified him for this mission, which was scheduled to last thirty months and certainly needed someone who could repair clothing. He certainly met the criteria of having experienced "hazardous duty on the Western frontier." These two factors certainly made him a valuable addition to the Greely expedition. For whatever reason, he volunteered for this duty and was selected.

William traveled to Baltimore, where he joined some of the expedition members. With fourteen others of the expedition, he departed from Baltimore on June 14, 1881, for Saint John's, Newfoundland, aboard the steamer Nova Scotain. They arrived in Saint John's on June 22, where others of the party were assembled and preparations were being made for their departure for Lady Franklin Bay. In a letter to his Aunt Mary in Seneca dated June 18, 1881, William stated that they had arrived in Halifax, Nova Scotia, the day before and that they were to leave St. John's, Newfoundland, for Lady Franklin Bay, in the Arctic seas, about July 4. He added, "I will be gone about 30 months; expect to have a little hardship, but hope to come out safe and well."

The final supplies were obtained and loaded aboard ship on July 7, and on that same day the steamship *Proteus*, with William A. Ellis aboard, departed for Lady Franklin Bay. William experienced seasickness on the journey. One of the expedition members, Jacob

Bender, wrote in his journal, "July 11th, 1881, The sea is smooth as piece of glass and all are well agin [sic], except Ellis." His Aunt Mary, Mrs. Edward Relyea, received a second letter from William, sent "from Fort Conger, Lady Franklin Bay, 606 miles from the pole" and dated August 18, 1881. It read as follows:

> Dear Aunt:
>
> After a moderate passage we all arrived here safely and in good health. We have had plenty of work since we have been here. We arrived on the 12th of August, and have been unloading ship ever since until this day. We will have our house up in about eight days more, and then I think we will have a very pleasant time.

The *Proteus* was discharged to return to St. John's the same day that William wrote his letter, August 18, 1881, as all supplies had been off-loaded. The steamer was to take back the mail that had been written, including the letter to Ellis's aunt. Because ice floes were continually blocking the path in Smith Sound, the crew had to wait until the sound cleared sufficiently for the steamer to leave. After a week of waiting, conditions in the sound improved enough to allow the *Proteus* to depart on August 25, when she steamed south toward St. John's, leaving the party with no contact with the outside world. As soon as the steamer left, some of the men begin moving into the house that they were building from precut lumber brought up with them on the *Proteus*. Private William A. Ellis shared an area about eight feet by ten feet with Corporal Nicholas Salor, Private Francis Long, and Private Jacob Bender.

The expedition planned to make many excursions, exploring around the region. Supply depots were built and stocked in order to accomplish this. Private Ellis assisted with the stocking of these depots. On October 23, 1881, Greely wrote, "While Lieutenant Lockwood and party were building the snow-house, Sergeant Gardiner and Private Ellis, with Jens, added a half-ton of coal, mined in Watercourse Ravine, to the supply at Depot 'A' [Cape Murchison]

On November 2, Private Ellis was part of a party to determine if it was practical to cross the ice across the sound to reach the Greenland coast and cache supplies there for a later trek to the north in Greenland. Later Ellis assisted in bring supplies to the depot. Greely writes, "From March 25 to 30 Sergeant Jewell, assisted for a portion of the time by Private Ellis, was engaged with his sledge in accumulating stores on the Greenland coast. There was no day on which the temperature did not fall as low as -40 degrees. On March 27 Sergeant Jewell was deprived of the services of Private Ellis, who, when sent to aid him from the home station, to Depot 'B', had unfortunately wet his feet from tidal overflow during the journey. Not exercising the proper precaution of changing his foot-gear, Ellis' imprudence resulted in his being seriously, though superficially, frost-bitten. Notwithstanding his condition, he made a journey, March 25 and 26, from Depot 'B' to the Greenland coast and back, and then in order not to interfere with the work, insisted on Sergeant Jewell permitting him to return to the station alone. Private Ellis showed remarkable fortitude and determination during the whole affair, which was especially creditable to him."

Private Ellis participated in another expedition trip in March and April of 1883. This party's primary function was to move rations and supplies to advance bases for future explorations.

After the resupply ship of 1882 and the relief ship of 1883 had failed to arrive, the Greely expedition party made their harrowing way southward in the fall of 1883, finally landing at Cape Sabine, some three hundred miles south of Lady Franklin Bay. Here they set up camp, called Camp Clay, with the meager supplies they had on hand. Ellis continued to support missions in search of caches of supplies. He was also instrumental in other areas. Sergeant Brainard wrote in his diary on December 15, 1883, "The water hole on the lake was again frozen up. Through the energy of Ellis it was re-cut." On December 23 Greely wrote, "Later, Brainard succeeded in getting water. Ellis worked long and faithfully on the hole, and on his return to the house fainted, from the effects of change of air from the extreme cold to the hut, and from his exhaustion by labor. Temperature, -25 degrees today."

The effects of the cold weather and the lack of food were beginning to show. On January 10, 1884, Brainard wrote, "Ellis complaining of illness. His speech is greatly affected by the excessive use of dried tea leaves and birch bark. Dr. Pavy had prohibited him and Ralston from smoking." The next day, Greely wrote, "Ellis somewhat better." But three days later, Brainard wrote, "Ellis, Linn, Ralston, Cross and Jewell are also badly broken down in strength. They seldom leave their bags unless coerced." Ellis appears to have been a person who felt a lot of compassion. Cross died on January 18, and on January 19, Greely wrote, "Ellis is the only one of the party who seems to be particularly depressed by Cross' death." And on January 27, Greely wrote, "Lieutenant Lockwood appears weaker. Ellis and Jewell are apathetic."

On February 8, while making plans to cross the sound to Littleton Island if an ice bridge should form, Lieutenant Greely entered the following in his journal: "Rice and Brainard to get up a list of weights which must be hauled, while Frederick, Schneider, and Ellis are to repair our clothing, sleeping-bags, etc." Here we notice that Ellis's skills are being used. On February 15, Brainard wrote, "Schneider, Ellis and Salor are sewing on boots, stockings, mittens, etc. for the crossing to Greenland." Within a few days Ellis seems depressed. On February 23, Greely wrote, "Ellis also remained in his bag, and did not work as he had promised. He is becoming indifferent and apathetic, and requires watching and urging to keep him in good spirits." Yet in early to mid-March, Ellis was active, helping outside with sledge hauling. And on March 22, Greely wrote, "Long and Jens hunting. Ellis carried out the Kayak for them." On March 27, Ellis complained of sickness; by April 6 he was again helping with the hauling, but soon he was down again. On April 10, Brainard wrote, "Gardiner is gradually drooping, and Connell and Ellis are beginning to feel to a marked degree the effects of this horrible life." The next day, though, Long and Jens shot a bear. It was to be their lifeline for the next few days. Ellis, along with others, retrieved the bear and brought it back to camp on a sledge. The comment made by Sergeant Brainard the next day in his journal was, "This fellow [the bear] is our salvation. Without him Ellis, Connell, Bender, Biederbick, Israel, Gardiner, Salor and Kislingbury would have been in their graves in two weeks."

But even with the bear, Ellis's condition seemed to worsen

within a few days. Brainard wrote on April 15, "Lieut. Kislingbury and Ellis are quite ill from over-exertion during the bear excitement on the 11th." From this point on, the journals of both Greely and Brainard point out the worsening condition of Private Ellis. On May 15 Ellis dictated his last will, and on May 19 he died. He was buried the next day on Cemetery Ridge, a burial ground for those who had died at Camp Clay.

His body remained there until the arrival of the rescue party a month later. His body was recovered and placed, along with others, aboard the ship *Bear*. The bodies were submersed in tanks containing preservative fluid.

When the ships reached St. John's, caskets were prepared, and Ellis's body was removed and placed in a casket. The casket contained a plate identifying him, including his age and date of death. His body was returned to the United States and shipped to Clyde, Wayne County, New York, for burial. His remains arrived in Clyde on August 9, 1884, and he was buried in the Maple Grove Cemetery in Clyde the next day.

Upon hearing of William's death, his widow, Mary Ione (Brace) Ellis, filed papers requesting that she be entitled to "administration upon his estate." As far as she knew, no will had been left by William, and his estate amounted to about six hundred dollars. She further stated that he had no children or other descendants left, nor a father. Their youngest son, Edward, had passed away since William had left. He also left his mother, Mrs. Eliza A. Vanderpool, residing nearby, and his brother, David, who was in military service.

In April the next year, however, the will of William A. Ellis, which he had made on May 15, 1884, four days before his death, was brought to the Wayne County, New York surrogate's office by Henry Biederbeck, one of the surviving members of the expedition and a witness to William making the will. In the will he left all of his back pay to his mother, Eliza A. Vanderpool, and to his son, Edward, to be divided equally. He was not aware that Edward had died. He outlined what bills he owed and said that he left his house to Mary Fulkerson. There is no mention of his wife, Mary Ellis, now Mary Pausley, in the will. William's mother, Eliza, filed papers requesting that she be entitled to administration upon the estate. She indicated in her filing "that the said testator left a widow, Mary I Ellis, now Pausley, Galen, N.Y. and left legatus, whose names, ages and places of residence are as follows: Eliza A. Vanderpool, residuary legatee of full age, Savannah, N.Y. Edward C. Ellis, residuary legatee who died before testator with out issue. Mary Fulkerson, legatee, Seneca Falls, N.Y."

A long process was involved in proving that this was William's last will. Sergeant David L. Brainard, another member of the expedition, was summoned to testify in a court in Washington, DC. The results were returned to a Wayne County, New York court, where the will was determined to be valid. Further results of the court have not been determined, nor has the relationship of Mary Fulkerson of Seneca Falls been decided. Possibly William, in his confused state of mind when he made the will, used the maiden name of his wife's mother, Fulkerson, instead of his wife's maiden name, Brace. Possibly, Fulkerson was the maiden name of his Aunt Mary Relyea, with whom he had a good relationship.

There had been rumors that cannibalism had been practiced in the later days of the Greely expedition. The New York Times reported on August 12, 1884, "When their food gave out the unfortunate members of the colony, shivering and starving in their little tent on the bleak shore of Smith's Sound, were led by horrible necessity to become cannibals." No source for such conclusions were published in the newspaper. Another news article, this one from Chicago on August 15, 1884, reads, "Dispatches from Rochester, N.Y., and Lafayette, Ind., state that the bodies of Private Ellis and William Whisler will be exhumed to test the truth of the Cannibalism stories." The body of Ellis was never exhumed. That Ellis's body was cannibalized is unlikely, as he died five days after a bear had been killed, which provided food for the survivors at the time of his death and for a week or two afterward.

Apparently concluding that her marriage in 1876 to John W. Pausley was invalid, as her lawful husband, William, was still living at that time, Mary Ellis married John W. Pausley again on August 30, 1884. John and Mary already had two children, Eva Margaret and Lulu B., by the time of their remarriage in 1884 and were destined to have another child, John. Later records show that Mary had six children in all, three of them having died before 1900.

Eliza, William's mother, was again widowed on the death of George Vanderpool on August 2, 1896. The following year, on September 12, 1897, she married Jacob Sager. This time her husband outlived her. Eliza died on July 12, 1914. Jacob died the next year. Jacob and Eliza are buried next to each other in the Maple Grove Cemetery in Galen, Wayne County, New York.

William's brother, David J. Ellis, married Susan A. Rarerick. Their children included Edward and William Allen, the latter likely named after David's brother. William died in 1897 and Edward in 1899. David's wife, Susan, also had a son from a former marriage, Arro, born in February 1884, and a daughter, May, born in April 1895. Susan apparently had another child who died prior to 1900. David and Susan, along with their surviving children, were living in Cleveland, Ohio in 1900.

William A. Ellis had a difficult childhood, but he did not let this hinder his dedication to his nation. He served honorably in the military during the Indian uprising in Dakota Territory and during the defense of our citizens' property rights in Texas. He returned home to find his marriage in a shambles and his son dead. He returned to the duties of service to his country and allegiance to his superiors, of which their journals attest, supporting them until the end of his life. There is no doubt, given the circumstances of his life, that William A. Ellis was truly a brave man.

24

Roderick R. Schneider

(1853–1884)

RODERICK R. SCHNEIDER was born Robert Roderich Schneider on June 29, 1853, in Dorfschellenberg (now known as Shellenberg), Germany, about ten miles east of the city of Chemnitz. He was the son of Friedrich Alfred Schneider and Agnes Amalia (Dietrich) Schneider. His father was born on December 13, 1823. His mother was born on February 27, 1823.

Roderick had two older brothers: Bruno Alfred, born on September 27, 1846; and Max Otto, born on January 9, 1848. He also had an older sister, Gertrud Amalie, born on September 5, 1849. He had two younger sisters who were twins, Emmy Johanne and Martha, born in 1859, and a younger brother, Felix, who was born in 1863. Except for his father and his oldest brother, Alfred, who were born in Dresden, Sachsen (now called Saxony), Germany, they were all born in or near Chemnitz, Sachsen. Roderick's father was most likely a farmer.

Roderick arrived in the United States in March 1870. He was just sixteen years old. By June of that year he was living with a couple, John and Eliza Mayer, in Walpole, Massachusetts. It appears that Roderick spent a good deal of his time after leaving Germany sailing. Greely wrote in his journal on September 8, 1883, "I directed Rice and Schneider, the most experienced sailors of the party, to examine the strip of water to the westward." On February 17, 1884, Lockwood wrote in his journal, "Schneider gave some personal reminiscences of the coast trade along the New England coast."

Roderick went back to see his family in Germany in about 1873 and was planning to go back again in 1878. He wrote an article for the Arctic Moon, a newspaper that was published in 1881 by members of the Franklin Bay expedition, in which he stated, "In the fall of 1878 I received a letter from my father asking me to come home to Germany to spend Xmas. I was employed at the time as clerk in a business house in New York and had been absent from home for five years." In response to this letter, Roderick decided that he would take the first steamship available out of New York. He booked passage on the *Pommerania*, a German mail steamer that sailed from New York on November 14, 1878, for Hamburg, Germany. About midnight on November 25, the ship was struck by another ship while in the English Channel. The ship sank within twenty minutes of the collision. Fifty-four of the 220 crew and passengers perished in the incident. The Newport Daily News (Rhode Island) carried an article pertaining to the incident in its November 27, 1878, issue:

> Roderick Schneider, a passenger, states that he was in the cabin reading at the time of the collision. He rushed on deck and got into the last boat just before the ship sank. The boat was whirled round and round, so he quite expected it would be drawn under. It was under charge of the first mate, and remained alongside of the sinking vessel until about two minutes before she sank. The captain, replying to repeated entreaties to get into the boat, asked them to stand alongside, when the mate shouted, "We have waited long enough." The captain told them to pull away a little and wait. Just then the vessel sank. As she went down Capt. Schwensen threw up his arms and exclaimed, "Oh God!" While the boat was rowing about we saw many people in the water with life preservers wrongly put on, so that the lower part of the body was floating while the head was under water. We did not pick them up.

In the 1881 Arctic Moon article Roderick says, "I was brought into Dover Harbor and from there went to London; here I found myself without money, clothing or anything." He wrote that he met someone who telegraphed home for him, and the next day he was aboard another steamer en route to Germany.

Prior to his trip to Germany, Roderick had been working for the New York firm Horstmann, Hein & Company as a clerk. He arrived back in New York on April 28, 1879. He apparently did not go back to work for the company, as he enlisted in the United States Army at Fort Columbus, New York, on September 15, 1879. His occupation was listed as clerk on his military papers.

The original orders, dated June 17, 1881, did not list Schneider as a member of the expedition. Instead, Corporal Paul Grimm of Company H, Eleventh Infantry was scheduled to go on the expedition. Paul Grimm, who was born in Baden, Germany, in 1851, had enlisted in the United States Army in June 1879. He was a telegraph operator. He did not show up for the departure from Baltimore on June 14, 1881, and was considered to have deserted from the army. Schneider was available as his replacement. Grimm returned to Germany, where he died in Dietinger on November 24, 1914.

It appears that Schneider was selected for the expedition based on two areas of experience, that as a seaman and as a clerk. Schneider supported many activities while at Lady Franklin Bay. These included moving supplies, hunting, hauling coal, and reading instruments.

By the time Christmas rolled around that first year in the Arctic, Schneider had gained a reputation as a dog handler. It was found to be a common practice for the dogs to seize and devour young pups, but although the bitches ate readily the litters of others, it never fell under their notice that a mother ate one of her own pups. The pups were placed in the care of Schneider, because in the opinion of the two Eskimos, these dogs could not survive. The original dogs sent on the expedition had been thinned out by diseases, and it was necessary for these pups to survive to become future sledge pullers. Schneider successfully raised fifteen of these puppies.

While Schneider's principal duty was recording the readings from the instruments and caring for the dogs, he also helped with hauling coal and supporting expedition preparations. In February 1882 two of the pups died. Schneider was heartbroken.

In September 1883, the departure from Fort Conger took place.

The dogs had been released from their pens, and as much food as was available for them was placed where they could reach it, for at least short-term survival. On August 9, 1883, the expedition members aboard the *Lady Greely*, with three boats in tow, sailed from shore. The dogs watched as the ship moved from shore. Then one of the dogs raced down toward the shore and across the ice and leaped into the water. Schneider was sure that it was Flipper. Flipper was one of the dogs born at the station, and Schneider had raised, fed, and trained him. Flipper struggled to swim through the icy water, heading toward the retreating boats. In a few moments, the dog sank beneath the water. Schneider was saddened.

Once they reached Camp Clay, their new camp, Schneider continued to help in all aspects, especially recording the instrument readings. By the middle of April and into May 1884, Schneider began to show signs of failing health. On April 18 Doctor Pavy wrote in his journal that Schneider was weak and his legs and face swollen, his heart fluttering. A few weeks later, on May 13, Schneider had to be relieved of cooking duty because of faintness. The doctor said that it was signs of scurvy. The next day Schneider made out his will, leaving his estate to his father in Germany. On June 7 Greely stated that Schneider was in a very feeble condition and seemed near death. A week later Schneider begged for opium pills with which he could end his life, but he found no help. Three days later, on June 18, 1884, Schneider died.

When the rescue ship arrived a few days later, Schneider's remains were placed aboard the ship, which sailed to St. John's. There his remains were placed in a casket and shipped to New York City. Once his father was contacted, his body was shipped to Chemnitz, Germany, for burial. A funeral was held, and he was buried at Chemnitz on August 2, 1884. As indicated in his obituary, Roderick Schneider was truly a brave man.

Roderick had another skill that deserves mention: he had talent as a violin player. The violin he played on the expedition was recovered several years later and found its rightful place in a museum.

Thirteen years after Roderick's death, his father, Alfred, died. His mother lived another ten years, and she died on September 8, 1907. Of his three sisters, Emmy died while he was on the expedition, on

August 16, 1882; Martha died just a few months after Roderick, on January 6, 1885; and Gertrud lived until January 2, 1927; all three of them died in Chemnitz. Of his three brothers, Bruno died in Dresden, Germany, on May 25, 1929; Max died sometime after 1904; and Felix died in Chemnitz in 1901.

25

Jens Edward

(1843–1884)

Jens Edward was christened Jens Edvard on August 30, 1843, in Kangersuatsiaq (once known as Prøven), an island off the coast of Greenland. The village currently has a population of fewer than two hundred people. He was the sixth of fourteen children born to Hans Immanuel and Beathe Asarpak. One of his brothers died as an infant, as likely did two of his sisters. Of his remaining family he had two older brothers, Samuel and Hans, and an older sister, Beathe. He had five younger brothers, Elias, Jakob, Paul, Martin, and Thomas, and two younger sisters, Lydia and Laurette. Elias and Martin died young, Elias in 1870 at the age of twenty-five and Martin in 1876 when he was twenty-three years old.

Jens's father, who was born in 1818, died in 1871 at the age of fifty-three. His mother lived until 1897.

On July 17, 1867, Jens married Anna Maria Frederikke Thorleifsen. They had four children. Niels Kristian Frederik Nikolaj was born on November 9, 1868. Rosa Kristine Rakel was born on August 20, 1871. Johanne Katrine Juliane Sara was born on October 21, 1874. Karoline Elisabeth Lydie was born on July 15, 1878.

In July 1881 the Greely party had reached Greenland. They were to pick up supplies, the prefabricated quarters, Dr. Pavy, Henry Clay, dogs, sledges, and dog-team drivers. The drivers that had been contracted backed out. Krarup Smith, the North Greenland inspector, recommended that two Eskimos, Jens Edward and Thorlip Frederick Christensen, be selected as replacement dog sledge drivers on the expedition.

The environment in which Jens lived was very different than any that we could imagine. The Eskimo houses were generally stone and turf structures lined with wood and provided with the usual wooden raised platform serving as a bench by day and for a bed at night. Any windowpanes the houses had were made from the intestines of seals. The houses were rarely tall enough to stand up in.

About three quarters of their livelihood came from hunting and sealing. A ship would occasionally arrive at their island and exchange other goods for seal meat, skins, etc. Jens was skilled at kayaking and seal hunting. He also knew how to care for and manage dogs for sledding. Dogs were important animals in North Greenland.

When the time came for Jens to decide if he would join the Greely team, he had to consider his family. His mother was a widow. He had an older brother, Hans Samuel Moses, and an older sister, Beathe Louise Margrethe. He also had three younger brothers, Jakob, Paul, and Thomas, as well as two younger sisters, Lydia and Laurette. So the family had been whittled down quite a bit by this time. Also his wife, Anna Maria, was pregnant with their fifth child.

But Jens accepted the offer and joined the expedition. The expedition party departed Greenland on July 29, 1881. They reached their destination, Lady Franklin Bay, on August 10, 1881. Jens shared a tiered bunk with his fellow Eskimo. It's likely that Jens never had it so comfortable, with a building he could stand up in, plenty of food and clothing, etc. His grasp of the English language was minimal; however, he seemed well able to communicate.

Immediately Jens's services as a dog-team driver were utilized. He was involved in exploratory trips, hauling coal, and caching supplies when needed.

As the winter set in, so did the gloom. Rice wrote in his journal on December 3, 1881, "Frederick, the Eskimo, has for some time appeared disheartened and has been making me the confidant of his gloomy projects, such as that of running away. Some days since Jens acted in the same manner, but we reassured them of their safety and security. They have both been treated with the greatest kindness by all the party, but as there has been little for them to do for some time past, they have become lonesome and homesick and doubtless imagine all manner of things."

Jens was obviously missing his family and his wife, who would have their fifth child in about a month. It was over nine hundred miles back to his home, over ice, open water, and rough terrain. There was no chance that he could make it back home; however, on December 13, 1881, just ten days after he stated that he wanted to run away, he ventured from the fort. Rice gave an account of the event in his journal:

> Today Jens the Esquimau, concluded he would vary the monotony of my life by absenting. His elopement was discovered at breakfast time. He had been seen in the early morning however, and we naturally concluded that he had not traveled far. After breakfast Lt. Greely instructed Brainard and I to start from a point outside the station and by walking in opposite directions discover his [Jen's] tracks leading from the station.
>
> It was about 8:30 a.m. when we started. Henry volunteered to go with me and Whisler went with Brainard. It was very dark, the sky overcast and no moon in the heavens. Fortunately for Jens a light snow had fallen the day previous so that his tracks could be readily found and distinguished from others. I soon found his tracks following the beaten path towards Dutch Island. We communicated with Brainard and Whisler who soon joined us and we proceeded at a rapid rate expecting to overtake the fugitive in a short time as the tracks looked fresh and we knew that he had not been very long on the road. After proceeding a short distance we thought it best to send back word to the station to follow us with a dog team in case Jens should lead us a long chase. Henry and Frederick, the other Esquimaux, returned. Brainard, Whisler, and I followed the trail expecting to catch up with Jens at any moment for one could see that unaided by any light, he could not be able to follow the path directly but wavered around off. With my lanterns we moved on very rapidly until Dutch Island, distance two

miles, was reached. Beyond that point the path is not well defined as it has not been traveled since the last party came in from Cape Beechy. We saw that our game had turned off at right angles towards the ice foot, so as to follow the coastline and avoid being lost in the ice. His tracks now became difficult to follow, much time being lost in keeping [illegible] of them. When about five miles from home, we were joined by Dr. Pavy with Frederick and dog team. We kept on at the most rapid rate practicable, two of us going in advance with lanterns, the others following the tracks as we found it. The ice foot was very rough and the darkness was so intense that it was impossible to select the most formable route for the sledge even if the erratic course taken by Jens allowed us it.

When near Distant Cape the progress was very slow and at one place I dropped behind to allow the doctor a better position behind the sledge. We had been walking behind it intending to rejoin him so soon as the point was passed. I had just left the advance and being able to hold on to the standards of the sledge and depend upon it for guidance I blew out the candle in my lantern to economize our light. As soon as I dropped behind the sledge disappeared in the dark and in groping my way after it I met with several severe falls. I did not go far before I slipped and was thrown violently against a projecting piece of ice. It was several minutes before I could move from my prone position on the ice. When I discovered that my shoulder was undoubtedly broken. I regained my footing and appreciating the importance of catching up with the sledge, I lit my candle under the great difficulties presented by the wind and the use of one hand only. I started at the best gait I could, suffering intensely and encountered several more falls, in one of which my light again went out and delayed me. I expected the sledge to wait for me at the moment they discovered my absence but, it appears, they were so interested in the chase that my absence was not noticed, as they thought I was following at my leisure. I plodded along, my candle burnt out. I overtook the party at a point a little south of Cape Murchison, distant about ten miles, but they had just concluded to wait for me.

On learning my condition, Whisler started to return with me. Brainard and [illegible] continuing on the way, intending to go as far as Cape Beechy and spending the night at the snow house if they did not find him, Jens, before. Whisler and I made but slow progress on the return as I was compelled to avoid jarring my shoulder. When near Distant Cape, Whisler began to complain of the cold. A few moments after, he began to talk incoherently and before we were half way to Dutch Island, he was delirious. My position was becoming rather unpleasant.

Whisler, overcome by the cold was entirely unresponsive and it took all my will and ingenuity to induce him to walk. He was continually falling down and could hardly resist the temptation to remain on the ice. I attempted to lead him, and carrying no light, our footing was so uncertain that I was continually jarred by missteps which caused me to suffer intensely from my shoulder. I had to cajole, coax, and command Whisler at every step to get him along. I began to fear for his life; if he refused to move he must have died in a very few moments.

We got so far as Dutch Island when Dr. Pavy, Brainard and the Esquimau overtook us with the dog sledge. I at once gave the doctor the state of affairs and told him it was necessary to get Whisler to the station as soon as possible. It was necessary to make him run behind the sledge and we learned on reaching the station that when near the station they had to place him on the sledge as he lost all use of his limbs.

Brainard and I reached the station at 4 P.M. We all had been out about 8 hours, traveled at least twenty miles with the thermometer -30 degrees on one of the darkest days of the winter. Whisler was delirious for several hours, his nose and cheeks frozen but otherwise he suffered no bad consequences. Dr. examined my shoulder and found fracture not complete but the bone evidently cracked and ligature injured. Jens was overtaken a short distance very near the point from which we started to return. He came back quite penitently but did not attempt to explain the cause of his strange conduct. Light snow was falling almost all day.

Jens continued providing sledge support for the expedition. He provided much support for trips that were to be taken during the summer of 1882. In one of these trips, designed to cache supplies for a future trip and where staying overnight away from the fort was necessary, Jens's consideration for others was recorded in Rice's journal:

> March 9, 1882—Linn gave me an instance of Jen's toughness. Linn, after one of the hardest days' work, traveling through a storm, was so completely tired out that he had at once crawled in the double sleeping bag and fell asleep. Jens, after attending to the dogs, came in the tent to sleep, but supposing Linn to be ill, laid outside the bag all night. He must have spent a terrible night as the temperature was below -40.

During a trip in April, when a sled runner broke some twenty miles from the fort, Rice and Jens carried the broken runner back to the fort for repair. The entire trip took eighteen or nineteen hours, in temperatures dipping below the minus forty-degree mark.

In July, Jens's youngest child, Samuel Johan Paul, whom he had never seen, died. Of course he had no way of knowing that.

Jens continued providing dog sled support throughout the summer of 1882 and into the fall of 1883, wherever it was needed. Once the party departed from Fort Conger and made camp at Cape Sabine, Jens's duties would change dramatically. The party no longer had any sleds or dogs. Jens now began to exhibit his skills at hunting and trying to catch seals.

On April 27, 1884, Jens tried to kill a seal that was on the ice. Jens missed the seal and was devastated. He showed signs of weakness. Two days later, on April 29, Jens and Long left the camp, Jens never to return. Greely gave the following account in his journal:

> April 29th.—A fatal day for us. Breakfast at 5 A.M., instead of 6, for accommodation of the hunters. Jens and Long got away at 6:45 A.M. in excellent spirits. Jens appeared to be in particularly good humor; and for the first time in many weeks came and shook hands with me before he left, laughing pleasantly during the while. At 2:30 P.M. Long returned, and reported that Jens was drowned at 11:30 A.M., losing the kayak and our only reliable rifle, the army Springfield. Every one grieves very much over the "Little Man's" death, not alone on account of the critical condition in which we are left as regards food, but on account of the strong affection we all had for his great heart, unvarying truthfulness and integrity. Long said they had been watching a seal on a floe which was separated from the fast ice, in the hope that the flow would drift in, but after a long delay Jens concluded to try and reach the seal, and started over the first pool of water in his kayak, taking a screen so as to crawl up on the seal. He crossed the first lead all right; and dragged his kayak up, and pushing it into the second lead, started across. It is possible that the kayak was cut by the new ice, as in the middle of the second pool Long observed that he suddenly commenced paddling very rapidly, and the rear of the kayak appeared to be inclined upward. Jens made an effort to jump with the kayak on the ice, which unfortunately was new and unable to bear his weight. The kayak remained in sight for an hour or two, during which time Long, at great personal danger, succeeded in getting within a foot of the body; but was compelled to retreat, after twice breaking through the young ice, by the drift of the floe, which, having touched the fast ice, was being separated for it by the tide. Long said that Jens was dead when he first came near to him, and that the kayak was filled with water.

Greely further stated in his journal, "Jens Edward, though an Eskimo, was a man and a Christian of whom no evil word was ever spoken, and on whom no shadow of fault rested in his three years' life with us."

A couple of weeks prior to his death, Jens risked his life to save that of Long, after Long had broken through the ice. Jens gave up his life while trying to provide a food supply for his comrades' survival. Jens was truly a brave man.

Jens's brother Hans died on October 4, 1897; his brother Jacob died on May 22, 1905; his brother Paul died on September 29, 1898; and his youngest brother, Thomas, died on November 29, 1902. His sister Beathe died on July 16, 1891; his sister Lydia died on June 19, 1891; and his youngest sister, Laurette, died on April 14, 1896. His mother died on May 20, 1897, at the age of eighty-eight. Jens's wife, Anna, died on June 16, 1902, at the age of fifty-four.

Jens's son Niels married Abigael Methea Cecilie Eva Christiansen on December 9, 1893. They had seven children. Abigael died on January 2, 1909, and Niels married Rakel Ane Margrethe Lene on April 12, 1911. Niels and Rakel had a daughter. Niels died on August 26, 1919.

Jens's daughter Rosa married Frederik Peter Lynge on August 8, 1897. Peter and Rosa had eight children. Rosa died on February 8, 1920, eight years after her husband's death.

Jens's daughter Johanne married Magnus Sigvard Mathias Christiansen on March 19, 1894. They had nine children. Johanne died on January 6, 1912.

Jens's daughter Karoline married Otto Christian Jens Svendsen on August 27, 1901. Otto and Johanne had two children. Johanne died on May 31, 1908, six months after the birth of her second child.

It is likely that many, if not most or all of the people currently living in Kangersuatsiaq, are relatives of Jens.

26

Thorlip Frederik Christiansen

(1846–1884)

LIEUT. LOCKWOOD, BRAINARD, AND CHRISTIANSEN RETURNING FROM 83° 24' N.

(From a photograph.)

THORLIP FREDERIK CHRISTIANSEN was christened Thorleif Frederik Christiansen on January 29, 1846, in Kangersuatsiaq (once known as Prøven), an island off the coast of Greenland. He was the oldest of eight children born to Christian Jensen Christiansen and Johanne Sigrid Thorleifsen. His brothers were Poul Nicolai Hans (born 1850), Gustav Johan Timotheus (born 1855), Lauritz Hans David (born 1860), and Frederik Andreas (born 1866). His sisters were Sophie Cathrine (born 1848), Mette Marie Frederikke (born 1853), and Amalie Elisa Pauline (born 1857).

His mother was born in 1824, and his father was born in 1825. His mother may have been born in Denmark, which would make Thorleif half Eskimo and half Danish. His oldest sister, Sophie, died in 1862, when she was fourteen years old. Both Thorleif's father and his brother Lauritz died in 1871. Lauritz was only eleven years old.

Thorleif married Wilhelmine Annine on April 14, 1872. Thorleif and Wilhelmine had two children, Casper Jens David Martin, born March 25, 1875, and Mathilde Louise Sara, born on April 21, 1879. Wilhelmine died a little after her daughter was born, on July 4, 1879. She was thirty-two years old.

Thorleif made his living by hunting seal off the coast in his kayak. Periodically a ship would arrive at the island, and seal meat and skins would be traded for other goods. Thorleif also had experience in driving dog teams used to bring in the seals. He probably lived in a dugout used as a house, as described in a previous chapter.

Life was not easy for these Eskimos. By 1881 Frederik (or

"Eskimo Frederik," "Eskimo Fred," or "Fred," the names he would be known by on the expedition) had lost his father, a sister, a brother, and his wife. At age thirty-five he was well above the age of many in his environment that had already died. It made good sense for him to go on this expedition, as he was already exposed to the Arctic winters and the hardships he might endure. Besides, he would receive, by his standard of living, a good monetary reward for going. He had no reason not to go. But on parting, both Jens (the other Eskimo on the expedition) and he shed tears that ran down their cheeks until they were out of sight of their homes. Communication would be only by expressions and hand signals, as English would be the language spoken on the expedition, and only a few of the other party members knew some German, and one or two could speak French. If Frederik knew any language besides the Eskimo language, it would have been learned from the Scandinavians that ruled Greenland and introduced them to the church.

Most of Frederik's duties with the expedition would be driving the dog teams to carry supplies and coal from the coal mine about half a mile from Fort Conger. During the fall and winter of 1881–1882 Frederik was on numerous trips. In September he drove the dog teams on two excursion trips. In October he drove the dog teams to bring back a load of musk-ox meat and to assist in building a snow house in which to store supplies for a later excursion. In November he drove the dog teams to bring ice to the fort.

In December, with much of the activity shut down, Fred seemed depressed. Rice wrote in his journal on December 3, "Frederik, the Eskimo, has for some time appeared disheartened and has been making me the confidant of his gloomy projects, such as that of running away. Some days since, Jens acted in the same manner, but we reassured them of their safety and security. They have both been treated with the greatest kindness by all the party, but as there has been little for them to do for some time past, they have become lonesome and homesick and doubtless imagine all manner of things. As Frederik appeared to be very much in earnest today, I sat up at night to intercept any attempt on his part to escape." Only ten days later the other Eskimo, Jens, walked off from the shelter with the expectation of walking back home. As it was several hundred miles to his home in Provo, during winter with temperatures reaching fifty degrees below zero or lower, with the ice and water lying between where he lived and Greenland, without food and other resources, it would have been impossible for him to get back to his home. A party went out and rescued Jens from this impossible venture.

Two days after Jens's escapade, on December 15, Fred exhibited a desire to follow his example. Following an evening in which Greely provided some interesting remarks concerning the "polar question," Rice wrote the following in his journal: "In a melodramatic maneuver he flourished a huge wooden cross in one hand and with the other on his heart bade the other members of the expedition goodbye and intimating that he was tired of life and about to immolate himself on the Shrine of the Polar question. He was, however, dissuaded." The term "polar question" may need some explanation. During that period, the generalized meaning referred to a question that could be answered with a yes or a no; but when it literally referred to the polar region, it took on a different meaning. It meant "to do or not to do"—whether to risk lives and resources exploring the polar region, or to stay away from there. In this case it appears that the polar question was whether Fred should survive through the dreary winter, or end it all.

During the months of January through April 1882, Fred was involved with at least ten trips as dog driver, most of them to cache supplies for the summer trip north. On one of these trips, a trip to Thank God Harbor, Fred severely froze his foot. The group, now consisting of Lockwood, Brainard, Jewell, Long, Jens, and Fred, traveled over a hundred and forty miles on this trip alone.

On April 2, 1882, Lockwood, Brainard, and Eskimo Frederik, along with a group of support teams, departed Fort Conger to explore the northern coast of Greenland. The advance parties carried supplies from the fort to depots that had been established the fall before and earlier in the spring. When they were about thirty miles from the fort, some of the party returned to the fort and some continued on. In about a week they had crossed the frozen strait and were on the Greenland coast. The party, now consisting of nine people, was about fifty miles from the fort when the runners of the sledge, which would be used to carry their supplies northward, became too badly worn to continue. Lockwood and Eskimo Fred volunteered to return to the fort to get new runners. The hundred-mile trip took them just over two days.

By April 28, after twenty-six days on the excursion, they reached Cape Bryant. This was where the support party of six would break off and meet Lockwood, Brainard, and Fred upon their return from their "farther north" exploration. Lockwood, Brainard, and Fred took twenty-five days of rations and other supplies with them. Altogether the supplies weighted about eight hundred pounds, which they had to haul on the sledge, with Fred as driver. They went toward Cape Britannia over the sea ice. On May 15, nearly a month and a half since they had left the fort, they reached their destination, about four hundred and fifty miles from the North Pole, and about fifty miles nearer the pole than any explorer had ever reached. The entire expedition, including all of the support teams, returned to Fort Conger on June 1, 1882. The entire journey was over a thousand miles and took two months.

It should be pointed out that Greely, Lockwood, and Brainard received historical credit for this achievement and Eskimo Frederik did not, although he placed himself in all the dangers and suffered all the conditions that the other expedition members suffered. He was an extremely important member of the expedition, enabling them to reach this historical point.

During the remainder of 1882, Eskimo Fred drove the dog-driven sledges on numerous trips. He was on six exploration trips, six trips to haul meat, four trips to haul coal, two trips to read instruments, and a trip to fire experimental shots to determine sound speed in the Arctic. In addition, he was involved in fishing and hunting. He shot at least four musk oxen, five hares, and a wolf.

In March 1883, Lockwood decided that he should try to reach a new "farthest north" record. His goal was to reach the eighty-fourth parallel, bettering the previous record of 83° 24½' north, a difference of thirty-five and a half nautical miles, or about forty statute miles farther north than his previous record. As before, Brainard and Eskimo Fred would accompany him. They departed Fort Conger on March 27. By the first week of April, after traveling through some pretty tough terrain, they had reached a point eighty miles from the fort. They continued on for several days; however, the drifts were so high that they had to cut a stairway of over one hundred steps to get over them. Eventually, to their disappointment, they found it necessary to retreat back to the fort.

For the remainder of their time at Fort Conger, Fred continued to provide dog sledge support, as he had been doing all along. When the expedition left Fort Conger on its way south, without the dogs and the sledges, Eskimo Fred's duties changed dramatically. He would now become a hunter instead of a dog-team driver. Even when the expedition was moving southward, Fred shot some seals, only to have them sink before they could be brought onto the ice floe. Soon after they had set up camp at Camp Clay, Fred shot several seals, but most of them could not be brought to shore. He had more success at shooting foxes.

Fred did his best to obtain game for the expedition, but it was insufficient to sustain them. Eventually his efforts and lack of nourishment turned into an illness. On March 20, 1884, Brainard wrote in his journal, "Fred is not feeling well. The late trip with Long has taken all his energy and despondency seems to have overcome his usual happy disposition." But Fred continued to hunt for the next few days. On March 28, Brainard wrote in his journal, "Eskimo Fred shot a ptarmigan on Cemetery Ridge, and returned to the hut immediately much exhausted from the exertion. He seems very despondent and says that he will never return to his home in Proven. Perhaps he is right." His health continued to worsen until the morning of April 5, when he died. Lockwood wrote in his journal, "Frederik Christiansen, Esquimaux, died unexpectedly to most of us at 9 A.M. this morning. He was taken suddenly worse last night, and everything done for him that suggested itself, I believe. He has been failing for some time past, but still I did not think there was any danger of his death. He was a good man and I felt a great affection for him. He constantly worked hard in my service, and never spared himself on any sledge trip. He was buried near Cross at 1 o'clock today, and a salute fired over his grave."

Fred's body remained buried in the ice until the rescue ship arrived some two months later. His body was removed to one of the rescue ships and taken to Upernavik, Greenland. The ship was met by many of the natives, who shed tears for their lost family members, Jens and Frederik. Governor Elberg, the inspector of North Greenland, was there to meet the ship. At his suggestion, the Americans decided to carry Fred's body south to Godhavn on Disko Island for burial. At the summit of a hill in the Christian chapel, the Danish inspector addressed his farewell to Frederik in English for the benefit of those few who knew him well and those who had brought him home. The inspector said, "As head of the Danish Government in North Greenland, I have received your body, and in the name of all the Danish and Greenland people I will say you farewell. Your last master, Lieutenant Greely, has said you were a good and brave man; he has promised me to send for your tomb a monument as a sign for your countrymen that he will never forget your service, nor will he ever forget the poor Eskimo who has lived and suffered as a comrade with the United States friends."

To Brainard especially, it was a moving experience to hear the Lutheran pastor of stolid Eskimo countenance deliver the funeral discourse before this mixed gathering, for his comrade of the assault party that had attained the "farthest north." The pastor said, "No man knows the thought of God concerning us. He whose soulless body we today are to bury, and the other, his companion, who perished in a kayak in the northern regions, did not think their days were numbered when they took leave of the wives they loved and the children who were to be their support in their old age. They thought they would be better able to support their families when they returned, and they begged them to pray for a happy meeting. But they were never to be made happy by seeing each other's faces. We pray to God that He will assist these strangers in the far country to whom the angel of death has also come. Peace be with their dust. In the name of Jesus, Amen."

In 1889, Frederik's brother Gustave, then just thirty-four years old, died. On June 14, 1891, his mother died at the age of sixty-seven. The next day, Frederik's brother Poul died; he was forty-one years old. Four days after Poul's death, his sister Mette died at the age of thirty-eight. Frederik's son Casper died on July 23, 1894, being only nineteen years of age, and another of Frederik's siblings,

Frederik Andreas, died five days later at the age of twenty-eight. His sister Amalie lived until she was fifty years old, dying in 1907.

As Greely voiced at the funeral service for Thorleif Frederik Christiansen, he certainly was a brave and dedicated man.

CPSIA information can be obtained at www.ICGtesting.com
Printed in the USA
LVOW13s0714081113

360278LV00003B/24/P